Tribal Economy at Crossroads

Tribal Economy at Crossroads

Edited by

S.N. Chaudhary

RAWAT PUBLICATIONS
Jaipur • New Delhi • Bangalore • Hyderabad • Guwahati

ISBN 81-316-0373-3

Published by
Prem Rawat for **Rawat Publications**
Satyam Apts, Sector 3, Jawahar Nagar, Jaipur 302 004 (India)
Phone: 0141 265 1748 / 7006 Fax: 0141 265 1748
E-mail: info@rawatbooks.com
Website: www.rawatbooks.com

New Delhi Office
4858/24, Ansari Road, Daryaganj, New Delhi 110 002
Phone: 011 2326 3290

Also at *Bangalore, Hyderabad* and *Guwahati*

Typeset by Rawat Computers, Jaipur
Printed at Chaman Enterprises, New Delhi

Contents

Foreword

Tribes are an integral part of our society. They are found in most part of the country. According to the 2001 census, they constitute 84.3 million or 8.2 per cent of the total population. It is said that 90 per cent of them live in or in close proximity to forests. The forests that remain in India today are mostly in tribal areas. And as per the Forest Survey of India Report (2003) about 60 per cent of the forest cover of the country and 63 per cent of the dense forests lie in 187 tribal districts.

Scholars may have different views about attributes of tribes today because they are not monolithic population in terms of bases of social stratification but there is near agreement among different stakeholders on economic dependence and backwardness among most of the tribal groups. In spite of various development initiatives by all the concerned only small number of tribes have been able to improve their socio-economic status. And this has become possible in their life due to modern education, political opportunity and participation and occupational mobility. Tribals at large have been associated with their traditional means of livelihood. Forest played crucial role in their economic and non-economic life. Local ecology occupied dominant role in their life. But gradually, due to number of historical reasons, the local resources have lost its importance. These resources are incapable to meet ever increasing needs and demands of tribal masses. This state of affair have forced many of the tribal groups to move towards non-traditional occupations. They are either wage worker at the local level or outside or they carry farm activities. But due to absence of required skill in wage work and lack of technological modernization in farm work they are not capable enough to come out of the trap of poverty and backwardness. Most of the poor and unorganized sector workers are still supplied from them. This state of affair put question mark on the effectiveness of the ongoing development schemes.

How process of tribal development may be made inclusive, functional and sustainable? How the inhibiting factors of development may be neutralized? How physical and social quality of life of tribal masses may be improved? How many tribes categorized under the umbrella of primitiveness may be brought out? How globalization and civil society initiatives may be made fruitful and functional for tribal masses? These were some of the major issues for the deliberation of which the two days national seminar on *Tribal Economy* was organized by the Rajiv Gandhi Chair in Contemporary Studies, Barkatullah University, Bhopal during February 11–12, 2009. Present volume is an outcome of this precious process. As was expected, the seminar reflected the variety of vision that dominated all discussions on *Tribal Economy.* Objective behind publication of this volume is to disseminate the deliberations of the seminar at different levels. I am confident that this volume will be useful for students of tribal studies, planners, policy makers and NGOs working for economic development and social change among tribal masses.

I congratulate Prof S.N. Chaudhary, Rajiv Gandhi Professor for editing this volume in a short span of time.

Prof. Ravindra Jain
Vice Chancellor
Barkatullah University
Bhopal

Preface

Tribal economy revolved around natural resources especially forests, at different stages of tribal development. Natural resources not only became source for their physical requirements but also it served as bases for the development of social institutions and cultural practices. But with the passage of time the nature of tribal economy became diverse and its impact on social and cultural practices also changed. Today tribal economy is not at all monolithic. There are some tribal groups who are still at the stage of hunting and food gathering but there are others who are settled agriculturist. Similarly a section of tribal population can also be seen in secondary occupations especially in urban situation but other groups are still termed as primitive tribe. In short, tribal economy which was earlier based on barter system at the local level is now significantly monetized. Near erosion of local level support base and their increasing exposure to outer world have contributed to the process of monetization among them. As a result of this process there is significant change in their social and cultural life. Similarly in the light of new socio-political formations there is change in their economy in terms of its nature, type and importance.

In order to examine the dynamics of tribal economy and its different dimensions especially since independence and its implications, a two day national seminar was organized by Rajiv Gandhi Chair in Contemporary Studies, Barkatullah University, Bhopal during February 11–12, 2009. Scholars and researchers across the country participated and presented research papers in this seminar. We have selected some of these papers and after necessary revision these papers have been included in this volume.

In course of organizing the seminar we received cooperation from different corners. At the outset we are thankful to Prof Ravindra Jain, Vice Chancellor, Barkatullah University, Bhopal for his cooperation at all the levels in the organization of this seminar. He was also good enough to write foreword of this volume.

Professor Vinay Kumar Srivastava, Professor Yogesh Atal and Prof Sachchidananda delivered keynote address, second Rajiv Gandhi Memorial Lecture and valedictory address respectively. I am obliged and thankful to them.

We are also thankful to all those scholars, planners, policy makers and NGO representatives, who participated in the seminar as a chair-person, co-chairperson, chief guest, discussant and paper presenters.

Last but not the least I am thankful to technical assistants, JRFs and research associate working under Rajiv Gandhi Chair for their day and night work to ensure success of the seminar.

S.N. Chaudhary

Contributors

D.C. Sah, Professor of Economics and Director, Madhya Pradesh Institute of Social Science Research, Ujjain, Madhya Pradesh.

D. Debnath, Associate Professor of Sociology, Indian Institute of Forest Management, Bhopal, Madhya Pradesh.

J.J. Roy Burman, Professor of Sociology, Tata Institute of Social Sciences, Mumbai, Maharashtra.

Jitender Prasad, Professor of Sociology, Maharshi Dayanand University, Rohtak, Haryana.

Kavitha Anbu, Guest Lecturer, Department of Sociology, Bharathidasan University, Tiruchirapalli, Tamil Nadu.

Neeta Tapan, Assistant Professor of Economics, Government Girls' P.G. Excellence College, Ujjain, Madhya Pradesh.

R.D. Singh, Professor of Economics, Department of Regional Planning & Economic Growth, Barkatullah University, Bhopal, Madhya Pradesh.

R. Shankar, Professor of Sociology, Department of Sociology, Bharathidasan University, Tiruchirapalli, Tamil Nadu.

S.K. Pant, Reader, Govind Ballabh Pant Social Science Institute, Allahabad, Uttar Pradesh.

S.N. Chaudhary, Rajiv Gandhi Professor, Rajiv Gandhi Chair in Contemporary Studies, Barkatullah University, Bhopal, Madhya Pradesh.

S.N. Tripathy, Professor of Economics, Gokhale Institute of Politics & Economics, Pune, Maharashtra.

Vinay Kumar Srivastava, Professor of Anthropology, Delhi University, Delhi.

Yogesh Atal, Professor of Sociology and Former Director UNESCO, Gurgaon.

Y.G. Joshi, Visiting Professor, Madhya Pradesh Institute of Social Science Research, Ujjain, Madhya Pradesh.

1

Introduction

S.N. CHAUDHARY

I

Historically, economic life was integrated with social and cultural institutions and practices in such a deep manner in the tribal world that it is rather difficult to comprehend it in isolation from these practices. All the economic and non-economic institutions were organically linked. They all contributed, nurtured and influenced each other. Many of the economic activities were constructed, conditioned and legitimized by socio-cultural activities and vice versa. And primarily the bases of formation and functioning of these economic and non-economic institutions were the local level natural objects, both animate and inanimate, which we call natural resources especially since the days of industrial revolution in England. Industrial Revolution and its aftermath not only changed the very concept of natural objects into natural resources and introduced capitalistic ideology for the maximization of output and benefit of these natural resources as a pre-condition for well-being of mankind but also it became the prime mover in many societies including tribal world. The process of acculturation may be old with reference to tribes of India because they were also in constant contact with several indigenous and non-indigenous civilizations till the coming of East India Company, but its motive, content and frequency definitely increased and expanded with British invasion. Introduction and expansion of missionaries, massive logging of wood for administrative and commercial purposes by the British Raj, coupled with classification of forests and formulation of Acts and provisions to manipulate forests, diversion of forest land for other purposes and introduction of Permanent Settlement in 1793 and such other arrangements for land management in the light of colonial interest, creation of middlemen from among tribal and non-tribal natives, various forest related proscriptions, etc., are few among many examples in this regard. These processes, including the old non-British process since several centuries, especially Hinduism and Islam, as well as local rulers and kings influenced tribal economy in terms of its autonomy, relevance and functions mainly in dysfunctional manner. This is supported by narratives documented in various Gazetteers reports and other literature. According to Manohar (2001), the rise of the Marathas from the mid-seventeenth century onwards for the first time led to serious inroads into the Bhils homelands. In order to develop trade and settled agriculture so as to boost their revenue they carried out sustained campaigns against the Bhils who refused to agree to this incursion into their lifestyle. Peasants and traders from Gujarat and Maharashtra were encouraged to settle in the Bhil regions and forests were cleared to bring land under the plough. Thousands of Bhils were massacred when they rose in revolt against this policy. According to Luard (1908), the British followed the policy of the Marathas and brought in Kunbi Patidar and Jat farmers from Gujarat and Rajasthan respectively and settled them on the Bhil lands in the plains so as to both increase the earning from land revenue and commercial agriculture and also to tame the militant Bhils. While some of the Bhils withdrew into the hills most others were converted into serfs or bonded labourers of these non-*adivasi* farmers.

Needless to mention that the net result of acculturation process of different varieties between tribal and non-tribal traditions was near breakdown of tribal autonomy of their both material and non-material culture. A new and alien way of life was gradually imposed on them, a significant part of it gradually became elements of tribal culture. The process of pauperization and ruinization among them, started during pre-British days by rulers and kings became common without any concerted and successful effort to stop this process during British period. Apparently *Raj* maintained distance with socio-cultural practices in principle but in practice its natural resources management mechanism was designed and introduced in such a fashion that it contributed to erosion of social and cultural heritage alongwith economic deterioration.

Towards the dawn of independence historical marginality of tribals was, however, recognized by the dominant change agents, especially by the state and civil society bodies. This realization led to formulation and implementation of different acts, provisions, policies and schemes for the protection and promotion of human rights of tribal masses especially in the light of problems and provisions of Indian Constitution. Many civil society organizations of different varieties, viz., protest movements as well as capacity-building oriented efforts, emerged for their development. Role of individual philanthropists and social reformers cannot be forgotten in this regard. Tribal's own cultural heritage, specifically indigenous knowledge relating to different aspects of life, custom and tradition, and seasonal outmigration, etc., also played role to encounter the process of pauperization and marginality. According to Srivastava (2008: 35), "Tribes have themselves done a lot for their own improvement – they have led movements for environment protection, saving their cultural and human rights, throwing the exploiters out of their territories, regaining rights over their lost land and other resources, closing liquor shops in their area a curbing practices of conspicuous consumption and putting a full stop to all those practices that reduce their respect in the eyes of other." Outcome of all these processes and its limitation especially with reference to the ongoing capitalistic model of development at the apex level and number of socio-political barriers operating at the local level was discussed in the seminar.

In the recent past, besides the ongoing tribal development schemes, some new initiatives, viz., Panchayati Raj, Self-Help Groups (SHGs), National Rural Employment Guarantee Scheme (NREGS), etc., have been launched to capacitate and empower poor, including tribes, from where there is maximum supply of poor. How these initiatives have influenced tribal economy? How and to what extent these interventions have positively and negatively influenced their income and expenditure, food security situation, saving and indebtedness, decision-making process, education and health and overall quality of life and so on? What is the nature and magnitude of class formation and inter-class relations among tribes in the light of these recently initiated initiatives? All these issues were discussed in technical sessions of the seminar.

Since 1991 India is formally going through the process of globalization. There is a general apprehension among a section of scholars that globalization is anti-poor and anti-tribal. And, as the process of globalization will get momentum tribals in particular will gradually loose their economic and non-economic identity. They will gradually loose their century old natural resources-based crisis management tradition and mechanisms such as herbs and medicinal plants and its value addition techniques which they are already loosing due to acculturation process and ever changing forest management strategies. Decreasing resource base and increasing dependence on the institutional arrangements for health management is a testimony to this. Growing individualism, formation and expansion of consumer culture, expansion of market forces and monetized economy, increasing degree of acculturation of different varieties, greed in favour of so-called modern lifestyle, etc., are likely to erode the two important bases of social capital, i.e., trust and reciprocity from among them. Needless to mention that presence of these two bases are must for crisis management especially among the groups which are deprived and underdeveloped in modern sense of the term. Globalization is contributing to mega development projects along with expansion of consumer culture in the tribal world as it is doing elsewhere, in such a massive manner that tribals at large are likely to be displaced from their economic, social, geographical and cultural domain. Increasing number of such projects in tribal dominated states like Chhattisgarh, Jharkhand and Orissa may be taken as an example. In the absence of forceful and sustained protest movement by tribal masses and apathy among change agents, gap between promises and performance at the time of displacement and rehabilitation is further likely to expand unchallenged (Chaudhary, 2002). Under the given scenario it is doubtful that how and to what extent tribal masses will save their damaged resource base, cultural identity and heritage especially from instrumental point of view as a crisis management mechanism. There is an apprehension that tribals cannot avail fruits of globalization led opportunities of development because they lack most of the requirements and pre-conditions of globalization. This apprehension seems true. How a poor, illiterate and ignorant tribe will get benefit out of IT revolution or what may be called 'mobile culture'? How they will get benefit out of five star schools and hospitals? Rather fortunate from among them can only associate themselves with SHGs and NREGS which can only bring marginal relief in their life in a non-sustainable manner. In the absence of all these resources, how their bargaining power will improve? Material and non-material resources available in tribal dominated areas will be manipulated by globalization forces unilaterally without extending any meaningful share and benefit to the tribal masses. They are incapable to question the state led capitalistic model of development which pleads national development at the cost of local level identity. The net result of all these processes shall be impetuous to the ongoing process of pauperization and marginalization. Those who are now less poor in comparison to the past, due to institutional intervention, they are further likely to become more poor and deprived in the current situation. Those small section of tribals who hails from middle or upper classes and who are the product of constitutional provisions and development measures, are likely to become custodian of globalization process as per their non-tribal dominant counterpart. Their growing inclination in favour of modern household assets like colour TV, VCR, mobile phone, two-wheeler, sofa, gas stove, alien food items, dress pattern, etc., support this proposition (Chaudhary, 2010). Due to growing individualism and lust in favour of consumer culture and modern urban lifestyle, tribal elites may keep themselves away from social concerns of tribal masses. In the functional sense state will also remain indifferent as it is today especially from the interest of tribal masses. Government may introduce many innovative projects for economic development but at the implementation or delivery level it may not be serious upto the desired level partly because of philosophical fault with model of development and partly due to the vested interests of change agents. As a result, all the negative forces may come together and it may slow the process of tribal development. Our (Chaudhary, 2004) experience at the panchayat level reveals that in spite of presence of large number of tribal leaders at all the three levels of panchayats in Madhya Pradesh, specific problems of tribal masses related to health, education, livelihood, indebtedness, land alienation, alcoholism, etc., are seldom addressed in an honest manner. Why it is so that in spite of presence of so many MLAs and MPs from tribal community at the state assembly and parliament level maximum number of poor and marginalized, illiterate, bonded and child labour, etc., are supplied from this community? Under the given situation, it is high time to watch from close quarter especially from field experience, nature and magnitude of interface between tribals and ongoing schemes for their development. The seminar attempted to locate and trace possibility of positive relationship between the two. There is need to trace success stories of relationship between the two from across the globe. One of the objectives of the seminar was also to search answer of these broad issues and suggest ways and means for economic development of tribal masses.

Even today, it is difficult to compartmentalize tribals economic life from their non-economic domain, in spite of the ongoing process of Monetization and opening of accounts in banks and post offices. Therefore, it is essential to uncover how development or deterioration in their economic life, including nature, type and sources of economy, which is large and primary in nature and there is change only from within in their economic life, i.e., from collection and marketing of NTFP and engagement in shifting cultivation to dependence on agriculture or wage work or both, is influencing their non-economic life. More specifically, the seminar aimed to examine changing patterns of tribal economy and its impact on their non-economic life, specially their physical and social quality of life and vice versa in the historical perspective.

The specific objectives of the seminar were the following:

1. To examine the nature of tribal economy and its autonomy in the historical perspective;
2. To find out interface between tribal economy in relation to state, civil society and globalization initiative;
3. To trace role of tribal social movement, tribal culture, science and technology, *mahajan* and migration in tribal economy; and
4. To suggest action agenda for strengthening tribal economy.

II

In the seminar a number of research based articles were presented. Due to various reasons, it is not possible to include all these articles in this volume. Only those articles were included which are directly related to either main or the sub-themes of the seminar.

Prof V.K. Srivastava delivered the keynote address. To him, in spite of the fact that earlier tribal economy had its autonomous character and gradually it has become part of the world economy, it is one of the most neglected issues of study of social scientists. He categorically narrated the process of erosion of tribal economy due to extraneous intervention over the time, and also remarked that tribal economy distinctively retained its salient attributes. He advised researchers to conduct studies on issues like the process of monetization of tribal economy, role of market in managing tribal economy, process of change, and relationship between tribal economy with migration, social movements, extent and nature of exploitation, state initiatives and so on. Finally he advocated in favour of multi-disciplinary approach in the comprehension of these issues and sub-issues.

Prof Yogesh Atal delivered Second Rajiv Gandhi Memorial Lecture on tribal issues. His paper deals with development of anthropology in India in the historical perspective. He talked about changing focus of anthropological enquiry. To him the focus is shifting from past to the present and future. He said that tribes are still the main issue of investigation by anthropologists. However, he said, there is need to reshape the methodology in the light of changing scenario in the tribal world.

Paper of Prof D.C. Sah deals with seasonal outmigration as a coping mechanism to deal with both economic and non-economic challenges among tribes of Madhya Pradesh. Proper focus have been done on both push and pull factors contributing to outmigration. To him migration along with short-term land transaction like share-cropping, fixed rent and land mortgage, etc., have played an important role in tribal society. The paper formulates two strategies to improve condition of migrants – both at the place of origin and at the place of destination. How to make the lives of migrants at the place of destination less stressful, provide them with amenities there, and make their position stronger in the labour market is as important as improving agriculture and increasing borrowing capacity of migrants at the place of origin, the paper stressed.

In his paper, Prof S.N. Chaudhary deals with dynamics of tribal economy with reference to a Gond tribe dominated village of Betul district of Madhya Pradesh. Attempt has been made to discuss different aspects of economic life, viz., farming, functioning of NREGS and its impact on economic life, wage work, functioning of SHGs, collection and marketing of firewood by tribal women, functioning of public distribution system (PDS), income and expenditure, saving and indebtedness and social implications of changes in economic life. It has been concluded that in spite of selective economic development in the village, changes in other aspects of life, viz., education, health, etc., is not taking place in the proper perspective.

Prof Y.G. Joshi in his paper discusses the situation of indebtedness among tribes of Madhya Pradesh and consequences of indebtedness in the form of land alienation. Degree of indebtedness as compared to income for repayment capacity, role of micro organizations and other institutional sources, degree of land alienation in covert and overt form to analyse reasons of indebtedness are also discussed in the paper. The paper is completely based on field data.

Prof Jitendra Prasad in his paper has discussed the impact of colonial rule in Santhals economy in today's Jharkhand. It deals with exploitative nature of colonial policies which still continues to be a part of their economy in one form or the other. Before the advent of colonial rule, Santhals had an autonomous control over the land and they had their own resource base. The British Raj prepared a scheme of administration on tribal land that endangered their existence. As a result, land came under the British control. With the enactment of Permanent Settlement (1793) land came under the direct control of the Raj and subsequently to the British sepoys. The non-tribal zamindars were authorized by colonial power to collect the rent on the land occupied by Santhals who had earlier cleared the forest and settled there. Their exploitative practices created land alienation and subsequently bonded labour system. They were now exploited by moneylenders, merchants, Britishers and zamindars. These structures of deprivation culminated into armed uprisings.

Prof R. Shankar and Anbu Kavitha in their paper deal with different aspects of tribal development in the historical perspective. They have highlighted the concept of tribe, process of continuity and change in their economic life, merits and limitations of National Tribal Policy, interface between tribes and different external forces and its implications, tribes and Indian Constitution, Panchayati Raj and tribes, question of food security, importance of medicinal plants in health management and so on. Towards the end, authors have suggested prescriptions relating to tribal development for all the change agents. Authors have also outlined some research topics for further studies.

Prof S.N. Tripathy in his paper has gone through globalization-led process of development and its implications in the form of displacement among different tribes across the country. His analysis is based on both primary and secondary source information. As per his findings in the process of rehabilitation, tall promises are made but in practice these are not translated into action. Issues like delay in the rehabilitation work, involvement of middlemen, corruption, etc., have been analysed in the paper. He concluded that net result of all these negative forces is national development at the cost of material and non-material culture of the local population.

Paper of Prof R.D. Singh tries to propose strategies and instrumental indicators of development and strategic approach to strengthen tribal economy. To him, efforts related to empowerment in the tribal economy should be based on the identification of the economic resources in regional perspective with a view to select key strategic indicators. According to him, without heavy dependence on micro perspective, development of tribes is not possible in a sustainable manner.

The paper of Prof J.J. Roy Burman discusses the relatively less debated process of conversion of faiths of tribal masses by Hindu proselytizers. This process is being justified by the statement that it is not a part of conversion but a matter of home coming. Main point in this article is to highlight politicization of the whole process of religious conversion and reconversion. Author gave the example of Christianization of tribes and subsequently their Hinduization. He cited the example of Friends of Tribal Society associated with Vishwa Hindu Parishad in Maharashtra. Following the pattern of Christian Missionaries Friends of Tribal Society they started schools, medical facilities, watershed project, plantation work, farming and such other activities which resulted in the conversion of tribes into Hinduism.

Debashis Debnath in his paper deals with strategies to reduce poverty among tribes of Madhya Pradesh by restructuring mechanisms of livelihood generation activities through forest resources. To him in spite of decreasing status of forest there is scope of livelihood for large number of tribals in the forestry sector. The paper deals with success story created by the Department of Forest, Government of Madhya Pradesh by introducing triple bottom line approach, viz., ecology, economy and social institutions. Success of this approach depend on proper management of watershed projects, respect to indigenous knowledge of tribals, sacredness of the areas, trees and water bodies, cultural practices, traditional livelihood mechanisms and effective functioning of organizations like Gram Panchayat, Gram Sabha, NGOs, SHGs and such other bodies. The paper concludes that if there is ecological sustainability, economic stability, social acceptability and institutional sustainability, it will provide both livelihood opportunity to ensure sustainable development.

Neeta Tapan attempted to examine merits and achievements of micro-credit system (SHGs) among tribes of Jhabua. To her, outsiders cannot develop tribals, they can only become facilitators. The credit needs of the rural poor are determined in a complex socio-economic milieu. It has been a well established fact that despite tremendous efforts, banks and formal credit institutions have been failed to deal with sections of society requiring small loans specially women. She dwelled upon the facts on the basis of her survey about the credit portfolios of women SHG members in Jhabua. She highlighted the pattern of internal money lending system, borrowing portfolio and status of repayment. The paper concludes that SHG is a potential mechanism with regard to economic empowerment of tribal women. It had provided self-dependency and reduced outmigration in a significant manner.

Prof S.K. Pant has observed that in the past efforts were made for socio-economic development of tribals but the output and implications is notional. Only few tribals have been able to avail benefits of development in a meaningful way. His paper suggests tribals model for their development. He pleads for popularization of micro finance model. It will empower tribal masses, especially those who are living in BIMARU states.

III

Some of the research and action-oriented recommendations, especially for researchers and change agents operating at different levels, which emerged out of the deliberations in two days national seminar, are the following:

1. Tribal economy having its own autonomous existence is gradually becoming the part of wider economy. There is a need to study tribal economy in relationship with the economy of outside world and its overall implications from the point of view of tribal interests. In this context specific aspects which needs to be studied are: How unmonetized societies are becoming monetized? How markets which were peripheral to tribals have gradually become central to the changes which are occurring in the societies? Reasons which contributes to outmigration and its economic and non-economic implications, role of the state and civil society efforts against the exploitation and overall consequences of this process on tribals.
2. Traditional knowledge, skills and practices of less known tribes should be documented and recognized. Potential of such tribal communities have not been recognized. Tribals skills should be introduced to the outside world to improve their economic

condition. It should be carefully patented. In the case of use of indigenous knowledge and material culture of tribal by others the former may be respectfully compensated. For this purpose suitable laws may be formulated.

3. Micro-finance model (especially SHGs) has the potential to improve the economic condition of the tribals. It has a capacity to empower the tribal community. This technique should be carefully popularized among them. Along with this they should be trained to manage their income in a meaningful manner.
4. Efforts related to improvement in the tribal economy should be based on the identification of local resources and planning. Local resources may be made fruitful and accordingly strategies may be suggested. These strategies must be ecology specific.
5. Economic development can be attained by distribution of power, provision of management skills and job opportunities.
6. While framing the policy for tribes, there should be uniform policy for their needs and a specific policy to conserve the cultural identity. Formulation of national policy of preservation of tribal identity was also suggested by some of the participants.
7. Globalization process cannot be reversed but safeguards should be made to preserve tribal interest and identity while prescribing interface between the two in the tribal world. For sustainable development perspective, besides an uniform national policy for all citizens for ensuring their survival, welfare and development needs supplemented with positive discrimination, there should be a separate policy for tribes for preservation of all distinct socio-cultural identities against impact of globalization and its consequential influences through mainstream lifestyles.
8. In spite of now decades-old history of reservation in employment, promotion and admission, its benefits have been availed by only few tribals. Why tribal masses are failed to avail its benefits? Necessary effort needs to be taken to trace and deal with these challenges.
9. In terms of access, utilization and equity of education the tribal India lags far behind the other communities. Factors responsible for this state of affair needs to be identified and analysed. There is need to universalise quality primary education among tribes because we are in the stage which is totally knowledge based. Without having proper knowledge, tribals cannot avail benefits of knowledge-based opportunities. For this purpose, the concept of residential schools may be popularized in the tribal areas.

10. Rehabilitation process should take into account the livelihood aspect, their culture and their sudden exposure to outside culture. No gap should exist between promises and performances while launching resettlement or rehabilitation schemes. In other words, globalization led process of development and its implications in the form of displacement in the tribal areas across the country should be addressed properly. If rehabilitation schemes are implemented honestly, tribal masses will become the direct or indirect supporters of globalization process, otherwise gap between rich and poor will further increase which may lead to protest movements and delay of development projects for many more years as it has happened with Sardar Sarovar Project in Madhya Pradesh and Gujarat. Attempts should also be made to reduce environmental/ecological cost of mega development projects especially in the tribal areas.
11. Protective legislations like PESA, poverty alleviation programmes and development programmes should be effectively implemented. For this purpose awareness programme may be launched among tribal masses on regular basis. Gram Panchayats may be trained and empowered to launch such schemes.
12. Strategies to be adopted to reduce poverty and increase livelihood generation work through forest resources and its protective and proper marketing.
13. Today, because of outmigration large number of tribes are living in the non-tribal areas. They are associated with non-agricultural activities. Their problems and challenges needs to be documented and accordingly effective strategies may be prescribed to deal with these challenges.
14. Tribal economy is traditionally agriculture and forest based. For that protective laws should be made effective and improved and advanced technology should be introduced. However, attempt shall be made to ensure benefit of modern technology to all sections of tribes otherwise only rich tribals will avail benefits of modern technology.
15. Livelihood issues of denotified tribes should be addressed. There is a need to frame plans according to the regional/geographical needs of the primitive tribes. There is need to investigate the question that why in spite of huge investment primitive tribes are incapable to come out of the trap of primitiveness? The structure, functions and implications of schemes meant for the development of primitive tribes needs to be thoroughly investigated.

16. Land alienation is another problem which tribals are facing due to their deficit economy. Land and forest on which tribal economy is based should not be affected while promoting mega development projects in the tribal world. As per the existing rule land owned by tribals may be purchased by tribals only. In one way this provision is harmful to poor tribals. Knowing limited alternatives the rich tribals purchase land of poor tribals at cheap rate otherwise the latter might have received higher price in the open market. This state of affair needs to be debated thoroughly.
17. Social capital formation is a pre-condition for tribal development. This is possible provided tribal masses are made members of political parties, NGOs, cultural bodies, watershed projects and so on. This effort will increase level of social networking among them which in turn will capacitate them to enhance their economic status.
18. Their dependence on agriculture and agriculture related wage work needs to be reduced. They should be associated with at least secondary occupations, if not the tertiary occupations at this stage. For this purpose training and orientation programme on constant basis may be organized at the block level. At the local level they should be associated with value-added activities in a significant manner.

References

Chaudhary, S.N. (2002): Harsud: A Study of Social and Economic Life, (Mimeo), Bhopal: NHDC Office.

—. (2004): *Dalit and Tribal Leadership in Panchayat,* New Delhi: Concept.

—. (2010): Development or Deterioration: Situation in a Tribal Village, (Mimeo), Bhopal: Rajiv Gandhi Chair, Barkatullah University.

Luard, C.E. (1908): *Central India Gazetteer Series: Western States,* (Malwa), Vol. V, Bombay: British India Press.

Manohar, D. (2001): *Bagh Ke Bacche Hai Hum (We are the Children of the Tiger),* Hosangabad: Disha Samvad.

Srivastava, V.K. (2008): "Concept of 'Tribes' in the Draft National Policy", *Economic and Political Weekly,* December 13.

2

On Tribal Economy and Society

VINAY KUMAR SRIVASTAVA

I

In a seminar that the Department of Anthropology, Andhra University, Visakhapatnam (Andhra Pradesh) had organized (on 30 and 31 January 2009) on tribal development with special reference to the problems and involvement of women, one of the sessions was devoted to listening to the voices of the tribal women, some fifteen of them who had come from villages contiguous with Visakhapatnam, two of them with their breast-feeding children. This certainly was not the first time that I saw tribespersons attending anthropology seminars, the focus of which was tribal problem and its solution, but certainly the practice of inviting the subjects of one's study to listen to the varied deliberations on them is quite uncommon in academic circles.[1]

Not all the tribal women, who had come to attend the seminar, spoke. Six of them came to the dais, but only three addressed the well-attended gathering, one of them with exemplary eloquence.[2]

The first submission of these women was that their land (the 'tribal land'), which has since been alienated, should be returned to them. They also noted a rise in the cases of marriage between tribal women and non-tribal men, as a result of which the land that the woman gets from her parents, either as a part of inheritance or gift, or is able to buy from a co-tribal, is appropriated by her husband. In this way, land slips out of tribal control.[3] Being simple and gullible, tribal women were unable to sense the nefarious ulterior motives of their non-tribal husbands. The women categorically stated that irrespective of the circumstances of acquiring the land and the cordial relations a tribal woman might have with her husband, tribal land should never be transferred to non-tribal persons. They strongly argued in favour of women getting an equal share of their family (or father's) property, but they should always be wary of non-tribespersons, even when they happened to be their spouses.[4] A woman must keep the land under her legal control, since with this she would be able to raise her children, in the event of her husband walking out of matrimony.

The women averred that their community was perennially faced with a shortfall of cash. They frequently faced contingent as well as other situations (such as illness in family, children's education, buying agricultural equipment) for which they required instant cash.[5] Since support for these did not come from the government, they perforce had to depend upon local moneylenders, who exploited them no end, charging exorbitant interest and mortgaging their land, jewellery, and house. In many cases, these were not returned, as tribal debtors were unable to pay off the loans with interest. Tribal economy was not surplus producing; people lived hand to mouth. Debts travelled from one generation to the next, which was one of the reasons of their bondage. Through the medium of the seminar, they urged upon the government agencies (banks, particularly) to be compassionate towards them and help them in times of exigency. Their entire life, they said clearly, was an existence of insecurity.

The functionaries in tribal areas were 'self-centred', solely interested in 'devouring the grants' that came from the government. Their proclivity towards corrupt measures of amassing wealth remained the same irrespective of the social category (tribe or caste) to which they belonged. Tribal elite was as 'money-minded' as were the 'others'. Rich tribesmen exploited their poor counterparts. Knowingly, the rich tribal people often distanced themselves from their 'humble and poor brothers and sisters', whom they looked down upon.

Police came to the aid of tribes if they had received 'gifts and bribe'. Whenever tribespersons went to police station to report a matter, the answer they usually received was that they should approach their own institutions (such as the traditional council (*panchayat*) for intervention rather than approaching the police. They were advised to solve the problem at their own local level. And, if it were a case of sexual exploitation, the patent answer was that they should not bother much about it since "it was the culture of tribes". What the authorities meant in this case was that since tribes were reputed to be lax about sexual mores, they should disregard (or take lightly) the instances of sexual harassment and immorality. The women unambiguously drew attention to the stereotypes that the outsiders – particularly government officials – nurtured about them.

II

My intention of succinctly describing what these tribal women shared with anthropologists and other intellectuals is that for them economy, and not culture, was a major concern. The issue of livelihood was central. One may argue that what these women said would have been what their men would have said had they been given the same opportunity to speak before the seminarians; and therefore, there is no distinct feminine perspective. Or, perhaps the patriarchal structure is so dominating that women think that when they speak in its terms and idioms only then they would be intelligible. Men talk about economy, and in order to be meaningful (and respectful), women also aim to speak about it, although it is likely that they may have their own distinct agenda and perspective, the 'true feminine view', to which they would not give vent in a predominant male congregation that a university seminar is expected to be.

For me, the issue here is not of disaggregating the gendered dimension of consciousness, but to submit that the economic condition of tribal communities has worsened to such an extent that it has cut through the gender distinction. Surely, women will have their specific charter of needs; and so would men, but where their points of view meet are the areas of economy, the issues of their basic survival. Rarely would tribespersons talk about building museums to keep their cultural artifacts; and not so often would they insist on the preservation of their dialects. Their first priority would be a survival with dignity and optimality. Like all of us, they wish to be gainfully employed, have enough for survival; they want their children to have good health, go to school, do well in studies, get a job and handsome salary, and live well. In other words, they would like to be a part of the 'mainstream', like the others, the images of which they know very well, courtesy the media machinery. It is wrong to think that tribespersons would like to remain as they are, or would like to cling to their culture irrespective of some of its non-compatible practices. All people critically examine their cultural aspects and change (sometimes radically) those that they find out of place in contemporary world.

All of us want good life, a life of satisfaction and security. Tribes are no exception to this. Development is not greed – certainly, it does not imply an excess of resources or power. For people, it means a secure existence, in which they have at their disposal what they require for their basic existence and survival. Security that thus emerges is the source of happiness. In this respect, tribal people are like all of us. The predicaments and fortitudes of humanity bind all of us, whether we are placed in one social category or the other that we (or our governments) have constructed. The unity of human concerns underlies all development and welfare programmes.

An aspect that makes anthropology nervous is the issue of defining the term 'tribe'. Although important, I shall bypass it, for it does not engage me here. Following Bates (1994, 1995), I shall say that those communities for which the colonial anthropologists and the authors of various compendia used the word 'tribe' came to be later known as 'Scheduled Tribes' with the advent of the policy of protective discrimination.[6] The students of Indian society are well aware of the continuities between tribes and non-tribes. In many cases, it will be nearly impossible to tap a person and say, "you belong to a tribe, or you belong to a caste".[7] Equally well known are the cases of tribes transforming into caste. There are also the cases of castes taking over the tribal characteristics or the appellation of tribe. Tribes and castes co-exist in the same geographical space, each having its own ethno-history of origin and migration. The unbroken continuity between tribes and castes in India is different from the separation one finds between the 'indigenes' (or the 'autochthones', 'minorities', 'ethnics', 'aborigines') and the 'migrants' (mostly Caucasians) who had settled down over time, as is the case of the Americas, Australia, New Zealand, and Russia.[8]

In the past quarter of the century, anthropologists and the others interested in tribal studies in India, have laid a lot of emphasis on the issues of development, exploring the contours of the 'right kind of development' for tribes and the other analogous groups. One of the consequences of this focus is that the studies of tribal economic systems have become fewer in number. Ethnographic accounts of changing tribal economies are almost out of fashion. What a survey of literature on economic anthropology yields are sketchy accounts of the processes of production, distribution, and consumption among Indian tribes. On many areas of interest – such as the household budget, response of tribes to money and market economy, impact of technological innovation on tribal economies – recent authentic information is non-existent. The theme of the autonomy of the tribal economic system and its integration with the outside (i.e., 'non-tribal') world that was investigated in mid-twentieth century and the later decades is no more a sought after and preferred area of research.[9] Just because the detailed studies of changing economic systems do not exist in the proportion in which they should, it is unsurprising that we still carry the image of tribespersons as unmonetized, exterior to market and trade situations, having no or negligible economic considerations, and depending upon their kinspersons and neighbours for all things pertaining to their survival. The tribal economic reality is, however, far different, and needs to be studied as a separate academic specialization rather than under the general rubric of development studies.

In spite of the continuities and morphological similarities between tribes and castes, wherever tribes live, they are different from non-tribes in various social and economic features. For instance, the percentage of scheduled tribespersons living below poverty line in 2004–05 was 47.2 in rural and 39.9 in urban areas. The corresponding figures of Scheduled Castes population was 36.8 and 33.3 respectively; for the other backward classes, they were 26.7 and 31.4 respectively; and for the rest, 16.1 and 16.0 respectively.[10] Take another example, this time of literacy rate among Scheduled Tribes: from 8.53 per cent in 1961, it has increased to 47.10 per cent in 2001; for the total population, it has increased to 64.84 in 2001 from 28.30 in 1961.[11] 47.8 per cent villages of Scheduled Tribes are not electrified; the corresponding percentage of Scheduled Caste villages is 21.4.[12]

If tribes have rolled down in these indices, in sex ratio, they are better than the overall population (933 females per 1,000 males); in 2001, they had 977 women per 1,000 men, and some of them have more women than men (like the Ho of Bihar and Jharkhand, who have 1,026 females per 1,000 males, according to Census 1981).[13] However, the studies also point out that as the interaction of tribal communities with the wider world is increasing, the patrilineal values are also finding a place among them, resulting in meting out discourteous and oppressive treatment to girls and women, thus eventually skewing the sex ratio.[14] Bride wealth, which is presumed to indicate women's high status, is found among 535 tribal communities in *People of India* project (Singh, 1994: 8).[15]

In other words, whether we take the positive or the negative indices, there is no doubt that tribes are different from the non-tribes. In terms of the index of deprivation, they are at the lower rung, at places almost overlapping with lower castes. Even those tribal communities that have the reputation of being assimilated with caste Hindu people and are placed considerably higher in local social hierarchy, such as the Mina of Rajasthan who equate themselves with the Rajput, Jat, Thakur, Mahajan, and Gujar of the area, are lower in economic terms in comparison to the communities with whom they claim equality.

III

A short visit to ordinary tribal settlements or a cursory glance at them will sadden anyone with the episodes of rampant poverty. The usual sight is of dilapidated houses, emaciated people with sunken faces, becoming grizzled in young age, draped in rags and soiled clothes, bony children toiling for livelihood, sometimes in highly perilous jobs, when in fact they should have been in schools, looking for a safe, bright, and secure future, sick remaining untreated, people just squatting, waiting for some job, howsoever small, to come through, taking up any task, illegal or life-threatening, to meet two square meal. Unemployment, hunger, deprivation, illness, and stagnation loom large. The stories of exploitation one hears in tribal villages, or of terror unleashed on them, are painfully unforgettable for years. Surely, this is not the description of tribal elite or the rich people among them, but in any case they constitute a minuscule of population. The vast majority of tribespersons is in want, poor, needy, and necessitous.

The second half of the twentieth century is a witness to several qualitative and quantitative accounts that have meticulously recorded and analyzed the miseries of tribesmen. Tribal areas have been fully explored for natural resources and biodiversity. The resource richness of tribal territories has attracted the powerful outsiders, who came with the sole intention of siphoning off the local wealth, which had scant meaning for the dwellers of that area. In this context, Sahlins' (1968: 367) following observation is relevant: "... to a hunting-and-gathering people, to Australian aborigines, say, coal is completely irrelevant: in the ground or no, it is not part of their environment; it has no selective impact on them", unless an Australian mine project found them to be 'squatting' on one of the biggest deposits of bauxite loads. And, the outcome of this was predictable: more and more outsiders came to 'search' for the resources that the aboriginal areas had, which could be useful for the 'civilized' man. Tribal world all over has witnessed its flooding by greedy and rapacious outsiders; the genesis of tribal problem lies in asymmetrical cultural contacts.

In his lecture on the future of anthropology (of 1959–60), Lévi-Strauss (1987) noted a dwindling of the 'primitive peoples' over time. Building of nuclear plants, experimental rocket ranges, and mining operations have decimated them dangerously. Their life-support systems were acutely paralysed. These changes were so ponderous that they left an inerasable imprint on their psyche.[16] Threatened by famines and ceaseless demoralization, Lévi-Strauss estimated that between 1900 and 1950, nearly ninety tribal groups had disappeared in Brazil. Against this background, he said, the concept of *indigène* (indigenous, native) was giving place to that of *indigent* (poor, needy, destitute). The former was presented romantically, depicting the bounteous beauty and charming aesthetics of the tribespersons; the latter was its opposite. It was an account of how the tribes were losing control over their habitat, its resources, and in their own land, which they colonized decades ago and where they were lords, they were becoming serfs, to be dehumanized, displaced, and driven out to lands unknown.

The state of indigence was an outcome of the asymmetrical contact situation the indigenous and local communities had with the outsiders. Initially, these contacts were infrequent and less impetuous. Local cultures were able to withstand any shock that came in the wake of these contacts, and continued to live the way they did, carefree and happy. Thus, when anthropologists conducted studies on these communities in the first half of the nineteenth century, they did not find among them those traits that characterized the western-industrial economies.

In his famous works on economic history, Karl Polanyi identified two meanings of economy, respectively called 'formal' and 'substantive', one that rested on the principle of the 'maximization of profit' and the other, on the 'fulfilment of one's needs'. The first was based on the 'laws of mind', of reason and rationality; the second, on the 'laws of nature', that is, 'if human beings have to live, they have to eat', and what they eat comes from their processing of the habitat around them. It was the second meaning of economy that was of relevance in tribal societies, which were neither profit-oriented nor believed in individualistic hoarding. Against this backdrop can be understood a number of ethnographies on tribal economy, in which people were described as free, having no surplus motives, and subscribing to the idea that nature has plenty in her womb and they would use only that bit of it which they need for their survival.[17]

In such systems, social relations were of primary importance; so was social esteem. If a Trobriander gardener produced much more than what he could possibly consume, it was not for maximizing his economic profit, for this concept did not exist in his society. It was to compete for the title of the 'best gardener', one that brought him prestige and esteem, which his king conferred upon the person who had produced the maximum.[18] Malinowski (1922) substantiated many ideas with the case of the Trobrianders, but one of them was that the 'primitive man', like the modern, was equally interested in his well-being, increasing his life-chances of survival, and gaining a high status. So, he would make every effort to promote his interests, although they are overwhelmingly social, and not economic. In his discussion of the Kula, Malinowski described the efforts and strategies (of wooing) that Trobriand men made to acquire the best gift from their partners, since it would raise their prestige among their community people. That is the reason why Malinowski is regarded as one of the first transactional theorists.[19]

A reading of the ethnographies on 'primitive societies' brings home the point that among them economy did not exist in the form it did in modern-industrial societies. Against this backdrop, some anthropologists proposed that instead of using the terms 'economic organization' or 'economic institution' for simple, pre-literate societies, since it would imply a state of differentiation, we should use the phrase 'the economic context of social behaviour'. These societies did not have 'economic men'; they had 'social men', who wished to ceaselessly multiply their 'social gains' (reputation, veneration, esteem, prestige, networks, respect). An understanding of this reality of 'primitive societies' – the social embedding of economy – was the salient contribution of economic anthropology. But, certainly it did not imply a state of utopia, people free from the pangs of scarcity and hunger, which in fact resulted not because of an inequitable distribution of resources or from a state of 'unfreedom', but because of natural calamities, technological inefficacy, low productivity, instances of war and raiding.[20] If they recurrently faced severe famines, they resorted to a lot of sharing of food among them (Evans-Pritchard, 1940) or learnt to live with scarcity and poverty (or developed what Oscar Lewis (1966) called the 'culture of poverty'). Well known are the practices and rituals by which the chiefs or kings of tribal communities distributed among the commoners the tributes (such as the material things or items of food) they had received by virtue of their position. Not only did the occupants of political offices and the other 'big men', but also those men who produced much more than the others were expected to generously feast their kith and kin and give them gifts, or contribute a larger share to the village granary, if they had one. Against this backdrop, we can understand the significance of the feasts of merit of the Nagas, or the pig-slaughter ceremonies of the Melanesians. The practices or rituals of what Polanyi called redistribution levelled the society and restricted the emergence of class distinctions.

IV

The observers have noted that hunting and food-gathering societies have less personal effects, only those that are essential for their survival. As said previously, they collect only that much food which they need for a couple of days. Although they claim to be the first settlers of the land, they are always prepared to dismantle their houses and move to another location, if need be.

Anthropologists have never interpreted this style of living as one of poverty. Having fewer personal belongings and living least ostentatiously does not imply living like poor people. Tribespersons were not poor; they were different. Living the way they did was their culture. Initially, it was thought that hunters, foragers, horticulturists, and shifting cultivators had fewer things with them because they were constantly on move, and obviously, they could not have accumulated much, for this would have greatly thwarted their perennial physical mobility. Later, when these people started settling down, they continued with a non-hoarding practice; their accumulativeness did not increase thereafter, guiding us to the conclusion that living a life of frugality is a cultural value among them, which will continue till the time they want its continuation. Because of the way they lived, with fewer things and exemplary parsimoniousness, they were, in some cases, believed to be leading a life of austerity and asceticism.[21]

Tribes were free to choose the way they liked. They were also free to alter it. This freedom illuminated their faces, endowed them with health, gave confidence in their cultural practices and lifestyles, and made them appear before the outsiders as proud inhabitants of their land. The happiness, joyfulness, pride, and satisfaction of tribes is well captured in the ethnographies produced during the first half of the twentieth century. The attitude of anthropologists towards tribal communities had also changed, even when they were working for the colonial government. This attitude was of a 'humble learner' of tribal communities, to learn from their differences and ways of living, and look at the western life critically against the background of the values of tribal living.

With the entry of the powerful outsiders in tribal areas, the freedom of people came to be curtailed. Although Malinowski (1922) did not pay much attention to the implications of the presence of white people in Omarakana, the Trobriand village where he had pitched his tent, he did notice that with the advent of missionaries, the Trobriand institution of youth dormitory (*bakumatula*) was being greatly undermined. Trobrianders preferred to conceal its presence among them, since they thought that the mission people would not like it and lecture them to stop sending their children to dormitories. We have umpteen examples in anthropological literature where people lost freedom to live according to their culture, which gave them meaning of life, with the coming of the outsiders in their areas. The Ho institution of marriage by elopement was interpreted as 'abduction', a legal offence according to colonial masters (Majumdar, 1944). Similarly, the Baiga man, who kept long hair, tying them as a bun on the occiput, was instructed to cut his hair, so that he looked like a 'civilized man' (Srivastava, 1991). Bride price was seen as 'buying a woman'. And, well known is the ban the colonial administration imposed on shifting cultivation, for it thought it was the practice in which 'wild men' engaged. A shift to plough cultivation also meant a civilizing mission (Vidyarthi and Rai, 1976). The cultural context in which these institutions needed to be understood was grossly ignored.

As the colonial rule expanded, it brought in its wake a large number of outsiders, who tacitly enjoyed the patronage of the rule.

They exploited the people, ousted them from their land and other resources. Since the people were unaware of the bureaucratic rules and procedures, they did not know how to get rid of the exploiters and how to get the land legally registered in their names. Alienation of land continued unabated, first to the outsiders, and second to the state.

This process continues till date; the state is the biggest alienator of tribal land, followed by the private entrepreneurs who are building housing colonies and office complexes on tribal land.[22] When a factory comes up in tribal area, the local people are forced to work for it, and if they do not, they are subjected to various ordeals. Tribal habitat is subjected to despoliation; the people have no option but to sit and watch, unless they start their own movement or some non-governmental organizations (NGOs) takes up their cause. Poor resource base that has resulted from untrammeled exploitation, negligible capacity to borrow money to start a new venture, no skills that the emerging market needs, have led people to migrate to towns and cities, where they lead a life of extreme destitution, in which breed vagabondism, deviance and crime, and the other types of wastefulness. The story of tribes all over the world is the story of deprivation of freedom and utter powerlessness.

Unsurprisingly, it has made anthropologists voice the concerns of tribes, their problems, and suggest viable solutions. Since the beginning of tribal studies, anthropologists have time and again argued that their contribution will be enfeebled by self-silencing. They should expose the structures of exploitation of local people, trying to save them from all sorts of nefarious elements. Against this light, if one reads the idea of creating a 'national park' as a temporary solution to the problems of the Baigas, one finds that it was borne out of Elwin's (1939) profound concern for tribal communities.[23]

Notwithstanding the theoretical position, anthropologists have always been sensitive to tribal problems and have committed themselves to finding a solution to them. That is the reason why anthropologists need to be engaged as activists, aid workers, policy advisors, and consultants. This however does not imply a compromise with the basic task of anthropology, which is reaching an objective and analytical understanding of social situations. Anthropologists have always been arguing in favour of an approach of partnership and participation, in which the tribes (and other down-trodden communities) have the freedom to choose the line and the programme of development they want, the way in which they would manage their natural resources; have the freedom to choose the leaders who would govern them in a participatory way; and have the freedom to protest against unjust systems and uninformed decisions. I cannot do better than to remember Sen's (1999) famous statement: "Development can be seen as a process of expanding the real freedoms that people enjoy."

V

Today's economic anthropology is concerned with the changing tribal reality and the differentiation of the economic system. No more does it bask under the romanticism of the substantive approach; it also is skeptical of the fuller application of the formalist viewpoint. Tribal economies are no more unmonetized; no more are their markets of ceremonial importance; no more are they part of the domestic economy.

Tribes have become aware of the importance and power of money; they also know the ways in which they have been systematically deprived of control over their resources; they also know that their unity and leadership will help them fight inequality and unjust systems. Tribes are becoming more conscious of their identity – it is a process whereby a 'tribe *in* itself' is being transformed to a 'tribe *for* itself'. Not only are the tribes busy in creating a self-image, consolidating their culture, but also in many parts of India they have started their own movements and founded their own organizations to combat injustice. Some of these micro-movements, at the local level, are creating ripples, the effect of which cannot go unnoticed for long. For instance, the tribal villages of Surat district have a group of thirty women lawyers from different tribes who take up cases of exploitation against the members of their community.[24] In another case, in the district of Ranchi, daughters and granddaughters of women who were once branded as witches are coming forward to root out the evil.[25] And, there are several cases from the north-eastern part of India where women have started movements against the evils of alcohol consumption and drug addiction (Narang, 2007). The Raika-Rabari have also become conscious of the fact that their contemporary state of acute debt-bondage has resulted from the custom of marriage-cum-death feast, which incurs a lot of expenditure and they have no option but to borrow money from merchants operating in their area, who charge exorbitant interest from them for the loan taken. In order to save them from indebtedness, they have started a movement to make these feasts humbler (Srivastava, 2007).

Anthropologists have become sensitive to the gender perspective; so have they become to the problems of old people. More and more social gerontologists are now focusing on the tribal old. But what has remained largely ignored is the paediatric perspective; for instance, what happens to the children when displacement occurs, or when a disaster strikes a community? In fact, there may be some information available on people who were displaced and how they coped with the new habitat, but when it comes to the impact of development and displacement programmes on the future generation, we have very little information, since this generally has not been the focus of study. Some NGOs have compiled data on tribal children, but proper anthropological accounts have yet to be written.

One such report pointed out that after the Chenchu, a primitive tribe of Andhra Pradesh, were displaced as a consequence of the building of the 'first temple of modern India', the Nagarjunasagar dam, their children started working as bonded labourers in stone quarries and mines. Tribal children work in these quarries as apprentices from a very young age and receive exceedingly low wages. Some of these children are agricultural labourers, rickshaw-pullers, and flower-sellers. Minor Chenchu and Lambada girls work as cheap agriculture labour in chilli and tobacco farms, where they are exposed to harmful chemical pesticides. Children are most prone to sexual exploitation; there are cases of Lambada girls sold for trafficking. Local NGOs have found incidences of HIV/AIDS among the Yanadi girls living around the temple and tourist town of Srisailam. Juvenile crime, which was non-existent among tribes, is now an issue of concern. As a consequence of these factors, the children fall prey to ill health, alcoholism and other vices.[26]

Economic anthropology is a vibrant discipline, with the potentiality to contribute a great deal to the understanding of tribal problems, and at the same time, supplementing and correcting the economist's understanding. Economic facts are inseparable from the other social and cultural facts. The impact of culture on economy is now a fact not just restricted to anthropology and sociology, but also economics has started accepting it.[27] People's decisions about resource management and distribution of gain are all influenced by their culture. Instead of disappearing or merging with the 'global culture', homogeneous and monolithic, each community's culture is able to withstand the tides of universal processes. The 'new economic anthropology', to borrow from John Clammer (1978), is concerned both with the contemporary dynamics of economic processes, the processes of class formation and conflicts, and the unremitting effect of culture on economy.

Acknowledgement

[This paper was presented as a Keynote Address at a Seminar on Tribal Economy that the Rajiv Gandhi Chair in Contemporary Studies, Barkatullah University, Bhopal (Madhya Pradesh) had organized on 10 and 11 February 2009. I am grateful to Professor S.N. Chaudhary for giving me this honour, and to the Vice Chancellor, Barkatullah University, for presiding over the Keynote Address. Data collection for this paper was facilitated by the research grant that the University of Delhi gave me in 2008–09 under its R & D programme.]

Notes

1. I attended a seminar (in 2002) on the cultural and social aspects of AIDS in which some HIV-positive patients were invited, who also took part in the discussion. Before that (in 1993), I attended a seminar in Jodhpur on pastoral communities in which their leaders also participated. On both occasions, I noted that the academicians and the members of the non-governmental organizations (NGOs) who had come to attend the seminars were more eager to speak to the 'subjects of their study', for they did not wish to lose this opportunity of collecting information.
2. What they said in Telegu (or their respective dialects) was translated into English by Professor Vijay Prakash, an anthropologist, who was also coordinating this session.
3. Although legally, land cannot be acquired by a non-tribal person, he can always enjoy its benefits. Moreover, he can always exercise political and money power to keep the land in his control, although he may not be its owner. See Singh (1988) and Xaxa (2004). Singh (1988: 3) also noted that marriages between tribal women and non-tribal men were not stable. Xaxa (2004: 362) writes: 'Often after such transactions (of land), non-tribal men have deserted tribal women. This in itself is an emotive issue among tribes in view of the long struggle that they have waged against the alienation of tribal land.'

4. In fact, as pointed out by Professor J.M. Naidu, this woman was not aware of the legal position that in Andhra Pradesh, girls have an equal right in the family property. But the important point to be noted here is that these tribal women were drawing attention to the difference between the 'rules on paper' and the existing practices. Surely, tribal land cannot be legally taken over by the non-tribal, but in practice, the cases of alienation definitely occur.
5. In his classical study of Bisipara, Bailey (1957) noted that the people sold their land in order to meet the 'contingent expenses'. The land had already been fragmented among different brothers after the death of the head of the household. Since there were no avenues to generate cash, they had no option but to mortgage or sell their land. Land, which was not a marketable thing, became a commodity to be sold and acquired in the market.
6. See Articles 342 and 366 (25) of the Constitution of India. Over time, many communities have been added to this list.
7. See Béteille (1975) and Pathy (1984).
8. Of 635 tribes and sub-tribes that Singh's People of India project covered, 409 (64.3%) claimed to be migrants to their present habitat. Singh wrote (1994: 7): "In fact all our tribal people have been migrants. Their migration is recorded in oral history and historical accounts. About eight per cent of the tribes recall their migration in recent years."
9. That economic anthropology has not attracted the attention of a number of writers in India is clear from the fact that so far only two titles with the name of this subject exist (Rao, 2009). One is N.K. Behura's *Anthropological Economics*, and the other is R.K. Gupta's *Essays in Economic Anthropology*. Both these books were published by the Institute of Social Research and Applied Anthropology, Bidisa, Midnapur, West Bengal.
10. Annual Report, 2007–08, Ministry of Tribal Affairs, Government of India, pp. 32–33.
11. Ibid., p. 31.
12. Report of the Task Force on Development of Scheduled Castes and Scheduled Tribes, Planning Commission, Government of India, March 2005, p. 39.
13. See Singh (1994: 404) and Xaxa (2004: 363).
14. See Singh et al. (1988), Unnithan-Kumar (1997), Government of India (2000, 2001). Except in states like Andhra Pradesh, Tamil Nadu and Uttarakhand, the Scheduled Tribes' sex ratio (as per Census 2001) was better than the general sex ratio (Annual Report, 2007–08, Ministry of Tribal Affairs, Government of India, p. 30).
15. Singh (1994: 8) also noted that the transition from bride price to dowry was slow. Here, the generally accepted idea is that tribes are known for

practising the system of bride price (or, bride wealth), whilst castes have dowry.

16. For instance, from a Hopi Indian, Don Talayesva, six hundred dreams were collected. Their analysis pointed out that they revealed less about the individual peculiarities than about the disintegration of the subject's society (Lévi-Strauss, 1987: 18). It is well known that many of them lost the desire to live, thus suffering from what is known as 'thanatomania'.
17. See Polanyi (1968); also see Dalton's edited volume of 1968 of the writings of Karl Polanyi; Humphreys (1969).
18. This reminds one of the distinction that Firth (1967) made between 'market mentality' and 'economic advantage'. The tribal communities definitely had the latter, but they were not market-oriented.
19. See Lewis (2003) on this point.
20. See Richards (1932, 1939). Also see Vernon (2007).
21. See Gardner (1982). He used the word 'ascribed austerity' for this.
22. Sah and Sisodia (2004:19) write: "In contemporary India, the tribals continue to be pushed in order to acquire land – their land – for large development projects ... . The demand for their resources – land, forest and water – is still forcing them out of their habitat."
23. Elwin wrote in 1939 (p. 519): "The gloomy future (of the Baiga) could be averted by the creation of the National Park ..., or at least by the handing over to the Baiga part of the great tracts of forest that can never be exploited commercially." Elwin's letter to *Vanyajati* (2[2], 1949) was: "I am ... vehemently in favour of opening communications in tribal areas. But I think that such roads should be made in the interests of the tribals and not for the benefit of those who would exploit them from the plains." Also see Sachchidananda (2009).
24. See *The Times of India,* 15 March 2006; also see *The Times of India,* 24 November 1993; for the short life sketch of C.K. Janu, a tribal girl, the president of the Southern Zone Adivasi Forum; for the role of Kalinga Nagar tribals who vowed not to vacate land for industries, see *The Hindu,* 11 January 2006.
25. A twenty-nine years old girl named Poonam Toppo, whose grandmother was once tortured for being a witch, has taken up cudgels to fight the crime of branding innocent people as witches.
26. See a report prepared by Samata in July 2008, pp. 67–69.
27. Writing on teacher truancy, an economist, Kaushik Basu writes: 'Culture is at least worth a try'. Economists today are seriously considering the importance of the concept of culture in economic analyses. See his paper in Jayaram and Deshpande, eds. (2008).

References

Bates, Crispin (1994): "Lost Innocents and Loss of Innocence: Interpreting Adivasi Movements in South Asia", in R.H. Barnes, Andrew Gray and Benedict Kingsbury (eds.), *Indigenous Peoples of Asia,* Ann Arbor: University of Michigan Press.

—. (1995): "Race, Caste and Tribe in Central India", in Peter Robb (ed.), *The Concept of Race,* New Delhi: Oxford University Press.

Béteille, André (1974): *Six Essays in Comparative Sociology,* Delhi: Oxford University Press.

Clammer, John (1978): *New Economic Anthropology,* London: Macmillan.

Dalton, George (ed.) (1968): *Primitive, Archaic and Modern Economies: Essays of Karl Polanyi,* New York: Doubleday.

Elwin, Verrier (1939): *The Baiga,* Delhi: Gyan Publishing House (Reprint, 1986).

Evans-Pritchard, E.E. (1940): *The Nuer,* Oxford: Clarendon Press.

Firth, Raymond (ed.) (1967): *Themes in Economic Anthropology,* London: Routledge and Kegan Paul.

Gardner, P.M. (1982): "Ascribed Austerity: A Tribal Path to Purity", *Man* (n.s.), 17: 462–9.

Government of India (2000): Women in India (A Statistical Profile), New Delhi: Planning Commission.

—. (2001): Report of the Steering Committee on Empowering the Scheduled Tribes, New Delhi: Planning Commission.

—. (2005): Report of the Task Force on Development of Scheduled Castes and Scheduled Tribes, New Delhi: Planning Commission.

—. (2007–08): Annual Report, New Delhi: Ministry of Tribal Affairs.

Humphreys, S.C. (1969): "History, Economics and Anthropology: The Work of Karl Polanyi", *History and Theory,* 8(2): 165–212.

Jayaram, N. and R.S. Deshpande (eds.) (2008): *Footprints of Development and Change: Essays in Memory of Professor V.K.R.V. Rao,* New Delhi: Academic Foundation.

Lévi-Strauss, Claude (1987): *Anthropology and Myth, Lectures 1951–1982,* Oxford: Basil Blackwell.

Lewis, I.M. (2003): *Social and Cultural Anthropology in Perspective: The Relevance of Social Anthropology,* London: Transaction Publisher.

Lewis, Oscar (1966): "The Culture of Poverty", in George Gmelch and Walter Lenner (eds.), *Urban Life,* Illinois: Waveland Press.

Majumdar, D.N. (1944): *The Fortunes of Primitive Tribes,* Lucknow: Universal Publishers.

Malinowski, Bronislaw (1922): *Argonauts of the Western Pacific,* London: Routledge and Kegan Paul (Reprint, 1992).

Narang, Mala (2007): Continuity and Change in an Angami Naga Village, Unpublished Ph.D. Dissertation, Department of Anthropology, University of Delhi.

Pathy, J. (1984): *Tribal Peasantry: Dynamics of Development,* Delhi: Inter-India Publishers.

Polanyi, Karl (1968): "Anthropology and Economic Theory", in Morton H. Fried (ed.), *Readings in Anthropology (Vol. II – Cultural Anthropology),* New York: Thomas Y. Crowell Company, (pp. 215–38).

Rao, P. Venkata (2009): Economic Anthropology, Special Assistance Programme (SAP) (of the University Grants Commission) Lecture, Department of Anthropology, University of Delhi (20 January).

Richards, Audrey I. (1932): *Hunger and Work in a Savage Society,* London: Greenwood Press.

—. (1939): *Land, Labour and Diet in Northern Rhodesia,* London: Oxford University Press.

Sachchidananda (2009): "Verrier Elwin's Anthropology", in Sachchidananda and Vinay Kumar Srivastava (eds.), *Social Anthropology in Eastern India,* New Delhi: Serials Publications (pp. 244–61).

Sah, D.C. and Yatindra Singh Sisodia (2004): "Editors' Introduction", in D.C. Sah and Yatindra Singh Sisodia (eds.), *Tribal Issues in India,* Jaipur and New Delhi: Rawat Publications (pp. 15–36).

Sahlins, Marshall D. (1968): "Culture and Environment: The Study of Cultural Ecology", in Robert A. Manners and David Kaplan (eds.), *Theory in Anthropology: A Sourcebook,* London: Routledge and Kegan Paul (pp. 367–73).

Samata (2008): *A Study on the Status and Problems of Tribal Children in Andhra Pradesh,* Visakhapatnam: Samata.

Sen, Amartya (1999): *Development as Freedom,* Oxford: Oxford University Press.

Singh, J.P., N. Vyas and R.S. Mann (eds.) (1988): *Tribal Women and Development,* Jaipur: Rawat Publications.

Singh, K.S. (1988): "Tribal Women: An Anthropological Perspective", in J.P. Singh, N. Vyas and R.S. Mann (eds.), *Tribal Women and Development,* Jaipur: Rawat Publications (pp. 3–10).

—. (1994): *The Scheduled Tribes* (National Series Vol. III), Calcutta: Anthropological Survey of India and Delhi: Oxford University Press.

Srivastava, Vinay Kumar (1991): "The Ethnographer and the People: Reflections on Field Work", *Economic and Political Weekly,* XXVI (22 and 23): 1408–11, 1413–4 and XXVI (24): 1475–81.

—. (2007): "Cultural Tradition and Child Marriage in India", *The Eastern Anthropologist,* 60(1): 45–68.

Unnithan-Kumar, Maya (1997): *Identity, Gender and Poverty: New Perspectives on Caste and Tribe in Rajasthan,* Oxford: Berghahn Books.

Vernon, James (2007): *Hunger: A Modern History,* Michigan: Harvard University Press.

Vidyarthi, L.P. and Binay Kumar Rai (1976): *The Tribal Culture of India,* New Delhi: Concept Publishing House.

Xaxa, Virginius (2004): "Women and Gender in the Study of Tribes in India", *Indian Journal of Gender Studies,* 11(3): 345–67.

3

Anthropology in the 21st Century

Need for Re-orientation and Fresh Perspectives

YOGESH ATAL

Preliminaries

I am grateful to the Barkatullah University for kindly inviting me to deliver the prestigious Rajiv Gandhi Memorial Lecture on a theme connected with the problems and concerns of tribal India. On two previous occasions I have spoken at this venue on this general theme, one focusing on the current concern for the preservation of indigenous knowledge, and the other on the issues relative to tribal development. As one who had spoken twice on the common theme, and under the same auspices, I feel diffident to make any different contribution other than reinforcing my stand. I am afraid the burden of my song is going to sound familiar. But as in a song, the more the line is repeated the better is its receptivity and the greater is the possibility of its being hummed by others. Let me hope that the fate of my recital would be no different and that I might enlist some from among you to sing the key line of the song in other settings so that the message reaches long distances and taken somewhat seriously.

Recently I was invited by the Department of Anthropology at Delhi University to address the participants of a national symposium on Rethinking New Paradigms in Anthropology. The theme chosen for that symposium is recognition of the need to revisit our theories and perspective with a view to assessing their relevance in the changing contexts. I am personally of the view that many of the old theories, and several of their attendant concepts, are gradually losing their utility. Their proclaimed universality is being challenged by the emerging structures and patterns. Such a situation demands not only more refined conceptual frameworks but also better informed perspectives to make meaningful analyses and offer do-able prescriptions to the policy makers and planners.

Tribes have bestowed to the discipline of anthropology its defining identity. It is, therefore, quite in order that we pay special attention to this segment of our society, and in doing so take steps to develop a proper framework rather than remain content with persisting stereotypes and join hands with the well-meaning but ill-informed philanthropists who see all wrong in the processes of change. Approaching the tribal societies as outsiders and behaving as their saviours we can only be the missionaries of charity, and advocates for the maintenance of status quo, rather than facilitators of the much needed change in the life-ways of the so-called backward brethren.

A concrete realization of this need for a fresh perspective came to me when I was invited by the Government of Rajasthan in the year 2007 to serve on the high-powered committee – known as the Chopra Committee – to examine the demand of the Rajasthan Gujars for inclusion in the category of Scheduled Tribes (STs). The key question was the very definition of the word 'tribe'. In our final report submitted to the Government of Rajasthan, we had strongly recommended that it should ask the central government to initiate a national debate not only on the issue of reservations but also on the definition of the concept of tribe. Unfortunately, the politics of ball game is throwing our report from one court to another in governmental quarters, and no heed is paid to the genuine concern expressed therein. Only a few days back, Colonel Kirori Singh Baisla has given signals of raising the issue once again, and of continuing the agitation until the demand is met. The solution to this crisis is not easy, and there is an urgency to attend to it which one finds missing in the decision-making circles. But more worrying is the point that social scientists, particularly those who have committed themselves to the study of the tribes, have also not woken up to this challenge. The Rajiv Gandhi Chair at this university should take up this task on a priority basis. Mine is a clarion call for this.

I take this opportunity to elaborate my deep concern over the issue of the definition of tribe. And in doing so, I shall like to take you to a brief sojourn in the past of the discipline of anthropology so that you can appreciate the urgent need for a rethink of the paradigm. I suspect that most of the speakers at this seminar might have not felt the need for such an exercise and, in their enthusiasm for the so-called 'poor' and 'backward brethren', come up with easily acceptable recipes and prescriptions in the old mode of thinking. Hopefully, my presentation would shake up this complacence. And I invite you to be merciless on my views.

I

The birth of anthropology in the second-half of the nineteenth century was in a way necessitated by colonialism and its growth was facilitated by Industrial Revolution. Described as general anthropology, it included physical anthropology, prehistoric anthropology, and social or cultural anthropology with due accommodation in it of philosophical and psychological anthropology. As Max Gluckman and Fred Eggan admitted in their 'Introduction' to the four-volume ASA monographs[1], "... by the 1930s the different disciplines were beginning to separate from one another ... (And as) each anthropological discipline separated out, its practitioners turned to other subjects ... Physical anthropologists depended more on the biological sciences; psychological anthropologists ... on psychology ... and psychiatry; and social anthropologists on sociology, history, political science, law and economics. Cultural anthropologists alone continued to draw on the biological, psychological, and sociological sciences" (1966: xi).

"Outwardly the common mark of social, cultural, and psychological anthropology was that they all continued to be comparative and cross-cultural in outlook, with an emphasis on the small-scale tribal societies of the world, and for many years the study of such a society was virtually the initiation ceremony which admitted a scholar into the ranks of anthropology" (ibid).

When my generation entered the university to specialize in anthropology in India, the orientation of general anthropology continued in the sense that we had to offer papers in prehistory, archeology, and physical anthropology; we also learnt serology, anthropometry, dermatoglyphics, and even photography. It was not only Hooton's *Up from the Ape* but also Grey's magnum opus, *Anatomy,* was a compulsory reading. While the focus on the tribes continued, a change took place in terms of fieldwork. We were directed to conduct fieldwork in the villages – rural India had entered into our curricula. But for the outsiders, anthropology was the synonym of the study of tribes. The senior batch in our department was taken by the then Professor of Anthropogeography to Bastar to be in the midst of tribals and conduct fieldwork – both groups those specializing in anthropology and in geography had such an exposure. By the time we arrived, four major books on rural India, all authored by anthropologists, had been published. The year of 1955 saw Dube's *Indian Village*, Majumdar edited *Rural Profiles*, Srinivas edited *India's Villages*, and McKim Marriott edited *Village India*. Indian anthropology was extending its scope to include village studies, employing 'holistic' approach and presenting the findings in the style of an ethnography.

Specializations did exist in the departments, and laboratories for anthropological research became part of the infrastructure. But as we grew in the profession, separation between physical and social anthropology began occurring on a large-scale. Those of us specializing in social anthropology were naturally getting exposed to other social sciences, especially sociology; our work on Village India brought us closer to rural sociologists, and caught the attention of the policy makers and planners who were engaged in the massive programme of community development.

At that time, the so-called puritans in anthropology treated us as 'defectors', and the puritans in sociology regarded us as 'intruders'. Social anthropologists did not, however, use any derogatory term for the physical anthropologists who were going down from Humans to Lemurs and Langoors, or moving closer to biological sciences; and I am not sure whether they were regarded as 'intruders' in those disciplines. The decades of 1960s and 1970s were characterized by discussions and debates on such separation and defections. It was heartening for us that some of the prominent social anthropologists were held as sociologists of international renown.

As I see the professional demography of the departments of anthropology today in India, I come to the rather dismal conclusion that the separation has led to a relative neglect of social anthropology. Recently, when I was invited by the Vice Chancellor of a prestigious university to address the staff and students of anthropology department the physical anthropology staff boycotted the event. There are also departments in other universities where social anthropology is taught by outsiders hired on a lecture-to-lecture basis. A discipline that grew out of an interdisciplinary coalition of ideas, and got the distinction of being specialist on tribal studies is now caged in its own web. Its greater affinity to biological sciences is distancing it from the study of those societies that were uniquely their domain.

I say this not to undermine the new signposts in the long journey of this discipline. Social anthropology has moved from the study of small and simple societies to the study of complex societies and civilizations. It is contributing its bit to the newly developing management sciences. What is worrying is that in the process it has virtually given up its old concern, namely the focus on the tribes.

Of course, such a shift is not all attributable to the increasing dominance of physical anthropology. The changes that are occurring in the tribal societies and the new challenges for application of anthropology to other areas of social interaction are equally responsible for such a shift.

II

As anthropology began its journey it came to be defined as the study of the 'past' and the 'primitive'. Evolutionary theories of the nineteenth century raised questions about the origin of man, and the voyages to distant lands facilitated by the Industrial Revolution of the times exposed the scholars to a variety of flora and fauna. The early encounters with the simple people, living exotic cultures, intrigued the scholars. Comparing them with their own culture they regarded them as 'primitive' and placed them at the lower rungs of the evolutionary ladder. The 'present' of these 'primitive' societies was regarded as some stage of their own 'past'. George Peter Murdock called them *Our Primitive Contemporaries.* Such a conceptualization gave strength to the colonial regimes to justify their rule by using the twin criteria offered by Darwin, namely, *Survival of the Fittest* and *Struggle for Existence.* Apart from such justification, the colonialists also wanted to understand their 'culture' – in the anthropological sense of 'way of life' – to be able to better administer them; and thus anthropology came to be defined as the study of 'other cultures'. At that time, ethnographies paid more attention to description, and less to theorizing. Ethnology, on the other hand, adopted the path of comparison and classification; in doing so, both the ethnographers and the ethnologists almost took the definition of the tribe for granted and refined constituent concepts related to family, kinship, religion and magic, etc.

With the end of colonial era and growing globalization and information revolution a new orientation for anthropology is now in order. The focus is shifting from the past to the present and to the future; and the processes of westernization, modernization, and now of globalization have brought in remarkable changes in the profiles of all cultures – primitive or modern. Ethnographies written in the idiom of 'eternal present' have become dated, and the tribal societies that were the subject matter of anthropology demand a new diction and a new grammar for their reportage. There is a demand for a definition of society that is universally applicable to all societies be they modern or primitive, living or dead. And in that definition, the definition of the prefix 'tribal' is being sought.

This is what I call re-invitation to anthropology. It is a call to revisit its original interest and contribute to the understanding of the change occurring in them. We must remember that whatever might be the private – that is internal to the discipline – image of ours, the public image of anthropology still remains the same, namely, the specialized study of the tribes.

The need to return to tribes was felt in Indian anthropology even in the 1970s. As Director of the Indian Council of Social Science Research (ICSSR), I convened a group to identify priorities for research in the field of anthropology. The group expressed its concern over the diminishing interest in the study of tribes, and also underlined the need for restudies as old ethnographies did not match the emerging profiles of several tribal cultures in India.

But not much was added in the subsequent years to our literature on the tribes from an anthropological perspective, although scholars belonging to other social science disciplines also began taking interest in them, thus breaking the monopoly of anthropology.

III

Why the need to return to the tribes? This is a legitimate question. Let me answer that question briefly in the Indian context.

India's policy of reservations and the special provisions that exist for the tribes and the oppressed castes has caused a number of demands from various communities for inclusion in one of the two lists. How does one determine whether a particular group qualifies to be designated as a tribe?

The most recent instance of such a demand is that of the Gujars of Rajasthan seeking the status of an ST. The demand was first raised in 1961, but it took a violent turn twenty years later, in 1981, and led to massive campaigns and huge rallies in the first decade of this century with horrifying incidents of violent clashes and death of agitators and policemen in the confrontations. While Gujars demanded a tribal status, those already included in the tribal category, strongly opposed this move. Others in the general public remained either neutral or joined one of the two camps.

The key question that is behind such agitations is the very definition of the word *Tribe* and its distinction from *caste*. It was natural that people looked towards anthropology for an authoritative response. Sadly enough, the discipline had no firm answer to provide. It is intriguing that in all the Commissions and Committees set-up by the Government of India from Kaka Kalelkar in 1950s to B.P. Mandal in 1980s no anthropologist or sociologist was ever appointed as a full member. The Mandal Commission did take assistance of Professor M.N. Srinivas but it was only for designing a questionnaire which, incidentally, had a poor response rate. The consequences of the Mandal Report are there in front of us. People challenging these reports signified their dissent on the definition on the one hand, and registered their protest against the policy of reservation, on the other.

The Constitution of Indian Republic recognizes the existence of tribes and has a schedule listing them for special treatment to facilitate their entry into the mainstream and enjoy the fruits of development. While taking this step, hailed by all as a well-intentioned policy, little attention was paid to the definition of the word 'tribe'. Perhaps the need was not felt as tribes were listed in the censuses since 1891. The 1931 Census – regarded as the last census that had enumerated population by caste – has listed 'Primitive Tribes', the list of 1935 talks of 'Backward Tribes'. Lifting these entries the Government of India prepared the schedule in accordance with the new Constitution, and included all without any exception thus erasing a distinction between a tribe and a Scheduled Tribe. Accordingly, the 1951 Census counted 212 tribes, constituting around 6 per cent of the Indian population. Over the years, this number has burgeoned to more than 700, although the percentage of population covered by ST category is around 8, not much different from the 1951 figure, taking cognizance of the fact of population growth. This increase in number of tribal communities, I must mention, is mainly caused by statewise recognition of the tribal groups – in other words, sub-groups of tribals have been given separate region-based identities with the result that a group that is considered a tribe in one state might have been denied that status in another. These anomalies were hinted by the Dheber Commission way back in 1961. For example: "The old state of Hyderabad (Nizam) did not recognize the Yenadis, Yerukulas, and Sugalis as Scheduled Tribes, whereas the old Andhra state recognized them as such and with abundant justification. Similar is the case of the Gaddis who are found in Himachal Pradesh and the adjoining Punjab Hills. In the Punjab, they are treated as Scheduled Tribes only in the Scheduled Areas where they do not live".

Examining the candidature of fresh applicants for the tribal status, the Lokur Committee, set up in 1965, firmly stated that: "... care was necessary in drawing up the Schedule in order to ensure that communities which had been assimilated in the general population were not at this stage invested with an artificial distinctiveness as tribes, and that communities which might be regarded as tribes by reason of their social organization and general way of life but which were really not primitive should not now be treated as primitive". The Lokur Committee categorically stated (p. 7) that "... in 1931 and 1935, as well as in 1950 and 1956, it was acknowledged that every tribe need not be regarded as requiring special treatment ...". It further said: "... we have considered that tribes whose members have by and large mixed up with the general population are not eligible to be in the list of Scheduled Tribes". They had dismissed the claim of the Gujars for a tribal status in the states of Himachal Pradesh and Jammu & Kashmir. The Lokur Committee also made it clear that Scheduled Tribes are not synonymous of tribes, as the ST category includes only those that are deserving of special treatment.

However, for some unknown reasons, such status was accorded to the Muslim Gujars in both the states, namely Himachal Pradesh and Jammu & Kashmir. Using the example of the two states, as also comparing their lifestyle with the Minas of Rajasthan, the Gujars of that state put forth their claim once again in the 1990s. Heeding to the demand of the agitating group, the Government of Rajasthan set-up a high-powered committee consisting of a retired Judge, an IAS of senior rank, and a social scientist. Thus, for the first time in the history of independent India, a social scientist was made a full-member to examine the case of a single community in the context of a single state, and full six months were given to the Committee to submit its report. Surprisingly for me, the onus fell on me to serve on the Committee as an expert social scientist. I should emphasize the point that the assignment came to me without any political connection or party affiliation. The fact that I come from Rajasthan and that I had studied a multi-caste village in Mewar that had Gujars as the numerically preponderant group must have influenced this decision. I regarded this assignment as a re-invitation to anthropology and I decided to face this challenge. Incidentally, the representative of the Mina community did file an appeal before the High Court asking it to have a representative of the Anthropological Survey of India on the Committee; perhaps they were not aware of my credentials!!

This assignment brought me back to my parent discipline and gave me a good opportunity to revisit both anthropological theory and the communities in rural Rajasthan. You can well imagine my plight when I did not find any significant guidelines either in anthropological literature or in official records for judging this particular case. Moreover, the Committee was bound to follow the broad definition of the tribe given by the Chanda Committee in 1965.

As I said earlier, pioneering anthropologists carried out their studies of primitive societies without bothering to precisely define the concept of tribe. This is not to say that there were no attempts at definition. I am merely referring to the lack of consensus. This is somewhat understandable if we went back to the beginnings of the discipline. When societies were classified into civilized and uncivilized – as savage or barbaric – the task was simpler. All uncivilized societies were preliterate, meaning thereby the absence of writing in them. That meant that the transmission of culture was through oral tradition, and the history of the society went as far back as human memory could take it. Beyond this was prehistory. With absence of history, oral transmission of society's knowledge pool to the younger generation, elementary technology, greater dependence on nature for survival, and faith in the supernatural described their way of life. Living in small hordes, and unaware of the world outside the narrow confines of the community, the geographically and socially isolated communities defined themselves as residents of a given territory, and as belonging to a specific racial stock. Initially, these students of 'other cultures' came to the non-Western societies and studied those small groups that were remotely located as 'little communities', cut-off from civilizational societies and pursuing primitive economic activities in settlements that were cradle-to-the-grave arrangements.[2]

Problems arose when countries like India were colonised. Described as an indigenous civilization, India got divided into the civilized and uncivilized sections, but belonging to the non-Western part of human civilization. In India, the original inhabitants got pushed into the remote tribal tracts by the groups that migrated from abroad at different phases of its history – as nomads and pastoralists, or as invaders who became conquerors of parts of the vast territory of India. Many such groups who came from the Middle East, Eastern Europe and Mongolia came as adventurers or nomads and gradually got assimilated with the local populace; this involved initial confrontation, accommodation, and, finally, integration into the main stream. Historians of the nineteenth century – mostly foreign, and primarily administrators or military officers of the Raj – called all such migrating groups as tribes – because of their common origin and a distinct identity. But they also acknowledged the process of their gradual assimilation into the Hindu fold.

It is important to note that there is no indigenous word for *tribe* in any of the Indian languages. In Sanskrit, there is a word *Aatavika Jana* (meaning *Banvasi* or forest dwellers) which was used to denote agglomeration of individuals with specific territorial, kinship and cultural patterns. Prior to the colonial period, they were also commonly referred to as a *jati* – caste. But, the colonial administration began calling them as tribes, and differentiated them from the other groups on the basis of animism. In this category, some food gathering groups and shifting cultivators were also included, though they lived closer to the villages. In the censuses, they were first called 'forest tribes'. In the 1931 Census, they were named as 'primitive tribes'. In 1935, the British began calling them as 'backward tribes'. Without questioning the nomenclature, the anthropologists, both foreign and natives, took those groups as subject matter of their study which were officially designated as tribes. It is interesting that in the 1931 Census, which had recorded castes for the last time, had given the listing of the tribes. But even in this Census, the groups that were identified by a distinct tribal name were classified in terms of their religion. Only those that were not converted to any religion – Christianity, Islam, Hinduism, or Jainism – were called tribals. Hutton went to the extent of calling tribal religions as residuals that were yet to enter the temple of Hinduism!

Let me quote, as an instance, the case of tribals of Rajasthan. The Bhils were classified into Christian, Hindus, Jain, Muslims and tribals; similarly, Grassia and Mina were classified into Hindu, Muslim and tribals. Classified this way, the tribal Bhils constituted only 23.62 per cent of the total Bhil population in 1931. Among the Minas, the conversion rate was so high that only 3.35 per cent of them remained tribals despite the fact that the total population of both the Bhils and the Minas was more than 6 lakhs. This can be seen from the following table:

Table 1

Tribals among Bhils, Minas and Grassias

Ethnic Group	*Total Population*	*Tribal Segment*	*Tribal (%)*
Bhil	6,55,647	1,98,005	23.62
Grassia	29,231	8,258	24.10
Mina/Meena	6,07,369	20,336	3.35

Source: 1931 Census.

The 1931 Census suggests that only 19 per cent of the Bhils were reported as Hindus in the 1921 Census; that percentage of Hindu converts rose within 10 years to 70. In case of the Minas the conversion rate was much higher. Both these groups are acknowledged by the Census as 'original inhabitants' and yet they were taken out of the tribal category on the basis of their religious affiliation.

Regarding the 1931 Census as the basis for identification of castes and tribes, the Indian government named them in 1948 as *Adivasis*, ignoring the religious distinction of the 1931 Census, and thus increasing their size. When the new Constitution of India was promulgated in 1950, all the *Adivasi* groups considered as backward tribes were included in the schedule for special privileges, and were named as Scheduled Tribes; their religious conversion notwithstanding. One is not sure whether any of the non-backward tribes remained excluded from the schedule. As a consequence, the distinction between a tribe and an ST got blurred, and the two terms became synonymous. Lokur Committee alerted to this fact and advised to re-introduce that distinction. The intervention of politics, however, did not allow this to happen.

It must, however, be said that the Constitution of India nowhere defines the word 'tribe'. Article 342 of the Constitution says just the following:

> The President may with respect to any State or Union territory, and where it is a State, after consultation with the Governor, thereof, by public notification, specify the tribes or tribal communities or part of groups within tribes or tribal communities which shall for the purposes of this Constitution be deemed to be Scheduled Tribes in relation to that State or Union territory, as the case may be.

Article 366 (25) defines the Scheduled Tribes as follows:

> 'Scheduled Tribe' means such Tribes or Tribal communities or parts of groups within such Tribes or Tribal communities as are deemed under article 342 to be Scheduled Tribe for the purposes of this Constitution.

When the two articles are read in tandem, one discovers the tautological nature of these definitions. Although the Constitution is silent about the definition, it is quite clear on one front, namely the eligibility for entry in the tribal fold. While in case of Scheduled Castes it says that *the castes, races or tribes, or parts of, or groups within castes, races or tribes* could be notified for inclusion in the category of Scheduled Castes, the scope for eligibility in the category of Scheduled Tribes is limited only to *the tribes or tribal communities, or part or groups within tribes or tribal communities.* Implicit in the formulation is the point that only those groups that were included in the category of tribes in the census of 1931, and in the following decennial censuses, qualify for inclusion in the category of Scheduled Tribes; no caste can be reclassified as a tribe.

The point I am making is that the 1951 list of Scheduled Tribes created several anomalies and encouraged many groups to push their claims for inclusion. Not finding any satisfactory guideline in the Constitution, or other available literature, a Joint Parliamentary Committee under the chairmanship of Anil K. Chanda adopted (1967) the following five criteria for judging the eligibility of any group as a tribe:

1. Indication of primitive traits
2. Distinctive culture
3. Geographical isolation
4. Shyness of contact with the larger community
5. Backwardness

The official documents nowhere provide any indicators for each of these variables to develop an objective index. Different people have interpreted each of these variables differently.

Let us now look at the five criteria that the Government of India still uses in judging the eligibility of a group for the tribal status. Objectively speaking, the first criterion, namely, indication of primitive traits, is broad enough to cover all the other criteria: the primitives are those that have a distinct culture of their own, live in relative isolation, and therefore fight shy of contacts with the outsiders, and as a consequence of their isolation, they have remained backward. What, then, are the additional 'primitive' characteristics to be included in the first criterion?

Primitiveness of a community is a comparative term, as it is opposed to modernity – yet another term which is variously defined. Broadly speaking, primitiveness indicates the lingering state of backwardness of a group and its inability to catch up with the mainstream in terms of socio-economic development. Primitiveness may be attributed to lack of education, narrow worldview or a *Weltanshauung*, ethnocentrism, cultural prejudices, lifestyle, and socio-economic inequities. No present-day society, however backward and underdeveloped, fits the nineteenth century stereotype of a 'primitive', stone-age culture. Construction of approach roads, opening of schools, use of modern means of agriculture (such as tractors, chemical fertilizers), use of national currency for monetary transactions replacing barter, and even the use of radio transistors, and now the mobile phones have changed the material cultural profile of the so-called primitive communities. What then are the key component variables of the concept 'primitive'? We also know that when several variables are included in defining an ideal type, they serve as 'indicators' on the basis of which an index is constructed. Such an index, by definition, is a scale with two polar ideal types. The real groups corresponding to the ideal types exist in between. That is why Robert Redfield talked of the 'Transformations' in the primitive world. He gave the concept of 'folk-urban continuum' that has much merit despite its somewhat evolutionary tones. The main point is that no real society corresponds exactly to the ideal type, and that no society is static; change is an inevitable phenomenon of all living societies. In such circumstances, how do we locate the 'pristine'?

The same is the difficulty with the concept of 'distinct culture'. Described as a multicultural society, India does not fit the western description of a 'melting pot'. That is why, many scholars have discarded this simile for India and call it a 'salad bowl' of cultures or as a veritable 'bouquet of flowers'. Indian national cuisine, for example, is a mouth-watering melange of *Idly-Dosa* from the South, *Tandoori* dishes from the Punjab, *Dhokla-Shrikhand* from Gujarat and Maharashtra, and *Rasgulla* from Bengal, and yet each one of these items forms part of the regional cuisine of the area from where they have gained national acceptance. As an indigenous civilization, India is regarded to be an amalgam of several thousand 'little traditions' to form the emerging national culture with a great tradition. One finds in the rural households not only the pictures and calendars depicting Hindu gods and goddesses but also the posters of favourite bollywood icons and stars. While traditional dresses are not altogether discarded, both men and women in the villages are found to wear modern attire and jewellery – Salwar-Kameez amongst girls and young women, and jeans and T-shirts among young men are a common site. Processes of universalization and parochialization[3] have created an impeccable salad bowl of Indian culture. In such a milieu, a search for isolated parochial cultures in terms of their distinctiveness is indeed a fruitless effort.

The criterion of 'geographical isolation' is also untenable. With increasing connectivity caused by tremendous improvements in the area of transportation and communication, there are a few islands of relative isolation with difficulty of access. Revolutionary changes brought about by advances in information technology have broken the communication barriers and reduced isolation. Democratic governance in the country has greatly contributed to the breakdown of isolation. The electoral process involves campaigning by various candidates in their respective constituencies including the village communities that are otherwise not regularly contacted. Such contacts not only break geographical isolation but also help enlarge cognitive horizons of the common people. They come to know of political parties, leaders, and political issues. And they are also dragged into the political process either as fellow campaigners or as candidates for posts for different legislative bodies and local self-governments, such as Panchayat Samitis and Gram Panchayats or cooperative societies. No doubt, geography still hinders effective interaction in some areas, but the situation is vastly different from the days when savagery and barbarism perpetuated because of lack of contact.

No groups fight shy of contact with others. Of course, shyness as a social norm of courtesy towards elders, or amongst people of opposite sex, is not to be confused with shyness that was exhibited by the people living in the non-civilized world. That is a matter of past. Sale of rural products, such as dairy items and cash crops in urban markets clearly indicate the entry of these people in the regional economy.

It is the concept of backwardness that seems, however, to provide a dependable list of variables for developing a suitable index. Since all groups covered in the three categories, namely, SC, ST, and OBC are characterized by backwardness, defined in terms of poor economic status and educational deficiency (illiteracy) it does not pose much problem except the point that while the letter C in OBC stands for 'Class', it is used as a synonym of the word 'caste', and has caused concern amongst those who are poor but are excluded from it because of their belonging to the supposedly higher caste. People living in geographically adverse areas that are characterized by difficulty of access, inadequate administrative back up, insufficient livelihood support, depletion of natural resource base, are still prisoners of primitive beliefs and superstition, and perforce dependent on traditional medicine and healing practices. Village life in such difficult living conditions certainly corresponds to a 'tribe-like' existence, though far from the idyllic portrayal of the bygone era. Here again, I would submit that backwardness is either an attribute of a territorial community or of individual families within it, and not of any biotic community.

I must mention that the new tribal policy draft document, issued by the Government of India in July 2006 acknowledged the redundancy of the five criteria. It boldly asserts: "... all these broad criteria are not applicable to Scheduled Tribes today. Some of the terms used (e.g., primitive traits, backwardness) are also, in today's context, pejorative and need to be replaced with terms that are not derogatory" (para 1.2). In para 20.4, it says that "Other more accurate criteria need to be fixed". It is significant that the tribal policy acknowledged the need for a process of 'descheduling' so as "to exclude those communities who have by and large caught up with the general population. Exclusion of the creamy layer among the Scheduled Tribes from the benefits of reservation has never been seriously considered. As we move towards, and try to ensure, greater social justice, it would be necessary to give this matter more attention and work out an acceptable system" (para 20.6).

Social situation in India has drastically changed over the years with several forces of change – planned or unplanned, endogenous or exogenous. And, the change has touched all sections of our society be they urban, rural or even tribal. If we stuck to our old definition then we should be prepared to take out those groups which earlier matched the definition but are now metamorphosed. To invent a new definition to suit the vested interests of the concerned groups is an exercise of little value. If the intentions of our Constitution makers were to include only the backward among the tribes in the schedule and make specific provisions for them so that their backwardness is removed then we should develop objective criteria for descheduling the groups, or individual families, that have shown improvement; and at the same time disallow entry of fresh groups on false pretexts. To insist on retention of the primitive traits is nothing more than conspiring to keep certain groups backward for all times. In today's context, tribal areas of the past can also easily be classified into urban, rural, and even tribal. In many groups the claim of being tribal is of historical significance only. Many individuals or families who belonged to these groups but who have changed their personal and social profile by acquiring good education, better employment, or a political stature should voluntarily opt out rather than wait for their ouster as a 'creamy layer'. One should ask as to when does a tribe cease to be a tribe. Or, do we take the view that once a tribe is always a tribe? The danger in the second option is that logically it would lead to all groups and communities to the backward path of history and reinvent their tribal past. The Gujar case hints at the emergence of a reverse process of *Sanskritization*. Colonel Tod's *Annals and Antiquities of Rajasthan* uses the term tribe almost as a synonym of caste – the Rajputs, the Brahmans, and all such groupings are mentioned as tribes. Do we take, then Tod as an authority and reclassify them? And then, imagine the chaos and crisis that this would create. I suspect that even Colonel Baisla realizes this, and therefore, his reformulated demand has the second part, which the Chopra Committee brought to the surface, that says that if "ST status is not granted to us, then the entire reservation policy should be carefully reviewed, and a national debate be initiated". This is exactly what our Committee had recommended. Let me hope that without waiting for the government to initiate action on our recommendation, the social science community would seize the opportunity and engage itself in this important task of national significance.

It is amply clear that the intention of the founding fathers of our Constitution was only to remove the backwardness of the groups, and not of preserving them as exhibits in an 'anthropological zoo'. But, the approach they followed of identifying specific groups rather than geographical areas as backward was at fault. In areas where the two coincided the problem did not arise, but in backward regions where people belonging to different groups were discriminated along lines of caste or tribe this strategy has failed. Rather than looking towards future, this policy has encouraged several groups to engage themselves in re-inventing their pasts. The groups who had moved towards acceptance of the elements of 'Great Traditions' of India, to use Robert Redfield's term, and putting claims for a higher status in the Hindu caste hierarchy, are taking a U-turn towards parochialization. When Gujars of Rajasthan, for example, were asked to furnish evidence of their being tribal, using the official five criteria they dug out whatever to them looked like primitive or tribal. They referred to their dressing pattern – but that was no different from other villagers in the same setting. They insisted on their being non-vegetarians whereas traditionally they are a vegetarian caste. They claimed to be addicted to drinking where in fact, teetotalism is the community norm. They asserted that they were believers in witchcraft and black and white magic, but this was no different amongst other village dwellers: worship of Bheru – a Hindu god – whose priest enters into a trance is a common feature of rural Rajasthan and of course, the priest is always a Gujar. It is also interesting to mention here that in the Hindu temples of Charbhujaji only a Gujar serves as the *Pujari.* The myth of Devnarayan contains references to Hindu gods and goddesses. To prove their being tribal, they even mentioned the prevalence of polyandry as if all tribes are supposed to be polyandrous. All this indicates the ambiguity that is found amongst the claimants as to what defines a 'tribe'. Dressing pattern, food habits, superstition and marriage practices are not enough indicators for a tribal status.

Our field visits to twenty districts in Rajasthan which have preponderance of the Gujars uncovered the fact that despite name semblance, people using the Gujar name belong to different endogamous groups, speak different dialects, and are not only pastorals but also agriculturists, and some of them have distanced themselves as a ruling class. The word 'Gujar' is an umbrella concept, perhaps referring to whosoever was a herdsman. The gotras among them include Hun and Kashana (an abrupt version of Kushan) indicating their entry with these two invading groups. Similarly, of the two divisions of the Gujar, namely, Lor and Khari, the latter can be traced to Iran where they are still known by this name and are primarily herdsmen. Gujar group has taken the character of a varna in the sense that like other varnas, the Gujars are also divided into several castes, and, leaving aside a small group in the district of Bikaner, all regard themselves as Hindus. However, we found some of the areas in the eastern part of Rajasthan where the lifestyle of the inhabitants could match the criteria of primitiveness. But then, these were the sites where people of other castes were also residing, and thus well-deserving of the special benefits. As a specific geographical sub-region such sites need development inputs without any discussion on the definition of the word 'tribe'.

The question that arises is: At what stage does a tribe ceases to be a tribe? Is it that a tribe remains a tribe for ever? It can be argued that all segments of the world population have remained at one stage or other tribes, and in due course of time, they merged their identities to form part of one or the other civilization. The concern for development basically implies efforts to breakdown isolation, expand their *Weltanshauung*, expose them to the developments in science and technology, and to ensure their participation in the national life. But if the doling out of privileges and a paternalistic attitude of charity continues, it would only reinforce tribal solidarity, and usurpation of benefits coming from the outside by the rich and powerful among them with total denial of these to their poor brethren. In other words, the time has come where poverty or backwardness needs to be treated as an 'economic' phenomenon rather than as an 'ascribed' status.

We must admit that both the words 'caste' and 'tribe' are non-indigenous terms that were used by the foreign writers while describing the Indian social structure as they understood it. That is the reason that the word caste is loosely used to refer to different kind of groupings ranging from Varna to Jatis, and even gotra (*Rishi gotras*, i.e., eponymous clans, and *Laukik gotras*) and to groups of people hailing from a particular region (such as Punjabis, Madrasis, Bangalis).[4] Similarly, there is no indigenous word for tribe. In vernacular languages, all endogamous groups were referred to by the word *Jati;* later prefixes like *Van* (forest) or *Jan* (folk) were used for the forest dwelling groups. Some others preferred the word *Adivasi*, for them to acknowledge their autochthonous and aboriginal character (oldest inhabitants)[5]. This appellation was officially employed in 1948[6] but this was replaced by *Vanyajati* or *Banvasi* by those who were interested in asserting that the majority group living in the Indian sub-continent is also original to this land, and, therefore, this epithet should not remain confined to the backward communities still leading a jungle life.[7]

While working on caste in the 1950s I also struggled with the problem of differentiating between caste and tribe, as the village in Mewar that I chose for my study had not only the castes, including the Gujar, but also representatives of the Bhil tribe who were treated as a caste and who distinguished themselves from the tribal Bhils by calling themselves as 'Gametis' (village dwellers) and occupationally identified as Chowkidars (watchmen). It was then that I wrote an article on the "Tribe-Caste Question".[8] In terms of core characteristics of a caste that I worked out, following S.F. Nadel, the Gametis qualified to be a caste as a unit in the caste system of the village. From this it occurred that the distinguishing attribute of a tribe is found at the level of the system and not as a unit. When a section of a tribe moves to be a part of the multi-caste village, it assumes the characteristic of a caste as a unit. But when the tribe lives a separate existence it has the core characteristic of being endogamous, but does not possess the feature of inter-caste relationships (hierarchy or occupational specialization, or commensual restrictions, etc.). I still feel that the distinction I offered then has validity even now. But my submission offered then went unnoticed which was not surprising in a country where status in the academic hierarchy decides the fate of a point of view.

In that article, I underlined the fact of continuous cultural contact amongst the tribals and the neighbouring members of the majority community, and suggested that the tribes should be seen as belonging to different stations in a continuum, and proposed the following classification[9]:

Tribal Communities Living in their Original Habitat

1. *Relatively isolated*: Retaining most of the characteristics of their social organization, despite some culture contact (the Kadars);
2. *Two or more tribal groups living in the same area:* Such groups maintain mutual contact, and yet remain isolated from other non-tribal groups, demonstrating some sort of cultural symbiosis (the Todas, Kotas, and Badagas);

3. *Living with other tribal/religious groups in the same community*: These have the subtypes:
    A. Followers of their own religion, retaining most of the characteristics of their social organization and culture;
    B. While remaining separate from other religious groups, accept the leadership and domination of the other groups;
    C. Those moving towards Hinduization;
    D. Hinduized
    (i) Tribes that have been forced the degraded status of untouchables;
    (ii) Those enjoying high status; and
    (iii) Those assigned status in the ranges of the Hindu hierarchy,
    (iv) Baptized in religions other than Hindu
        (a) Towards conversion; and
        (b) Converts

Tribal Groups Living Away from their Original Habitat

1. *Settled in neighbouring villages:* These could also be classified into five categories as in I (c):
    A. Followers of their own religion, retaining most of the characteristics of their social organization and culture;
    (i) While remaining separate from other religious groups, accept the leadership and domination of the other groups;
    (ii) Those moving towards Hinduization;
    (iii) Hinduized
        (a) Tribes that have been forced the degraded status of untouchables;
        (b) Those enjoying high status; and
        (c) Those assigned status in the ranges of the Hindu hierarchy,
    B. Baptized in religions other than Hindu
    (i) Towards conversion; and
    (ii) Converts
2. *Living in separate villages in other areas,* such as Bhoksa of Nainital; and
3. *Settled in industrial centres or cities, or in tea plantations, military recruits, and others.*

This distinction of the original habitat, seems to me, to be very much relevant in the sense that such groups are not migratory and, therefore, there is greater degree of territorial attachment. Like the Maoris in New Zealand, such indigenous people have ancestral claims, and despite their getting modernized their autochthonous roots cannot be challenged. As against these, the migrating communities lose their attachment to their parental land and show greater degree of adaptability. All those who constitute the mainstream have a queer mix of the great tradition and the little parochial traditions. Their being tribal is a matter of past; that is why Colonel Tod or Sherring calling all groups – Rajputs, Brahmans, Gujars – tribes becomes less significant in the context of today because they have entered the fold of civilization and even contributed to its richness. Even illiteracy does not block this transition. Those who are part of the civilization also have stratification in social, economic and political terms.

IV

By way of conclusion let me say that here is an invitation for us as social scientists to 'rethink' our frameworks and reorient our perspectives relative to the tribal population. We need not jump on the political bandwagons, or over-demonstrate our philanthropy by pleading a case for the protection of the primitive cultures by raising the bogey of endangered cultures or social structures. There is a need to ensure scientific objectivity in our approach and to stick our necks out when needed rather than towing the lines of the ill-informed political leaders or rule-bound bureaucrats.

Let me hope that this lecture will instigate some of you to rethink and revisit our paradigms and theories and develop new protocols for handling problems or issues of development.

Notes

1. Edited by Michael Banton and published by Tavistock in 1966.
2. Robert Redfield defined the *Little Community* in terms of four attributes as under:

   Quality of *distinctiveness* where the community begins and where it ends is apparent. The distinctiveness is apparent to the outside observer and is expressed in the group consciousness of the people of the community. *Smallness*: "So small that either it itself is the unit of personal observation or else, being somewhat larger and yet homogenous, it provides in some part of it a unit of personal observation fully representative of the whole". "A compact community of four thousand people in Indian Latin-American can be studied by making direct personal acquaintance with one section of it". Community is ... *homogenous.* Activities and states of mind are much alike for all persons in corresponding sex and age positions; and the career of one generation repeats that of the preceding. So understood, homogenous is equivalent to 'slow-changing'. "As a fourth defining quality it may be said that the community we have in mind is self-sufficient and provides for all or most of the activities and needs of the people in it. The little community is a cradle-to-the grave arrangement".

3. The terms popularized by McKim Marriott in the 1950s. See, McKim Marriott (ed.) (1955): *Village India*, Chicago: University of Chicago Press. His article in the book titled *Little Communities in an Indigenous Civilization.*
4. It is interesting to note that in some of the older reports on Backward Classes, Bengalis have been mentioned as a caste, even in the context of Rajasthan.
5. In the Indonesian and Malaysian language, aboriginal groups are called *Orang Asli* – meaning original people.
6. Government of India published a book by that name at that time.
7. The replacement of the term Adivasi was disputed during the debates of the Constituent Assembly – drafting the Constitution of the Republic of India. A tribal leader, Jaipal Singh asked President Rajendra Prasad: "I wish that you would issue instructions to your Translation Committee that the translation of Scheduled Tribes should be Adivasi (meaning original inhabitants or indigenous peoples). The word Adivasi has a grace ... . Why this old abusive epithet of Banjati (forest dwellers) being used ...".
8. Yogesh Atal (1963): "The Tribe-Caste Question", *Bulletin of the Bihar Tribal Research Institute,* Vol. V, No. 1.
9. Ibid.

4

Migration as a Coping Strategy

Evidence from Central Tribal Belt of India

D.C. SAH

Sah, Bhatt and Dalapati (2008) reveal that incidence of chronic poverty in central tribal belt of India is alarmingly high. About half of the households in this tribal belt are categorized as poor. A fourth of poor are chronic poor. A large part of chronic poverty is due to access failure to production resources, population pressure and declined landholdings, recurring droughts and access failure to land-based livelihood and lack of off-farm employment avenues and consumption loan from moneylender that result in a debt-trap that pushes people into chronic poverty. Seasonal migration in this tribal belt is regarded as an essential coping mechanism especially in response to a shock, including crop failure, son's marriage, serious sickness, etc.

The objective of this paper is to analyze the observations relating to seasonal migration from the central belt of India.[1] We have tried to establish in this paper, that (i) a shock can induce a complex socio-economic processes like access failure to food, debt-trap and depletion of assets, repayment, short-term land transactions, and migration; (ii) all locations and households do not respond in the same pattern: for some, migration means livelihood option, for others it means savings, asset formation and technology transfer; and (iii) locational disadvantage in a shock can be overcome by investment in agriculture. We have used both qualitative and quantitative methods in data collection. The quantitative data were generated for 1,614 sample households that provided information relating to incidence and intensity of seasonal migration, income and saving from migration and the correlates of migration.

Conceptualizing Migration

A voluminous literature is available explaining migration that mirrors the discipline and ideological underpinnings of the researcher. Although sociologist like Lee (1966) conceptualized migration as the play of negative and positive forces that respectively push a migrant from the place of origin to migrate and pulls him to the place of destination, neoclassical economists constructs dominated the explanations. Locating migration decisions at the household level and arguing that such decisions are based on opportunities and constraints that the households face, the neoclassical theorists propagated human capital theory (Sjaastad, 1962; Todaro, 1969, 1980). This construct argued that inclination to migrate is determined by difference in income between source and destination of migration, and may result in equating expected income. Given their skills, decisions about where to live are based on where individuals can optimize the present value of their discounted stream of expected future earnings. Migration according to Saxena (1977) may be motivated by a desire to seek skill and leads to development, urbanization and socio-economic transformation. In the same vein, Stark (1980) identifies transaction cost, imperfect information and imperfect credit, land and labour markets as main determinants of migration. On the other hand, researches driven by Marxist ideology (Breman, 1985; Olsen and Murthy, 2000) identified structural constraints of capitalist system as main source of exploitation of migrant labours. In absence of alternatives, in extreme cases, monopoly creditor also becomes a monopsony buyer of migrant's labour (Olsen and Murthy, 2000). But the recognition that seasonal migration also provides a respite from interlocked credit, land and labour transactions was never missing. Breman (1985) also shows that while for resource poor, migration is a coping mechanism that provides means for debt servicing, for the well endowed it increases households' earnings, creditworthiness and ability to manage crisis. Breaking away from the neoclassical interpretations of determinants of migration, Mosse et al. (2002) argue that migration is not an external factor impinging upon or undermining agrarian society. Existing social relations and inequalities, which define differential opportunities, constraining experiences and social outcome, profoundly shape it. Moreover, migration contributes to continuation and intensification of agriculture and social networks on which it depends. Insufficient land, larger dependency within family and poor are more likely to seasonally migrate than others. Sah (1999) argues that access failure to resources as well as constraints on markets influence seasonal migration.

In a resource-poor economy, the existing economic hierarchy collapses during a shock like crop failure, drought, sickness, death, son's marriage, *Notra* (gifts in social ceremonies), Jhagda (dispute settlement), population pressure[2], etc. In this situation, heads of even larger landholding households also have to borrow to meet the eventualities. In order to repay such loans some of the family members of the household have to migrate. In what follows, we try to establish that during a shock depletion of assets and related borrowings have strong positive influences on intensity of migration. Postulate a village consisting *'n'* households with per capita calorie intake of the ith household c_i such that during normal situation the available food stock with the households G_i is able to support the intake at the minimum per capita per day acceptable level c^* for all, M_i of its members for rest of the d_i days till the new harvest arrives. During a shock there are, however, households whose per capita intake falls short of c^* by an amount s_i for remaining D_i days. Under such circumstances, in order to maintain the minimum level of intake, m_i out of M_i members of household migrate for D_i days in such a way that:

$$c^*. (M_i - m_i) D_i + c^*.M_i. (d_i - D_i) < G_i$$

The following implications relating to seasonal migration may be noted. First, the decision to migrate is not taken by any individual in isolation; seasonal migration is a group decision taken by the household as a whole, perhaps even by several households together. The cost of information relating to destination, movement of the group, type of work and wage contract, dwelling at the destination and payment to middlemen, etc., may be shared by households that perceive seasonal migration inevitable for the larger interest of their families. During a shock existing food stock are augmented to s_i by taking a loan from the local *bania.* Second, the duration of seasonal migration is controlled by households' perception about the shortfall in consumption s_i. As soon as the shortfall is overcome and borrowed loan repaid, the migrating members are free to rejoin the family, i.e., no sooner $m_i.c^*$. $D_i = s_i$ in such a manner that savings from migration are enough to repay the loan, the time to return is opportune. Third, after the decision to seasonally migrate has been taken, there may not be many households whose intake falls below c^*. In fact, among the '*n*' households in the village, those opting for seasonal migration may be the ones with relatively higher intake levels. It can be seen from the above construct that if the migrating members from a household choose to stay for more than the required days at their destination the per capita intake of the remaining members of household may be maintained at higher levels than c^*. In a scarcity situation, it is highly probable that the calorie intake of the remaining members of migrating households is higher than of the members of non-migrating households in the village. These households may also have some savings and assets. Lastly, the decision to migrate could confer larger societal benefit provided: (a) the consumption levels of migrant is maintained at least at c^* level at the destination without adversely affecting the wage rate; or (b) the state intervenes to support the minimum consumption of the migrant through (i) food for work, or (ii) public distribution system support, or (iii) creating investment climate for additional employment. None of these options is closed in an economy where policy makers are sensitive to the emerging crisis of displaced households. But in remote rural areas, such public actions are too diluted and too delayed. Although it is difficult to establish fully the above construct, evidence provided by our research indicates the operation of the process.

Extent and Pattern of Migration

There has been a long tradition of tribal migration in search of employment from the region (Baviskar, 1997). There are evidences that even in early 1970s, up to 40 per cent of total working populations of the eastern tribal belt of Gujarat migrated seasonally in search of livelihood (Bureau, 1974). Breman (1985) describes such seasonal migration as marginal tribal farmers' efforts to prevent a slide down in the agrarian ladder. Evidences that are more recent reveal that over a period of time, intensity of migration in terms of number, duration and distance has increased (Patel, 2001). This increase in migration can be attributed to both push and pull forces operating in the tribal economy;

access failure to food in the village pushes the tribal out to seasonally migrate whereas the expansion of labour demand in irrigated agriculture as well as in the urban-industrial sectors in Gujarat and Maharashtra pull them to migrate in search of higher wages. But such explanations will be partial, for at societal level a complex process operates that governs migration.

Agriculture is the main economic activity in both in this tribal during normal years. But agriculture does not provide sustenance for whole year for a sizeable number of households even during normal years. Poor quality of land, insufficient landholdings and low productivity are the main reasons that force households to resort to labouring in and around the villages. This also forces some households to work in brick-klins and labourer in industries nearby township and in neighbouring states as seasonal migrants. In abnormal situations, about 33 per cent of households from underdeveloped villages and about 20 per cent of households from developed villages have reported seasonal migration of some of their family members. The major reasons for larger migration from underdeveloped in comparison to developed villages are remoteness, its difficult and undulating terrain, poor soil and indifferent agricultural productivity, access failure to commons, lack of employment opportunities and larger borrowings to meet the current consumption. Relative remoteness of underdeveloped villages in terms of its physical distance from agro-processing and industrial markets has resulted in significantly higher reliance on seasonal migration of households. But migration in underdeveloped villages is not in one stretch; migrants like to return to the village after some time and migrate again after staying in the village for a few days. In contrast, seasonal migration in developed villages, which are relatively less remote, is highly spread starting from non-farm employment opportunities to industrial Gujarat, Maharashtra and mines in Orissa and Jharkhand. About 86 per cent of migration is reported as rural-to-urban migration, 62 per cent of the migration is outside the state. Land owning class in the village considers seasonal migration a degrading option in a shock; medium size landowning households have reported that they would rather do labour around the village than migrate. Extent of migration is significantly different in different states (Table 3); while Madhya Pradesh, Rajasthan, Gujarat and Jharkhand have reported sizeable migration, Chhattisgarh and Orissa have relatively low migration. About 48 per cent of tribal households in

1990s in Jhabua (West Madhya Pradesh), Banswara (South Rajasthan) and Panchmahals (East Gujarat) had to opt for seasonal migration for their livelihood (Mosse et al., 2002).

Drought not only has repercussions that disrupts the economy but also has socio-cultural implications. Apart from depletion of milch animals, reduction in availability of food and fodder increased, the households also faced serious non-economic problems like withdrawing children from school, doing work that in normal situation they would not have preferred, sending out old members of the family to relatives, inability to settle hospitalization bills, etc. (Sah and Shah, 2003). Migration owing to drought, with whole family and taking care of siblings, were main reasons for withdrawal of children from schools. Significantly, drought affected families opted for larger out migration both in terms of number of members migrating and duration of migration. Some migrants, in distress, remained outside the village even during festivals like *diwali* and *holi.* Food availability alarmingly reduces during monsoon when food stock depletes and current harvest would reach the hearth after nearly four months. For a large number of poor households, boiled cereals, called *rab*, becomes staple food. Non-availability of fodder and malnutrition resulted in loss of milch animals whereas goat and sheep herds deplete because of additional demand for cash. Borrowings from *bania* located in markets increase. In order to repay the loans, the intensity of migration – duration of migration and number of family members who would migrate – increases. Sah and Shah (2003) also observed that the effects of drought were significantly harsh on migrant in remote tribal areas than non-remote. Although both remoteness and bad agriculture super-impose each other, subsequent analysis would establish that unsustainable agriculture is relatively more important than remoteness in explaining the migration[3].

The effects of drought were significantly harsh in underdeveloped villages than developed (Table 1). For example, the odd-ratios for shortage of food and fodder are 1.4 times more in underdeveloped than developed villages. Similarly, the incidence resorting to degrading works, which a household would not take in normal situation, is 1.4 times higher in underdeveloped villages than developed villages. The adverse effects of drought on migrant families were much harsher than non-migrating families; as withdrawal of child from school, increased debt, increased intensity of migration, mortgaged land and have sent their elders to relative relatively were significant more in the case of households that had resorted to migration than those that did not migrate. On the other hand, those who have not migrated in the reference year have faced more food shortages than migrants.

Table 1

Drought and Its Implication

	Per cent Household Reported	*Odd Ratio Across Villages*[a]	*Odd Ratio Across Migrant*[b]
Withdrawn children from school	6.8	NS	*** 5.80
Started degrading work	42.6	*** 1.4	*** 0.59
Sent elders to relatives	1.4	NS	** 3.60
Mortgaged land	7.4	NS	* 1.60
Severe food shortage	72.6	*** 1.5	*** 0.67
Livestock depleted	12.2	NS	*** 3.10
Borrowing increased	32.5	NS	*** 3.50
Migration rate increased	18.0	NS	*** 28.0
Could not pay hospital bills	4.7	NS	*** 3.4
Fodder shortage increased	35.2	** 1.4	** 1.4
Sold land	1.3	NS	NS
Sold trees	8.9	* .59	*** 0.25

[a] Odd ratio across developed and underdeveloped village.
[b] Odd ratio across migrant and non-migrant households.
Significance *10 per cent, **5 per cent and ***1 per cent, NS: not significant.

The seasonal migration forced about a third of the family members remaining out of village for 43 and 132 person days in developed and underdeveloped villages (Table 2). Female usually migrate along with the male in the area; the percentage of female migration was about 33 per cent of total migration in developed villages and 40 per cent of total migration from underdeveloped villages respectively. But the high female migration is not abnormal; studies (Mosse et al., 2002; Sah, 1999; Breman, 1996) have also found that migration of family groups in order to maximize the productivity of their labour is quite common in the Western tribal belt.[4] What is revealing from Table 2 is the fact that households that have resorted to migration have relatively poor resource base. Their silver possessions depleted 3 times more, their land holdings are smaller, irrigation investments, agricultural production is two-thirds of non-migrants, expenditure and consumption behaviour is significantly constrained in comparison to households that have not migrated and their food stock lasts 40 days less than that of non-migrants, their consumption expenditure is lower and unpaid social debts are three times more than non-migrants. To top the deprivation, the size of the family of migrant households is significantly larger than non-migrant households. The implication of this resourcelessness is forcing upon the households.

Table 2

Migration, Migrant and their Resource Base

	Developed Village	*Underdeveloped Villages*	*Difference Between*	
			Village F	*Migrant F*
Total family size	5.42	5.66	**	Migrate larger
Workers	2.49	2.25	***	NS
Land in acres	2.67	3.03	NS	Migrate less
Gross cropped acre	3.04	3.05	NS	NS
Irrigated acre	1.08	0.50	*	NS
Silver possession (Rs)	2,169	2,723	**	More among migration
Depletion of silver	316	698	***	Three times more among migration
Animals	7,993	8,758	*	NS
Depletion in animals	1,178	1,689	NS	NS
Consumer assets	3,536	2,689	**	Less with migrant
Depletion of land (Rs)	43,186	40,732	NS	NS
Migration intensity	43	132	***	–
Male migrants	0.24	0.46	***	–
Female migrants	0.12	0.29	***	–
Agricultural income	10,415	8,598	**	70% of non
Produce lasts (days)	257	258	NS	Intensity less by 40 days
Per capita expenditure	445	436	NS	Migration smaller
Unpaid debt	5,127	4,880	NS	Migrant three times more
Agricultural credit	1,521	4,739	NS	NS

Significance * 10 per cent ** 5 per cent *** 1 per cent, NS: not significant.

Consequently, a large majority of migration is reported to have taken place every year irrespective of shocks; over a half who have migrated reported that land fragmentation is the cause and about forty per cent migrated because their income could not sustain their consumption levels. Exigency of additional funds to meet the shock forces the number of migrants from a family. As coming back from migration depends on their need in farms and with the advent of monsoon bulk of migrants return home. Those who come back early, do so owing to either adequate earnings or because of work contract was over or on information that local labour opportunities exist in the village. About 20 per cent of the migration is around the district vary within 40 km to 80 km from the village. About 20 per cent of total migrants had moved outside the district. For about 86 per cent of migrants the main economic activity is labouring in mines and industrial belts; only 14 per cent of migrants in the study villages reported that they were employed as agricultural labour (Table 3). The non-farm opportunities are generally created through middlemen (*Mukadam*).[5]

Table 3

Some Characteristics of Migrant Households in Different States

	Madhya Pradesh	*Chhattis-garh*	*Orissa*	*Jharkhand*	*Gujarat*	*Rajasthan*	*Total*
% Migrant households	56	3	10	15	32	89	26
% Migration within district	17	75	21	20	35	10	21
Outside district	3	17	63	25	59	16	20
Outside state	80	8	15	55	5	74	59
% Urban migration	89	33	84	78	83	96	86
Migration to same place	56	45	65	68	62	66	62

Findings relating to pattern of migration can be summed up as follows: (a) seasonal migration in the study villages is forced by access failure to food and unsustainable agriculture: the more the unsustainability in agriculture, the more is seasonal migration; (b) average migration is about three members per household, and such households that resorted to migrate, remain out for about 13 to 18 man-months per household; (c) the remoteness of the area creates paucity of off-farm employment in the nearby areas, forcing the migrants to move to agriculturally vibrant areas and for labouring in mines and industry; (d) migration in the last few years is more for survival rather than for supporting capital formation; (e) female migration is about half of male migration; and (f) migration is a group activity which attracts households in distress taking certain decisions relating to such matters like choice of destination, movement, stay and coming back between to look after remaining family members in the village.

The movement generally is organized not as individual migrants but is in the form of a close kin-network of families. A close relative, like brother or cousin, provides information about labour demand, wage rate and living conditions prevailing at the destination. The migrants, in order to find work especially in distant locations, form a group of 5 to 6 families that stay together. One member, more often the one who had no family members in the village, would come back to village to look after the remaining family members of the group. He replenishes the food grain stocks and other supplies and repays to the *bania* from migration earnings. The accumulated savings are remitted once a month, at least, in this way. This person, who brings the savings back to respective families of the group, has also an important task of meeting the sharecroppers who manage their land in their absence.

The remittance back home depends on the extent of migration in man-months a family has, the number of days the migrants could find employment, and cost of stay at the destination. Household income and savings from migration are significantly higher if total number of migrants was more. However, the income and saving across different size class of holding is not significantly different (Table 4). On an average, a migrant family earns an additional sum of Rs 3,265 per year from migration. After meeting the day-to-day expenditure at the destination, replenish food supply for remaining members and some purchases (clothes, shoes, transportation expenses, etc.) while returning, the net savings accrued due to migration was about Rs 1,926 per family.[6] Migration income of underdeveloped villages is two times higher than developed villages. The migration income significantly varies across poverty profile, remoteness and in different states (Table 4).

Table 4

Income and Saving from Migration

	Income	*Savings*	*Migration Intensity*
	Rs per Household		*Person Days*
Poverty profile			
Chronic poor	5,355	3,242	143
Non-chronic poor	3,561	2,091	104
Transitory non-poor	3,240	1,749	83
Always non-poor	1,893	1,145	45
Remoteness			
Developed village	1,968	1,181	42
Underdeveloped	4,473	2,622	132
Across States			
Madhya Pradesh	8,098	4,721	234
Chhattisgarh	170	92	3
Orissa	347	205	7
Jharkhand	2,118	1,186	47
Gujarat	4,029	2,360	135
Rajasthan	9,751	6,377	214
Total	3,265	1,927	189
F across poverty profile	12***	14***	8***
F across villages	42***	46***	44***
F across states	65***	87***	40***

Significance ***: at 1 per cent.

Those migrants who opted to stay within district earn much less, as wage rates are depressed in there. But those who had moved to outside state earn more, for wage rate are significantly higher. The savings from migration are usually created in harsh environment like humiliation by land and factory owners, unhealthy and inhospitable staying many times under open sky, poor health facilities, isolated living and lack of educational facilities for children, etc. Given the hostile and insecure environment outside, the migrant finds it difficult to break away from the social lineage with the rest of the communities back home, which is the only dependable capital they have in the event of a major disaster. Besides these, opportunities for getting employment for longer period of time are also doubtful. Hence most of the households do not prefer to migrate for a longer time if the option for borrowing is still open.

Table 5 gives borrowing for social purpose for the reference year. Expenditure on dowry and consumption are two important purposes that bring together the *bania* and the tribal most often. But *bania* also supports expenditure on feast in marriage, death and *jhagda* (conflicts), etc. *Bania* has first access to earnings from migration; as migrants repay consumption loan directly from the migration earnings when someone comes to replenish the food stocks of the households. Finding on borrowing for different purpose shows that marriage and sickness as a purpose of borrowing was significant. But a shock in the form of death, drought (borrowing for food) and conflict could force household in to debt trap. Occasions for borrowing under shock are random hence there could be significant variations in these across poverty profile.

Table 5

Distribution of Debt per Household for Social Purpose (last five years)

	Marriage		*Notra*	*Birth*	*Death*	*Sickness*	*Food*	*Conflict*	*Others*
	Son	*Daughter*							
Poverty profile	**Rs per household**								
Chronic poor	6,564	1,263	218	460	445	882	633	90	455
Non-chronic poor	2,815	426	0	129	207	496	432	2	30
Transitory non-poor	2,619	1,650	0	342	975	1,899	406	286	209
Always non-poor	1,384	815	2	93	327	1,054	393	10	72
F across poverty profile	***	***	*	***	***	***	**	*	NS
Remoteness									
Developed villages	2,791	913	4	145	352	1,008	543	89	95
Under-developed	3,005	694	61	229	366	750	359	8	153
All	2,02	800	33	188	359	874	447	47	125
F across remoteness	NS	NS	NS	*	NS	*	***	NS	NS

Significance level *** at 1 per cent, ** 5 per cent, * 10 per cent; NS: not significant.

Credit and migration work as supplements as well as substitutes to each other. Absence of 'good' credit support is seen to be the major cause of migration, at least of distress type. However, in the case of the resource-poor (i.e., those with limited land as well as irrigation resources), migration is clearly a more effective option because of the limited credit worthiness' of the migrant. In fact, migration in a dynamic context might help enhancing the credit worthiness, especially by improving the repayment schedule among these households. This would imply that given the limited land base and the uncertainty associated with the stream of income flowing from the land based activities, migration becomes inevitable for most of the poor households. A 'good' credit support could reduce the burden of migration, whereas a 'bad credit' system might increase it. But credit support per se can hardly be a substitute for migration unless both the household's resource base and the corresponding 'credit worthiness' are enhanced. Occurrence of a shock or lumpy borrowing for social events like death, son's marriage and at times sickness may further turn the equation against the poor borrowers.

Correlates of Migration

Table 6 presents the findings of linear regression analysis taking intensity of migration (total person-days of migration from the household) as dependent variable. The variations in intensity of migration across household is explained by variations in the following explanatory variables: family size, days the home produce lasts, borrowings for non-agricultural purposes, asset depletion, leasing land, income other than migration, benefits from schemes, consumption expenditure, investment in agriculture, poverty and relative remoteness of location. The regression analysis is done for all the 1,614 households irrespective of the status of migration, dependent variable taking value zero for non-migrant households. About 19 per cent of total variations of dependent variable are explained by the explanatory variables when all households were considered in the analysis. The analysis had considered dependency ratio, landholding, loss of animals, agricultural borrowings, land leasing by the households as explanatory variables. But the variations in these variables do not explain the variations in migration intensity. This indicates that during an abnormal year, larger agricultural land and depletion of assets could contain seasonal migration for some but for others migration was a major coping mechanism. What these findings, however, reconfirm is that unless a critical minimum area is available in dry land conditions, many of the households even with relatively larger cropped area but without enough creditworthiness or savings to meet implications of a shock like crop failure, may have to resort to other measures.

Table 6 reveals that in distress situations, family with larger members resorts to large outmigration for more months than smaller families. Other factors remaining the same, as silver assets of the household depleted, the intensity of migration increases. But asset losses could work as coping mechanism only in initial phase of successive scarcity years. Once the households in the tribal belt face consecutive droughts, there remains hardly any valuable that could be mortgaged or sold. This is a negative imperative of a complex process of additional cash need under few livelihood opportunities during a shock. The consumption behaviour during a shock is revealing; households that have food stocks for longer period, resort relatively less to migration compared to households whose food stocks last for shorter period. On the other hand, households that resorted to seasonal migration had higher consumption expenditure compared to non-migrants. A shock reduces food consumption of the affected household but those who stay put in the village and do not resort to migration had to suffer a welfare loss in terms of consumption; more migrants from a family and migration for longer duration tend to help in making the household's consumption in distress period towards normal. On the other hand, factors like reduction in milch, draught power and poultry, fall in operated land have no direct impact on intensity of migration.

The relative importance of remoteness vis-à-vis investment in agriculture in explaining migration intensity is caught by intercept dummy variables D_1, D_2 and D_3. Although weakening in effect of remoteness and improvement in private investment in agriculture both significantly reduce migration, the reduction due to investment in agriculture is far more significant than that of weakening the effects of remoteness. The constant represents the average intensity of migration in remote area with no private investment in agriculture. The sign and the significance level of dummy D_1 reveals that intensity of migration does not reduces significantly from the level that is in remote villages with households with no investment situation, if the households are the one that have invested in agriculture even in relatively remote areas.

Table 6

Factor Explaining Intensity of Migration[a] (All households)

Factor[b]		*Coefficient*	*Significant*	β^c
X_1	Family size	24.5	***	I
X_2	Depletion of silver	.003	*	
X_3	Panchayat benefits	-27.7	***	
X_4	Unpaid debt	26.2	***	VI
X_5	Total income (-migration)	-0.003	***	II
X_6	Cereal produce lasts	-10.2	***	
X_7	Debt owing to death	-.0.02	***	III
X_8	Total expenditure	37.8	***	IV
X_9	Literacy	-35.1	***	
X_{10}	Poverty	-23.5	*	
	Constant	11.8	NS	
	D_1	10.1	NS	
	D_2	-59.9	***	V
	D_3	-55.9	***	
	$\bar{R}^2$	18		
	F	29.3	***	
	Number of observations	1,609		

a Based on linear regression analysis where:
Dependent variable is migration intensity in person-days.

b The correlation between explanatory factor is low.

c β is standardized coefficients that provide relative importance of different factors in the $\bar{R}^2$.

X_1: 1 = up to 4; 2= 5 to 6, 3= more than 6.

X_2: Depletion of silver in Rs in last 5 years.

X_3: Rs per household 1 = nil, 2= up to Rs 1,600, 3= more than Rs 1,600.

X_4: Outstanding social debt 1 = nil, 2= up to Rs 4,000., 3 = more than Rs 4,000.

X_5: 0 = poor, 1 = non-poor.

X_6: Produce lasts 1=up to 90 days; 2=91 to 150 days, 3= 151 to 310 days, 4=more than 310 days.

X_7: Number of times missed both the meals.

D_1, D_2 and D_3 are intercept dummies.

D_1 = 1 for households located in underdeveloped villages but had invested in irrigation, 0 for rest.

D_2 = 1 for households located in developed villages but not invested in irrigation, 0 for rest.

D_3 = 1 for households located in developed villages and with private investment in irrigation, 0 for rest.

On the other hand, a reduction in intensity of migration is higher when the household is one that is located in relatively developed villages but with no investment in agriculture; the negative and significance of D_2 imply this fact. In other words, intensity of migration would have been higher but for the weakening of the effect of remoteness. The size of D_3, though significant, has reduced, indicating that compared to developed villages with no investment in agriculture, the intensity of migration does reduce significantly if the households have invested in irrigation. But the effect of the process of weakening of remoteness reduces migration to larger extent compared to investment alone. This is so because investment in agriculture in remote areas only supports an individual's agriculture and his capability to circumvent the debt trap during a shock but the process of weakening of remoteness through infrastructure and market development influences many. The beta coefficients reveal that though four most important factors in explaining are size of the family, income other than migration, social debt, the importance of weakening of remoteness is more important than individuals' investment in agriculture.

The above analysis identifies the individual factors that have influenced the migration. However, it is interesting to note that it is the shared play of factors, rather than individual factors, that influences

Figure 1

Interaction between Factors

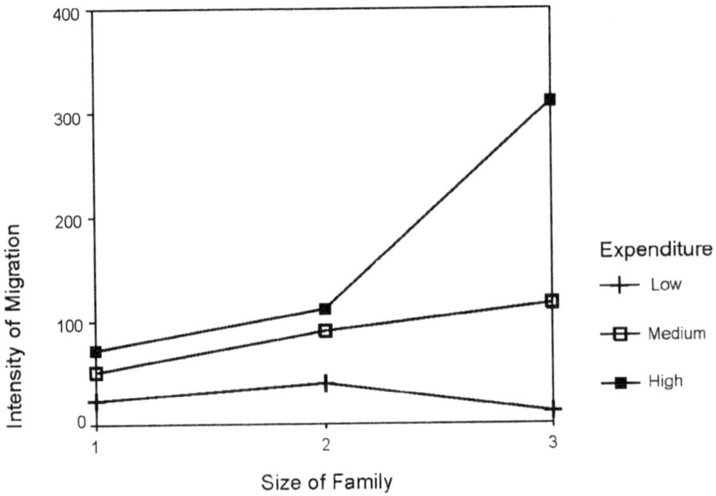

intensity of migration. Results of Analysis of Variance (Appendix 1) reveal that interaction between (a) family size and consumption expenditure; (b) income and family size; (c) income and consumption expenditure, have significantly influenced the migration intensity. The significance of the interactions also means that individual factors like the size of family, consumption expenditure, income, etc., though may be significant, have no impact in governing the migration. What matters are the combined effects of the two. For example, it is neither size of family nor the expenditure alone that has significance in governing the migration pattern but if large families also have higher consumption expenditure then the intensity of migration increases dramatically (Figure 1).

Two different processes influence the well-being of the households, one supporting the intensity of migration and the other restraining it. Seasonal migration becomes inevitable during a shock in order to have command on resources to improve food consumption and to meet non-food expenditure of the remaining members in the village; in the process it is inevitable that some members of the affected household to migrate. While the income generating processes like operational area, access to employment in nearby areas, improved access to food, benefits of government schemes are able to restrain intensity of seasonal migration, but these processes during a consecutive period of drought create market failure for individuals both as producers as well as consumers. The extent of migration that takes place during a normal year is not always a distress migration. It provides access to additional capital and knowledge for investment in irrigation, new inputs and agricultural technology. Although sale and mortgage of silver and bullocks may provide necessary cash in hand, it also brings into operation the much-defamed *bania* who provides them cash or would do so for replenishing the depleted assets and draught power, or fresh agricultural loans for next season. Consequently, the *bania* has first access to migration savings.

There are also some households that have relatively lower income. As a result, their resourceless forces them in perpetual web of debt, inability to service their debt and distress migration. The process is particularly severe for 50 per cent of households that have less land with no irrigation. For these households, access to cash for preparing for migration, especially for purchasing some food grains for remaining members, is a process where the silver depletion is the only way to have access to some cash. On the other hand, access to cash, even during a shock for a large landowner with some irrigation is much easier. The *bania* does not necessarily demand a mortgage-deed from them in anticipation of a good crop next season. But for both the above groups, resource poor and resource rich, the access to output market is restricted because of the credit provided by the *bania*. This interlocked market becomes severely exploitative. The *bania* not only charges high interest but also restricts free sale of output.

Seasonal migration also results in short-term land transactions like sharecropping, fixed rent and land mortgage. Some market institutions like labour and credit markets are well developed in the region. But in absence of land market, the land related institutions – working for bringing tenant and owner together – have developed. These institutions have come up to minimize the cost of negotiating agriculture under resource constraints. *Dhans,* a sort of exchange of bullock and labour between kin-groups, has also developed in response to market failure of the two important resources. The main role of short-term land transactions is not only to share risk of farming but it also optimizes labour use under a shock; poor quality of land and need to move out and engage the family in some economic activity other than agriculture, forces such land transactions. While these institutions are likely to have existed over a long period of time, the recent changes in the functioning of these institutions due to increased incidence of droughts need to be probed further. Similarly, importance of such land transactions in making the migrant family's representation in social hierarchy would be worth discussing.

An important facet of migration relates to a process of maintaining individuals' position in the social hierarchy.[7] This is one of the important investments in a society where social networking, rather than quantum physical assets, decides the worth of individuals in the society. What, however, is relevant to note is the fact that if the society is traditional, social relations and investment on maintaining social relations become important for the survival of the individual. In the process, leasing out land by migrant engenders his symbolic presence in the village and his representation in social hierarchy without his being physically present. The power to till land of a migrant protects economic interest of both the migrant and the tenant but in the exchange, the migrant also obtains control over his social interests. The most preferred arrangement is crop sharing because it makes migrant's links with the community preserved. In order to force the contract in terms of labour use and sharing output, the migrant has to make a number of trips to village, especially during peak harvest season.[8] That reinforces his severed interests in the social set-up in his absence.

The expansion of cultivated land in the village after a shock is also not uncommon. In order to repay accumulated loans, migrants often start cultivating wasteland that had not been under cultivation. The untapped land resources in this tribal belt come under pressure because the debt-trap forces the migrants to supplement their land resources. This additional land has low productivity and can sustain only traditional crops like *kodai, kudki* and pulses on the one hand and often have serious environmental implications. Generally, the outer slopes are the only available areas but bringing such areas under cultivation creates favourable setting for soil erosion. Once under cultivation, the steep slopes deplete the natural grass cover that binds the soil and the expansion in cultivable area leads to washing off top-soil. Population pressures and land fragmentation owing to succession also create pressures on land. Migration and expansion of cultivated area in this remote tribal region often trigger an environmental crisis. But migration for a few is a source of saving, investment and agricultural transfer.

The change in the form of technologically driven agriculture, though restricted to about 25 per cent of cultivated area, is not entirely an outcome of state intervention. It happened because of seasonal migration. Seasonal migration for the tribal is not coping with shocks alone;[9] it is experiencing development that has by-passed them.[10] What a tribal learns during his stay as a migrant labourer – either on irrigated farms of plains of Orissa, Jharkhand and Chhattisgarh or on the farms of irrigated HB cotton growers of Khandesh or on the fields of irrigated paddy and sugarcane growers in south Gujarat – is a main source of agriculture technology transfer. How to energise the well and distribute water, how to grow irrigated fertilizer-responsive cotton, soybean and wheat, and utilization of post-harvest technology of these market-oriented crops. etc., are learnt during seasonal migration. No matter how much the left-oriented non-governmental organiztion[11] discredits it, this process of production of knowledge has created space for non-tribal institutions, that is, inducing conversion of subsistence way of agriculture to a market-driven agriculture. The process is, however, internalised without any state support. In irrigated areas, the *bania* provides agricultural credit without any security. The tribals are also able to repay the loans promptly at least during good agricultural years. But in the process, they have started attaching a high degree of dependence on non-tribal institution they loathed the most, the market.

In unsustainable agriculture where population pressures have reduced wages, improving agricultural productivity by investing on soil and water conservation could be an important way of checking seasonal migration. Next section presents a successful experiment that has influence on seasonal migration during normal years. While the state has also made some interventions in the form of check dams in the study villages, outcome of these has been indifferent due to factors that are generally associated with low performance of such interventions. Against these, there are success stories of watershed programmes in the region that have reduced migration.

Migration and Investment in Agriculture

Despite consistent efforts of state to improve tribal agriculture, problems like uncertainty of agricultural production and access failure to food have forced a large population of the tribals to adopt alternative avenues of livelihood.[12] It can be argued that these efforts are not only target-oriented and top heavy but also lack people's participation.[13] Not only benefits of these projects have reached a few but also the structures have short life owing to poor construction and maintenance problems. There is, therefore, an urgent need for a paradigm shift in the process. Unlike the state, an influential non-government organization always acts with communities with understanding and satisfies their most felt needs. Sadguru Water and Development Foundation (SWD Foundation) is actively involved in creating alternatives through sustainable development of common property resources in tribal areas of Madhya Pradesh, Rajasthan and Gujarat.[14] The SWD Foundation, in these tribal areas, intervenes with a design to improve carrying capacity of land so that agriculture becomes capable of providing sustenance to the needy.

The inevitability of making groundwater available to agriculture in a sustainable manner has been recognized by SWD Foundation. It has also recognized that only small water harvesting devices, such as check dams, would be able to harness water in these difficult areas. These devices harness surface and groundwater resources that flow through as run off. Thus, obstructing this runoff and diverting it to enter into pitches of soil rocks through gravity is the major strategy of the Foundation for harnessing water for irrigation. Eventually, this underground water is lifted through tube wells for irrigation. Theoretically, this source of irrigation is renewable as long as groundwater recharge is in excess of its depletion. The Foundation forces this equilibrium to be in favour of water recharge by institutionalizing water lifting and its use, and maintenance of the physical structure through farmers' irrigation cooperatives. Each cooperative, organized by the Foundation, comprises of 35 to 45 tribal farmers. The executive committee of the cooperative has main task of providing irrigation to its members in equitable and sustainable manner. This is done by putting community pressure for (i) optimizing water use by extending irrigation only to low water using crops like cereals, pulses and short duration vegetables; (ii) maintaining irrigation infrastructure so that water availability in the command area is uninterrupted to all of its members; and (iii) maintaining water distribution, water lifting cost and revenue proceeds from sale of water at levels that are conducive for sustainable use.

The impact of such a water-harvesting programme in tribal areas is seen from two angles. The first is on macro economic aspects of the region, and second at the micro level on socio-economic conditions of tribal beneficiaries. The macro impact is felt on (Shah, 2000) increased groundwater table, changes in land use pattern, and increase in area under irrigation by various sources, improvement in soil quality and crop productivity. At the micro level, impact of SWD Foundation's water harvesting programme is observed (Shylendra and Umarani, 1999) in the following areas: first, (a) disappearance of mixed cropping, increase in cropping intensity and area cultivated in *rabi* and summer; (b) cropping pattern changes and increase in productivity; (c) increase in farm income and profits; (d) strong forward and backward market linkages; (e) increased access to farm residual for fuel and fodder. Secondly, there is significant reduction in distress migration, especially female migration. Lastly, there is significant improvement in food consumption and access to social infrastructure of the villagers. All these changes initiated by the SWD Foundation have improved the quality of life of the beneficiaries with a strategy that is also highly viable.[15]

Such positive interventions have raised expectations that replication of such experiments in tribal areas would be a panacea for the ills of the tribal society.[16] But such positive impact is also accompanied with counterproductive processes when physical structures are created without people's participation (Sah, 1994; Patil, 2000). When such physical structures do not accompany an institutional structure, they often prove beneficial for a few influential that take advantage of the system by extending irrigation beyond the command area and cultivate high water using commercial crops at the cost of the other tribal farmers. Consequently, groundwater depletion is faster than its recharge. In the process, both equity and ecological considerations are at stake. Nevertheless, replicating the SWD Foundation intervention can ensure equity as well as sustainability of such development efforts. The important question, however, is: Can a programme developed by intensive understanding of local conditions and needs be replicated by state through its National Watershed Development Projects for Rainfed Areas (NWDPRA) approach in other tribal areas?

Equally important is sustainability of water harvesting technology, especially in the remote tribal areas when such structure depends on rainwater. Consecutive droughts render such structures useless and the economy of the region owing to failing agriculture resorts to migration.[17] Evidences from SWDF command area, that witnessed consecutive droughts, have shown the efficacy of such structures in severe drought years. And hence, the policy implications of these water-harvesting experiments need to be understood and used in greater details.

Summing up

Tribal migration in search of employment has a long tradition. Recent evidences reveal that the intensity of migration has increased over the years. Migration from tribal areas is not uniform; some locations have large seasonal migration whereas some locations have relatively less migration. Both remoteness and unsustainable agriculture superimpose each other in forcing migration. Unsustainable and stagnant agriculture is relatively more imposing than remoteness in explaining the migration. Although, in recent past migration has been caused by harvest failure, a shock can activate a complex socio-economic process leading to migration. Apart from population pressure, reduction in availability of food and increased debts increases intensity of seasonal migration. The households under shock also face serious non-economic problems like doing work that in normal situation they would not have preferred; other problems that emerge in the process are inability to service their debt and missing meals, etc. Borrowings from *bania* located in markets increase. The intensity of migration seems to have strong links with borrowings for meeting current consumption needs; to repay the loan, the migration increases. Seasonal migration does supplement investable surplus when cash needs are more and sources of institutional borrowings are few. In fact, credit and migration work as supplement as well as substitute in the remote tribal society. On an average, a migrant family saves rupees five thousand per year from migration. But a large part of the savings goes for servicing the debt.

Evidently, in abnormal years larger agricultural holding is unable to neutralize the risk of harvest loss. Unless a critical minimum area is available, a household with relatively large cropped area but without enough savings needs to resort to migration. Interactions of factors like large family, higher expenditure, low income (other than migration), depletion of silver and thus borrowings at exuberant interest, lower access to state schemes result in increasing the intensity of migration. More migrants for longer duration from a family help in pushing food consumption of the remaining members to normal during bad agricultural years. Consequently, households that do not resort to migration have lower in food consumption and more days without meals. Migration along with short-term land transactions like sharecropping, fixed rent and land mortgage has played an important role in the tribal society. This not only reduces the risk of farming but also optimizes the efficiency of family labour. Some of these land transactions also strengthen social links that maintain individuals' position in social hierarchy even in their absence. But for some resourceful, migration has become the major source of agricultural technology transfer, savings and investment in this remote tribal area.

Migration in absence of a sustainable livelihood has become unavoidable in remote rural areas. A way of reducing the incidence of migration is to intensify investment that conserves the soil-moisture and makes agriculture sustainable. Evidences reveal that civil society initiatives in tribal areas have reduced seasonal migration significantly. Replicating such efforts may be helpful for the hapless migrants. Our findings have demonstrated that a shock can push even a well-to-do tribal household into a debt-trap and has to resort to migration as a coping mechanism. But for a large section of households that are resourceless owing to population pressures, migration is the only coping mechanism. Therefore, the processes that facilitate migrants in the course of migration are as important as reducing migration. How to make the lives of migrants at the place of destination less stressful, provide them with amenities there, and make their position stronger in the labour market, is as important as improving agriculture and increasing borrowing capacity of migrants at the place of origin. Breaking the debt-trap that triggers migration and strengthening agriculture of the area are two important interventions that may result in reducing migration.

Notes

1. This analysis is based on data generated from randomly selected 1,614 household from central tribal belt comprising Gujarat, Rajasthan, Madhya Pradesh, Chhattisgarh, Jharkhand and Orissa.
2. In tribal society, agriculture is the way of life and also its major economic activity. Population pressures result in depletion of agriculture land due to marriage of children and thus division of family. The newly formed households are relatively resource deficient and rely not only on social networks but also on migration for survival.
3. The remoteness of underdeveloped villages and poor agricultural base has resulted in relatively large population to rely on migration as a coping mechanism compared to developed villages.
4. This society has relatively high female work participation rate than that of non-tribal. Moreover, those who have paid dowry price of Rs 20 to 25 thousand, in 2006 prices, would like to get the money back through migration.
5. Unlike rural to rural migration, where destinations are known to the groups as, some of the members have past experiences of working there, rural to

urban migration depend on middlemen, known as *mukadam*, who guides movements towards city. A *mukadam* is a middleman-cum-supervisor who has well developed network in the areas from where migration originates. He provides some advance to migrant groups, arranges for basic facilities at the destinations and negotiates with prospective employer.

6. There could be an overreporting in migration savings, as the qualitative investigation reveals that on average migration brings clothing, footwear and consumer items from this income.
7. Moral hazards are involved in share cropping. The tribal who is leasing out land would like to ensure that the tenant, as agreed, has applied labour and inputs on the field for he has to share the out-of-pocket cost. Similar is the case when the crop would be harvested and shared for, the landowner has to ensure that he receives the portion of crop output as agreed earlier. For enforcing these, the landowner migrant has to either make a number of visits to the village or leave all these monitoring in trust on the other party. In this area the first option is more prevalent, not because of lack of trust but because it re-establishes his ties with the community.
8. Tribal economy is based on reciprocity. Apart from performing economic transaction under market failure conditions, the short-term land transaction, especially share cropping and fixed rent create social trust that works as metaphor for social return in exchange of economic gains. This latter (social)-function of this exchange is an important as its formal (economic) function of exchange.
9. A number of villages in this tribal belt have come under submergence of Sardar Sarovar Project in Gujarat and Madhya Pradesh. This is equally true in other states of the central tribal belt where mining, industrial projects and big dams have displaced large tribal population. The scars of relocation and play of civil society institution have made the inhabitant weary of outsiders on the one hand and created trust and solidarity amongst them on the other hand (Sah, 2003).
10. In drought prone areas, migration also works as asset formation device. Successive droughts render agriculture as unsustainable livelihood option and forces even large farmers to join the queue for doles. Rains have failed in the last four years in this area. Landless labourers and marginal farmers do save some money owing to migration. But such savings are major source of repayment to *Bania* on consumption loans taken to meet the scarcity. The debt-trap and dependence on non-institutional sources for consumption loan creates a socio-economic process in which migration becomes a major livelihood option.
11. Civil society movements have strong presence in this tribal belt. Control over forest is a major contention that has brought into play institutions like the Adivasi Mukti Sangathan (AMS). Displacement due to large dams in

the region has rationalized the presence of the movements like Narmada Bachao Andolan (NBA), an NGO that has provided alternatives to the existing development paradigm. Both these movements have created a strong social capital base in the area. For details see, Sah (2003).

12. Working as wage labour and seasonal migration are the most widely adopted livelihood strategies in tribal areas.
13. These official irrigation schemes are carried as if their creation is an end in itself. These official programmes are operating without institutional arrangements necessary to enforce equity and ecological considerations. Consequently, the checks and balances needed for water use efficiency are missing. Planning for these programmes are not only target-oriented but also lack understanding on various constraints, which resulted in past failures of the programmes.
14. Sadguru Water Development Foundation is working in about 375 tribal villages of Gujarat (Panchmahals and Dahod), Madhya Pradesh (Jhabua) and Rajasthan (Banswara). By the end of 2000–01, 195 lift irrigation projects and 187 check dams were operational in the project area irrigating about 37,000 acre land; for detail see Foundation (2001).
15. A study by Kumar et al. (2000) has estimated that the economic benefit-cost ratio of check dam-lift irrigation schemes turns out to be highly viable in tribal regions. The economic cost in the project included construction cost of 6 check dams on Mahhan river located in Dahod (Gujarat), Banswara (Rajasthan) and Jhabua (Madhya Pradesh), plus capital cost of 6 lift irrigation schemes and operation and maintenance cost. The benefits from the project included increase in agricultural income owing to irrigation and income earned from water charges. The capital cost of check dams and lift irrigation schemes put together was Rs 17.37 million. The scheme irrigates about 690 acre of land per year. Increase in agricultural income owing to irrigation net of maintenance and operation cost, plus the water charges received by the project were estimated at Rs 3.12 million per year for next 20 years. The present value of this income stream at 12 per cent discount of was Rs 23.25 million. When compared against the capital investment, the benefit-cost ratio turns out to be 1.33, which for irrigation project, is very high economic rate of return. If social benefit of drought proofing is added to it, the benefit-cost ratio would go further up.
16. The strategy, however, is not a solution for all situations. Drought proofing in recurring monsoons failure has its own problems. During last three years dry farming in Madhya Pradesh, including its tribal belt, saw three consecutive crop failures, not only food security has adversely been affected but also seen a prolonged drinking water crises, especially in the tribal region including areas covered under water harvesting structures.

17. Harnath Jagawat, Director SWD Foundation, has emphatically said that under severe rainfall deficit years though the watershed interventions do provide drinking water to the inhabitants in the command area, the structures are unable to sustain normal agriculture.

References

Baviskar, A. (1997): *In the Belly of the River,* Delhi: Oxford University Press.

Bureau (1974): "Final Report of the Survey of Seasonal Migration of Labour in Panchamahals District", *Quarterly Bulletin of Economics and Statistics,* Vol. 15.

Breman, J. (1985): *Of Peasants, Migrants and Paupers,* Delhi: Oxford University Press.

Breman, J. (1996): *Footloose Labour: Working in the Indian Informal Economy,* Cambridge: Cambridge University Press.

Deshpande, R.S. and V.R. Reddy (1991): "Differential Impact of Watershed based Technology", *Indian Journal of Agricultural Economics,* Vol. 46 (3).

Deshpande, R.S. and A. Narayanamoorthy (1998): "An Appraisal of Watershed Development Programme across India", *Arth Vijnana,* Vol. 12 (4).

Foundation (2001): Annual Report for the Year ending March 31, 2001, Dahod: Sadguru Water and Development Foundation.

Kumar, M.D., V. Ballabh, R. Pandey and J. Talati (2000): "Sustainable Development and Use of Water Resources", Working Paper 150, Anand: Institute of Rural Management.

Lee, E.S. (1966): "A Theory of Migration", *Demography,* Vol. 3 (1).

Mosse, D., S. Gupta, M. Mehta, V. Shah and J. Rees (2002): "Brokered Livelihoods: Debt, Labour Migration and Development in Tribal Western India", *Journal of Development Studies,* Vol. 38 (5).

Olsen, W.K. and R.R.V. Murthy (2000): "Contract Labour and Bondage in Andhra Pradesh", *Journal of Social and Political Thoughts,* Vol. 1 (2).

Pandey, R. (1998): "Water Harvesting Need and Strategies", *Journal of Rural Development,* Vol. 17 (4).

Patel, Arjun (2001): Study of Migrants of Dangs and Dahod, (Mimeo), Surat: Centre for Social Studies.

Patil, B.R. (2000): "Pani Panchayat in Pune District: An Experiment of Water Management for Sustainable Agriculture", in B.C. Barik (ed.), *Resource Management and Contours of Development,* Jaipur: Rawat Publications.

Patil, D.K. (2000): A Study of Economics of Percolation Tanks and their Impact on Agricultural Development, Ph.D. Thesis submitted to Shivaji University, Kholapur.

Sah, D.C. (1994): Midterm Evaluation of Shree Niketan Rural Development Project, (Mimeo), Surat: Centre for Social Studies.

—. (1999): "Pressure on Land, Employment and Migration", *Review of Development and Change,* Vol. 4 (2).

—. (2003): "Commons and Community: Evidences from South-western Tribal Belt of Madhya Pradesh", Working Paper 7, CPRC (India), New Delhi: Indian Institute of Public Administration.

Sah, D.C. and Amita Shah (2003): Chronic Poverty in Remote Rural Areas of South-western Madhya Pradesh, Ujjain: Madhya Pradesh Institute of Social Science Research and Ahmedabad: Gujarat Institute of Development Research (Mimeo).

Sah, D.C., Ashish Bhatt and Tapas Dalapati (2008): Chronic Poverty in Remote Tribal Areas: Evidence from Central Tribal Belt of India, Ujjain: Madhya Pradesh Institute of Social Science Research (Mimeo).

Saxena, D.P. (1977): *Rural Urban Migration in India: Causes and Consequences,* Bombay: Popular Prakashan.

Shah, Amita (2000): "Promoting Small Water Harvesting Structures in Dryland Regions", Working Paper No. 115, Ahmedabad: Gujarat Institute of Development Research.

—. (2001): "Who Benefits from Participatory Watershed Development", *Gatekeeper,* Series No. 97, International Institute of Environment and Development.

Shylendra, H.S. and Umarani (1999): Development Intervention and Its Impact: Evidences from a Village Study in Panchmahals, (Mimeo), Anand: Institute of Rural Management.

Sjaastad, L.A. (1962): "Cost and Returns of Human Migration", *Journal of Political Economy,* Vol. 70 (5).

Stark, O. (1980): "On the Role of Urban-Rural Remittance in Rural Development", *Journal of Development Studies,* 16 (3).

Todaro, M.P. (1969): "A Model of Labour Migration in Less Developed", *American Economic Review,* Vol. 59 (1).

—. (1980): "Internal Migration in Developing Countries: A Survey", in R.A. Esterlin (ed.), *Population and Economic Change in Developing Countries,* Chicago: Chicago University Press.

Vaidyanathan, A. (1986): "Labour Use in Rural India: A Study of Spatial and Temporal Variations", *Economic and Political Weekly,* Vol. 26 (45).

Appendix 1

ANOVA Results Explaining Variations in Migration Intensity*

Source	*Sum of Squares*	*Degree of Freedom*	*Mean Square*	*F*	*Sig.*
Intercept	70,13,269	1	70,13,269	109	
Family size	1,22,45,529	2	6,12,276	9	.000
Expenditure	23,54,396	2	11,77,198	18	.000
Income	81,07,425	2	40,53,712	63	.000
Family size* Income	22,15,861	4	5,53,965	9	.000
Expenditure * Family size	27,22,501	4	6,80,625	10	.000
Expenditure * Income	10,63,835		2,65,959	4	.000
Error	1,36,236	53	64,192		
Total	13,45,05,174	94			

* R^2 = .16 (Adjusted R^2 = .0.15).

5

Changing Patterns of Tribal Economy and Its Implications

Case Study of a Betul Village

S.N. CHAUDHARY

Historically tribal economy, the nature of which was primary, informal and local, revolved around basic requirements of food and shelter. It was by and large non-monetized with having legitimacy and support from local ecology and socio-cultural traditions. However, with the passage of time, as the process of acculturation with non-tribal traditions increased, the tribal economy largely retained its informal character upto British invasion, but within its boundary there was continuity and change. Among many tribes forest was the main source of livelihood but with the passage of time their dependence on agriculture and subsequently on wage work increased. And with this in many cases forest ceased to remain the main or the only source of their livelihood. Today, there are tribes among whom due to interplay of all these sources of livelihood, there is visible economic development. They have not only moved from one to more than one sources of income but also there is a trend in favour of monetized economy. These sources have functional implications for many. But these implications are exogenous as well as unsustainable, because neither these sources nor its economic and non-economic implications are tenable. Given the situation it is high time to comprehend nature and dynamics of tribal economy in the historical perspective and suggest ways and means to retain the changing trend. In the light of these two broad objectives this study was conducted. More specifically, the study is directed to search answer of the following questions. What are the specific sources of income? What is the situation of continuity and change? How change in income influence economic and non-economic life in terms of possession of household and agricultural assets, saving and indebtedness, health management, education, entertainment and lifestyle?

I

Methodology

The study was conducted in Pathai village of Sahpur development block of Betul district. Logic behind selecting Betul district and Sahpur development block was heavy concentration of tribal population in the area. The district and the block consists of 40 per cent and 64 per cent population of Scheduled Tribes respectively. Historically tribals have been residing in large number, for instance 44.99 per cent during 1921, in this district. And in the village under study more than 98 per cent population is of tribes. In the neighbouring villages of Pathai both Gond and Korku reside but in Pathai it is only Gond who live. The village is located at a distance of about 4 km from Sahpur. There are 201 households in the village. All of them participated in the study.

Some of the specific features of Pathai is that here it is the illiterate who outnumber the literate, non-workers outnumber the workers, marginal workers and agricultural labours outnumber the cultivators, female outnumber the male population and average number of persons in each household is six. So far as availability of basic facilities inside the village is concerned out of 38 such items listed by us which are related to day-to-day life 11 are available in the village itself. These are: Panchayat office, sub-health centre, metal road, electricity, Anganwadi centre, primary and middle school, Kirana shop, PDS shop, flour mill, tube well/handpump and *Jhar-Phunk* facility.

Interview schedule, case study, information from secondary sources, Right to Information Technique (RTI), group discussion and interview guide were the techniques used to collect relevant information from different stake holders. Fieldwork was done in 2008. Findings of the study are as under.

II
Findings and Discussion

Today tribal economy revolves around agricultural activity, wage work within and outside the village through migration, marketing of firewood and other forest related activities. Hardly some of the tribals are associated with secondary or tertiary sector activities for their livelihood. Patterns of saving and indebtedness have also changed over the time which have affected both quality and number of household and agricultural assets. Public Distribution System (PDS), Self-Help Groups (SHGs), National Rural Employment Guarantee Scheme (NREGS) and other development projects are also providing economic opportunity. The net result of interplay of all these local and non-local sources of income and livelihood is that it has impacted economic life of tribals in a significant manner. Economically, they are at the crossroads. And change in their economic life have also influenced their social life. This is apparent from findings and discussions presented below.

Farming

Tribals are historically associated with land as a source of their livelihood in different ways. They are either owner, they have taken land on share-cropping basis, taken land on mortgage or lease and many of them are partly landowners and partly wage earners and some of them are totally wage earners. Of 200 households 25. 32 per cent have land upto 2.5 acres, 23.5 per cent possess land between 2.5 to 5 acres and there are 19.5 per cent (39) households who possess above 5 acres of land. 75 per cent (150) households are landowner and remaining 25 per cent are landless.

Of the total landowners, 84 (56%) have their total land unirrigated, 43 (27%) have all their land irrigated, 13 (9%) have half of their land irrigated, five have one-third part of land irrigated, three have one-fourth part of land irrigated, one has three-fourth part of land irrigated and remaining two have about one acre of land irrigated. This means, most of the agricultural land is unirrigated in Pathai.

If we see relationship between annual income of households (HHs) and landownership of 150 landowners 139 (93%) HHs have either or less than Rs 11,000 annual income. Of 150 households with having land, about 72 have land paper (*Patta*) of all the lands possessed by them. There are only three who do not have *patta*. There are 20 per cent households who have land but name of their father, father-in-law, mother, and wife is mentioned on *patta*. In most of the cases they are son-in-laws and they have settled with their in-laws. Most of the land is cultivable. It is relatively cheap. About 22 per cent respondents could not estimate cost of their land but about half of the total landowners (75) individually possess land only upto Rs 1.5 lakh. There are 16 families who possess land costing around Rs 3 lakh or above individually. 16 households have received government land during last few years. Most of them could not recall both year of land allotted to them as well as scheme under which land was distributed among them. Only two could recall that they were allotted grazing land. Size of land allotted to them differ from one acre to about 4 acres. About half of them (8) have name of their female members on land patta. The cost of land allotted to them differ from Rs 10,000 to either or more than rupees one lakh. Cost differ only because of difference in size otherwise quality of land in terms of its productivity is by and large the same.

Villagers themselves cultivate their own land. This is a general trend but not universal in Pathai. While some (34%) cultivate on all the land they have there are respondents between 3 to 6 per cent who cultivate only some part of their land. Only 10 households do not cultivate land at all. Ox and plough is the main or the only instrument for cultivation. Almost 85 of them have their own arrangement to plough land. Remaining obtain it on rent basis. And the rent of ploughing differ on the basis of season and labour demand. The standard rate is either between Rs 100 to Rs 150 per acre or between Rs 100 to Rs 200 per day. There are 18 households who occasionally use tractor for ploughing. And its rent is Rs 200 to Rs 300 per hour. There is no tractor in the village. It is obtained on rent from Sahpur. Some (5) have leased out their total land. Villagers do not have land outside the village boundary. Only five have. Cost of their total land outside the village is upto Rs 50,000 per household. Majority feel that they do not have good quality of land in terms of productivity. Only some have taken steps to improve productivity, i.e., seven did fencing, three removed stones, four planted seedling of big/small trees and four used proper amount of bio-fertilizer to improve productivity. Only two opted for test of soil but this effort also could not extend any meaningful benefit to them.

This description help us to conclude that in spite of the fact that villagers at large have land, but state of quality of land, irrigation facility and efforts to improve land productivity is almost invisible in the village.

Land on Contract/Share-cropping

During 2007–08, 35 villagers took land on contract/mortgage or share-cropping basis. All the lenders and receivers are tribals. Number of reasons are held responsible for taking land on share cropping/mortgage.

1. Rajkumar Thatia took 3 acres of land on contract basis for cultivation. He took land at the rent of Rs 1,200. Other expenditure relating to ploughing, fertilizer, seed, etc., took Rs 1,600. Hence, total expenditure made by Rajkumar was Rs 2,800. He planted Soyabean, *jwar* and *tuar*. But due to lack of irrigation facility production was poor and he could not cultivate other crop. His experience was not pleasant.
2. Basant Pardhan has taken 3 acres of land on share-cropping basis from his parent. He could not produce as per expectation due to lack of irrigation, but he received compensation from government because the village was declared as a famine affected area in 2007–08.
3. Rajendra Wadeba has taken 2 acres of land on share-cropping basis from his mother. His effort was successful because he had net profit of one quintal maize and 2 quintals wheat.
4. Kisan Gond took 2 acres of land on share-cropping basis from Phundan. He took land on this basis with the hope that it will provide sufficient food and he will be able to save income from wage work for other purpose. He is happy because he achieved the goal and he could gain 2 quintals of *tuar* and gram as a net profit.
5. Maniram Uikey took 2 acres of land on share-cropping basis from Phundan Dhurve. His effort was also successful because he could produce 2 quintals paddy, 6 quintals maize and 2 quintals gram. He is pleased with the total outcome. He also took 1 acre of land on contract basis for one year from Gunda Parte at the total rate of Rs 1,200. He had to spent Rs 500 on good variety seed and fertilizer. He could gain half quintal soyabean and half quintal gram from the land of Gunda Parte.

In course of study it was observed that villagers take land on contract or share-cropping basis to ensure food security. Their purpose is not at all to produce and market the produce in a massive way, although occasionally they do not hesitate to sell surplus farm produce. Most of those engaged in this process are also wage earners. Food security provide them an opportunity to save their income from wage work and in many cases they spent their saving to obtain household and agricultural assets. The increasing number of assets of different types in the last few years support this argument. The total number of transportation and communication facility was only 34 upto 1999 in the village the number of which increased upto 152 after 1999.

Table 1

Transportation/Communication Facilities

Assets	*Available with Households*	*Year of Purchase*		*Total Number of Items*	*Cost (Rs)*
		Upto 1999	*After 1999*		
Telephone	6	–	6	6	2,380
Mobile phone	9	–	9	9	18,700
Radio	16	3	13	16	2,800
Tape recorder	11	2	9	11	12,950
B&W TV	20	5	15	20	45,250
Colour TV	5	–	5	5	28,500
CD player	15	–	15	15	22,550
Cycle	96	23	73	98	1,24,101
Two-wheeler	8	1	7	10	1,93,000
Total	186	34	152	190	4,50,231

Except cycle most of the items, which are modern in nature, were purchased after 1999. This shows growing atmosphere in favour of consumer culture and modern way of life. Barring few, say for instance, 14 cycle which were received as a dowry item, most of these items were purchased from personal saving.

Land under Cultivation

During 2007, 298.21 ha of land was under cultivation, i.e., 249.21 ha under kharif and 49 ha under rabi crop. Hence, kharif is the most preferred crop than rabi in Pathai. Data reveal that soyabean production was preferred by most of the villagers today. Of 249 ha land under kharif, under 147 ha of land soyabean was produced. Other food crops under kharif were maize, *Jwar* and paddy. The traditional crops like *Kodo, Kutki, Sama,* etc., is still produced but only by few farmers. Because of low productivity of Kodo and Kutki on the one side and inclination in favour of non-traditional serials farmers do not prefer to produce the former. Production of crops like Kodo, Kutki, Sama, etc., have significantly decreased over time. Under rabi crop wheat and gram is the most preferred crop.

Table 2

Production of Kharif and Rabi Crop in Pathai during 2007

Name of Crop	*Land (in ha)*	*Percentage*
Kharif		
Paddy	16.00	6.42
Jwar	25.00	10.03
Maize	30.00	12.03
Kodo/Kutki/Sama	12.00	4.81
Tuar	14.00	5.61
Urad	2.30	0.92
Mung	0.17	0.06
Soyabean	147.53	59.20
Peanuts	1.00	0.40
Teel	1.20	0.48
Total	249.21	100
Rabi		
Wheat	40.00	81.63
Gram	28.00	57.14
Peas	1.00	2.04
Mustard	2.00	4.08
Total	49.00	100

Source: Information provided by Senior Agriculture Development and Extension Officer, Shahpur on December 10, 2008.

If we see cropping pattern in the historical perspective in Betul district it is apparent that over the time production of traditional crop like Kodo, Sama and Kutki which was the most preferred crop during 1907 have drastically decreased, production of wheat have retained the trend although production of red wheat has totally been replaced by white wheat and production of soyabean has tremendously increased since 1975. Today soyabean is the most preferred cereal in comparison to any of the crop.

Table 3

Dynamics of Cropping Pattern in Betul

(in acres)

Crops	*Years*					
	1891–92	*1901–02*	*1911–12*	*1921–22*	*2002–03*	*2006–07*
Wheat	1,53,235	1,12,218	1,78,394	1,23,277	2,07,664.94	2,31,798.86
Paddy	–	–	–	–	1,01,408.45	1,00,672.1
Jwar	–	–	–	–	1,30,286.63	1,12,485.79
Maize	–	–	–	–	79,271.065	1,18,606.38
Gram	57,682	36,923	43,137	38,396	69,809.73	78,408.69
Tuar	–	–	–	–	54,047.44	68,977.02
Urad	–	–	–	–	30,504.07	24,398.32
Sugarcane	9,272	3,08	4,016	3,356	17,118.85	19,945.63
Vegetable	–	–	–	–	15,127.25	28,727.45
Spices	–	–	–	–	5,421.29	11,549.29
Peanuts	–	–	–	–	15,698.64	14,096.86
Til	17,928	28,143	46,334	36,186	2730.41	563.38
Soyabean	–	–	–	–	3,97,435.14	4,297,47.96
Cotton	–	–	–	–	2,829.25	3,162.83
Kodo-Kutki	1,48,140	1,34,151	1,40,708	1,38,872	insignificant	insignificant

Source: Gazetteer of India, Madhya Pradesh, 1999, pp. 286–88 and Districts Statistical Hand Book, Betul, 2007, pp. 24–28.

Use of Fertilizers

Modern fertilizer like urea and DAP is frequently used in the village in comparison to bio-fertilizer. Former was used by about 150 farmers and the latter by 58 only. However, many of them use both bio- and chemical fertilizer. Most of the tribals in Pathai in particular obtain HYV of seed and fertilizer from Sahpur open market. At Sahpur there are seven private shops of seed and fertilizer including one shop run by cooperative society. Prateck traders is the biggest shop. According to shopkeeper, of the total sell only 5 to 6 per cent is purchased by Pathai people. This is extremely low. To him possible reasons are poverty and lack of awareness. People at large do no know where, why and how to use fertilizer. Most of the fertilizer shopkeepers said that because of lack of irrigation facility, lack of interest in farming, availability of bio-fertilizer, villagers use little amount of fertilizer. Urea is also used for liquor making. While making liquor, urea is mixed with *mahua* flower.

However, the in-charge of Adim Jati Sewa Cooperative Society (AJSCS) Sahpur had different story to narrate. To him the AJSCS is functioning in 36 villages. Pathai people rarely take fertilizer. Of 200 households only 14 are registered and of 14 only three farmers left fertilizer on irregular basis. Most of these farmers own between 2.5 acres to 9 acres of land and most of them are either illiterate or mere literate. In comparison to OBC beneficiaries tribals lift fertilizer and improved seed insignificantly in Sahpur villages.

Factors responsible for insignificant use of fertilizer as narrated by shopkeepers above was also supported by Agriculture Development and Extension Officer as well as Sarpanch of Pathai Panchayat Smt Rajni Dhurve. To them poor or pitiable economic condition, lack of skill to avail government provided benefits, availability of cow dung made bio-fertilizer inside the village, availability of non-farm means of livelihood especially road construction and head load of firewood, seasonal outmigration for wage work, lack of assured irrigation facility are the main factors responsible for low level use of chemical fertilizer. There is also system of marketing of cow dung made bio-fertilizer in Pathai. Its current rate is Rs 500 per tractor or Rs 200 per bullock cart. To meet contingent expenditure some of the tribals also sell it to non-tribals from outside Pathai.

Marketing of Farm Produce

Of 150 landowners there are 33 (22%) who sell food grains produced by them. This shows that in spite of radical shift from traditional crop to so-called modern crop farm production is primarily made for consumption by most of the villagers. Some of them (17) sell 100 per cent of soya produced by them. There are five who sell 75 to 90 per cent of the produce. 11 households sell between 25 to 50 per cent of their produce. This shows that for significant number of households availability of food grains is not problematic. Some households sell soya to purchase other food items. Maximum number of them sell it at local Sahpur market and all the shopkeepers at Sahpur are non-tribals.

Relationship between Annual Income and Landownership

There is relationship between the two. Of 50 landless 38 are from below the poverty line. Their annual income is either or less than Rs 11,000. Only 12 have either or more than Rs 11,000 annual income. This means most of the landless are poor. In case of remaining 150 households with having land, 107 are from below the poverty line but they are both from the category of marginal farmers and farmers immediately above the poverty line. There are 38 households who have either or more than 5 acres of land but here also about half of them are from below the poverty line.

Table 4

Landownership

Annual Income	*Landless*	*Up to 2.5 Acres*	*2.5 to 5*	*Above 5*	*Total*	*%*
Up to Rs 11,000	38	51	30	20	139	69.5
11,000+	12	18	13	18	61	30.5
Total	50	69	43	38	200	100

Maximum number of landowners with having different size of land are from below the poverty line. It is primarily due to poor income from their main source of income, i.e., land. Other sources of income is also not effective to bring them out of poverty trap. Needless to mention here that main occupation of male heads of the household is either wage work (37%) farming and wage work (52.5%) and farming (7%). In short, none of the current sources of income in its present shape, is capable enough to bring villagers out of poverty trap and contribute to economic development in a sustainable manner. They have also number of expectations from government in order to bring improvement in farm work. Except landless 50 households, all the remaining 150 made either or more than one advise for improvement in farm activities. For maximum number of them (88) irrigation issue is the main challenge before them. Government should come forward and solve this problem by increasing number of wells/tube wells, diesel engine, provide pump sets, etc. Many (29) want more land and those who have land without proper paper, they want proper land paper so that a sense of permanent ownership may emerge. Some (19) want free fertilizer. Similar number of them want ox, plough, *bakhar* and other agricultural equipments on subsidized rate. There are 10 who opine that they do not have information about schemes meant for tribal farmers. It should be made available to them in the interest of effective utilization of development schemes.

Table 5

Expectation From Government for Agricultural Development (multiple response)

Response	*F*	%
Well/Tube well/Irrigation	88	43.13
Ox/Plough/Bakhar	8	3.92
Electricity	4	
Land/Land Patta	29	14.21
Free fertilizer/Fertilizer on subsidised rate	19	9.31
Agricultural assets	12	
Diesel engine/Pump	21	10.29
Information about schemes	10	4.90
Loan facility	3	1.47
Levelling of land	7	3.43
Job	3	1.47
Total	204	100

Institutional Intervention for Agricultural Development: Kapildhara

Under National Rural Employment Guarantee Scheme (NREGS), there is a provision of *Kapildhara* as one of the sub-schemes directed to provide irrigation facility to those who are marginal farmers. Under this scheme there is a provision of digging and construction of pucca well. The construction cost of well differ from year to year and during 2007 an amount of Rs 82,400 was allotted to each of the beneficiary household through village panchayat. Panchayat releases the sanctioned amount step by step examining progress of well construction work. Needless to mention that under this scheme villagers, including the beneficiary, are provided wage work because under the NREGS each of the households have right to get employment at the local level for at least 100 days in a year.

When this news spread in Pathai that well will be constructed free of cost significant number of marginal farmers (47) assembled in a meeting organized by panchayat on 19 August, 2007. There was discussion in the meeting and as a result of that 18 villagers were identified for this benefit at the first stage. Their names along with required papers were forwarded to Janpad office which was subsequently accepted. But this process took more than 4 months. However, digging work started since middle of January 2008. In one of the cases digging work continued for 15 days and 9 wage workers were hired for this purpose. As per information provided by panchayat secretary the digging cost took Rs 43,764 still about half of the amount was available for making the well pucca and making it user-friendly.

In the case of a villager named Phoolchand, the quality of soil was soft and because of this well was constructed properly and in time. We observed that as per the scheme well should not be less than 12 metre deep, but panchayat representative seldom follow it. Phoolchand said that about 12 wells were constructed during 2008, but as soon as water appeared digging work discontinued. To him well was not constructed upto pre-fixed level. Needless to mention that instead of a well with having 36 feet deep well of only 12 feet was constructed. As a result, cost of digging of 24 feet was saved by panchayat. Some villagers know that their well should be 36 feet deep but partly because of lack of assertiveness and partly due to powerfulness and assertiveness of Sarpanch and secretary the system of malpractice continues. Needless to mention that well is constructed under the direct supervision of panchayat.

The vary purpose of irrigating land is largely defeated because when beneficiary need irrigation especially in summer, there is no water in the well. Due to lack of proper deepness water is only available when there is no severe need of water. Here it was also observed that as per the guideline well construction work is to be completed before rainy season. But in actuality it is not completed during the stipulated period. As a result, panchayat discontinues digging work as soon as water appears inside the well and as soon as monsoon begins. The incomplete wells are damaged during rainy season due to soil erosion.

In one of the cases Sarpanch said that cement work was not done because stone plates were very costly and they decided to obtain it during the rainy season when its price goes down. Unfortunately in some of the cases semi-structured well looses its identify. Today, one of the wells appears almost like a 5 feet deep nallah. In one of the cases when the beneficiary approached panchayat office the reply was that well will be made pucca after the rainy season because money is still available but beneficiary family has to bring that nalla into the shape of well by himself or from their own resources. This reply frustrated the so-called beneficiary. It was also observed that amount sanctioned for the construction of a well is much higher than the amount actually required. In course of a question one of the tribal beneficiaries replied that he might have constructed a suitable well along with cement work had he been asked and allotted only Rs 50,000 for this purpose. This narration clearly reflect that how an innovative scheme directed to the empowerment of marginal tribal is diluted by change agents.

In order to provide irrigation facility and employment opportunity within the village itself under NREGS during 2008, 21 households of Pathai were allotted well. Towards the end of the year, 11 wells were completed and 10 wells are in the process. Details of these wells in relation to profile of beneficiaries and extent of water use are as under:

The cost of construction of well differs from year to year. For instance, during 2006–07 cost of construction of one well was Rs 73,000. It increased up to 82,400 in 2007–08 and Rs 1,30,000 during 2008–09. One of the pre-conditions to get benefit of this scheme is that the beneficiary must have at least 2.5 acres of land. In case, one household do not have that amount of land there is a provision to allot one well to two beneficiaries on joint basis on boundary of their land from where both of them may use water.

In Pathai as yet 11 tribal households have availed benefit of this scheme. *Details* of these beneficiaries are as under:

1. Jondu s/o Shambhu was allotted Rs 73,000 for well. The well is now complete and it has about 5 feet deep water. But he could not use this water for irrigation during 2007–08. He do not recall the

total land which he possess because he lives in joint family and currently the legal owner of the land is his father and not Jondu.

2. Ram Prasad s/o Ratan has 3.25 acres of land. He was allotted Rs 82,400 for well. His well is complete with having 4 feet water during December 2008. He also could not use water for agricultural purpose.
3. Shankar s/o Phuntu was also allotted Rs 82,400 for this purpose. The well is yet to be properly cemented. In this well also there is about 4 feet water. He has about 10 acres of land. He could not use water for irrigation on his own land rather it was used by his neighbour for irrigation.
4. Bundiya w/o Shukh Lal was also allotted Rs 82,400 for well. She has about 5 acres of land. Nearly 4 feet water is available in her well. She has constantly used well water to irrigate wheat, gram and peas crop during 2008. She has pleasant experience of this experiment.
5. Balmat s/o Bake Singh was also allotted Rs 82,400 for well. His well is still to be completed. There is no water in the well. His land is almost barren due to lack of irrigation facility. He even do not know how much land he has.
6. Kanhaiya s/o Roshan was allotted Rs 82,400 for well. His well is ready but it is not complete with boundary. About 3 feet water is available in the well. He has about 3 acres of land but he has not started taking benefit out of the well.
7. Rando Bai w/o Durkasa was also allotted Rs 82,400 for well. Well is complete but water is not sufficient. She has about 6 acres of land but only small fraction of it is under irrigation from the well.
8. Manohar s/o Rantu was also allotted the same amount. Officially his well is complete but it has to be made deep. He has 5 acres of land and he was only capable to irrigate land under wheat during 2008. If the well is made deep Manohar will be happy to irrigate other crops with the availability of sufficient water.
9. Santri w/o Kadak Singh was also allotted similar amount. Well allotted to her is at the stage of completion. It has 3 feet water but it was not used for irrigation during 2008.
10. Milap s/o Punnu was also allotted well. He has about 6 acres of land. About 3 feet water is available in the well. In 2008 it was used to irrigate wheat crop.

11. Kishori w/o Swamu has also completed well under her possession, but there is no water in the well. Till date she has not availed any benefit out of the well. And, there are 10 tribals whose well is still to be completed.

Of all the completed wells few were completed before rainy season during 2008, but it was not cemented. As a result, soil erosion took place and well lost its identity. Similar incident has happened with well owned by Phul Chand. It has water but it has lost its shape and size due to soil erosion.

If we analyse these wells in terms of benefit it is not very visible and apparent today. This is because 2008 was almost like a famine year for people of Pathai. The magnitude of water fall was almost half of the earlier years. For instance, during 2006–07 the average rainfall in Sahpur was 1,200–1,600 mm. But during 2007–08 it reduced upto only 714 mm. This situation inhibited many villagers to use their land for cultivation. Even those households who have received well facility they have realized limitation of well water for irrigation purpose. This prohibited them to use most part of their land for cultivation purpose.

Land in Market

Land is not in market in the village. During last five years only a single household have sold one acre of land. He sold land in order to meet expenditure on treatment. It was sold to another tribal at the cost of Rs 10,000 only. Three households have purchased land during last 5 years. They purchased it from tribe themselves. One purchased two acres of land at the rate of Rs 4,000 only per acre and other purchased five acres at the rate of Rs 5,000 only per acre. Other one purchased 2.5 acres of land at the total cost of Rs 6,000 only. They purchased land because (a) land was on sell, (b) his own land was not leveled and he was in search of leveled and more fertile land, and (c) he was earlier landless. Except one household whose land was encroached about 10 years ago by the government for canal construction, there is no case of displacement from land.

Farmers Status: Mixed Perception

Since this is an agriculture and wage centred society and full-time or part-time wage worker wish to become farmer, and the existing full-time farmers do not have food problem therefore, their perception about farmer's status is mixed. About 81 per cent respondents have high regard for the status of farmers. The reason is that they have not to bother for food, they command high respect among co-farmers in the village and locally, they are self-reliant, they have pleasure of good cropping and so on.

Table 6

Factors Responsible for High Status of Farmers

Response	*F*	%
Respected by all	23	13.93
Sufficient food	39	23.63
Sufficient grass for cattle	2	1.21
Can lend grain	4	2.42
Self-reliant	28	16.96
High status	7	4.24
Sufficient production	16	9.69
Food security	5	3.03
Can sell grain	5	3.03
No wage work	3	1.81
Unclear	7	4.24
More investment more benefit	4	2.42
Good cropping	13	7.87
Profitable	3	1.81
Saving	1	0.60
Entertainment of guest	1	0.60
Happy life	2	1.21
Proper production in own land	2	1.21
Total	165	100

But there are some (25) who perceive farming in a negative way. To them it is risk ridden, inferior in comparison to job and many times farmers are looked down in the society.

Although many respondents rate farming positively but there are 77 (39%) who preferred government job for their children. Agriculture was preferred by only 29 respondents. Business and wage work is not the preferred occupation.

Table 7

Preferred Occupation for Children (Single response)

Wage	7	4
Agriculture	29	15
Wage and agriculture	36	18
Job	77	39
Business	2	1
No reply/Not applicable	49	25
Total	200	100

About 70 respondents narrated reasons for not sending their male child in farming. To them decreasing productivity in land, decreasing quality of land, decreasing social status of farmers in comparison to government job, farm work being disliked by educated children, insufficient amount of land or due to near landlessness, division of land among brothers, poor and insecured income from land, etc., they do not wish to see their male child in farming.

Regarding occupation of their daughters too only 100 respondents expressed views and 70 per cent of them wish to see them in government job. Remaining, however, preferred occupation where they themselves are, i.e., wage, farming or both. In short, tribals at large have developed strong inclination in favour of government jobs for their sons and daughters. Their interest in favour of traditional occupation especially for their children is decreasing rapidly.

Wage Work

Wage work is an important source of livelihood for landless and near landless villagers. Almost 185 villagers, i.e., 108 men and 77 women (16%) are full time wage workers. Besides them many more men and women are occasional wage workers. Their main source of wage is government initiated works within and outside the village. Within the village they are engaged in road construction and well digging and repair work. They are also hired for personal work. It is also reported that some of the villagers engage wage worker at one point of time but at another point of time they themselves are wage workers. There is seasonal outmigration among them. Many of the wage workers go to the neighbouring districts such as Hoshangabad, Itarsi and Harda, for harvesting work.

Table 8

Wage Rate

Wage Work	*Within Village (in Rs)*		*Outside Village (in Rs)*	
	Female	*Male*	*Female*	*Male*
Wage rate	40	50	80	80
Crop harvesting	5 Kg raw grain	5 Kg raw grain	10 kg raw grain/Rs 80	10 kg raw grain/Rs 80
Crop irrigation	40	50	80	80
Tomato plugging	–	–	80	80

Note: Rate of wage differs on the basis of change in demand as well as seasonal variation. Many times rate goes up to Rs 100 in the case of wage work outside the village.

However, since the introduction of NREGS frequency of outmigration have decreased because workers get wage opportunity at the local level. Their period of outmigration is usually for 2 to 3 months in a year. Most often food grain is paid as their wage. They earn sufficient grain which provide food security to them for more than six months. However, most of them showed inability to move out of the village on regular basis in case they get wage work at the village/local level.

Self-Help Group and Economic Development

There are five self-help groups (SHGs) formed between 2001 to 2006. These groups are Tara Mahila Mandal (2001), Nov Jyoti SHG (2006), Suraj SHG (2006), Roshni SHG (2006), and Jai Ambe SHG (2006). There are 67 members in all these groups. Their main functioning is to manage mid-day meal, construction of family-based toilet, well construction under Kapildhara Scheme and so on. Case study of Jai Ambe SHG is presented below.

Jai Ambe Self-Help Group (SHG) was formed in 2006. Head of this group is Dharm Das, a non-tribal. There are 11 members from both tribal and non-tribal communities. This group was formed to increase income of villagers even by living in the village. To form the group, number of informal meetings were organized and all members were prepared to form the group.

Members are between the age group of 20–35 years. All the members deposited Rs 100 per month and they have a bank account in

Shahpur Central Bank. Today the group has a saving of Rs 18,000 in their joint account. Members of this group are engaged in wage and agricultural work, but wage work is the primary source of their livelihood. This group was also graded high and a loan of Rs 3,14,000 was sanctioned to it of which Rs 1,25,000 is the non-refundable money and on the remaining Rs, 1,89,000 they have to pay 11 per cent interest. Today they have returned back maximum amount and only Rs 55,000 they have to return. They are eager to return this amount but manager of the said bank informally discourage them to return it before one year because bank will loose interest. Group members organize meeting in each month to discuss several issues including money matter. Group provide loan to the needy, no matter whether they are member of the SHG or not. However, the rate of interest differ. For group members interest rate is 2 per cent and for non-members it is 5 per cent. Of the loan amount taken from bank all the members were provided financial support for income generation. For example, five members were provided loan to purchase ox, three to obtain she goat, two for opening Kirana shop, two to built brick and one to purchase irrigation machine. President of the group said that if he and any of tribal members in particular goes to bank individually in order to get loan for income generation he feels frustrated because nobody listen to him but through SHG it is very easy to get loan. SHG have made them self-reliant and confident.

Besides the above, the group has undertaken number of social activities during the past. For example, with the help of Public Health Engineering (PHE) the group launched Total Sanitation Campaign (TSC) in the village under which number of family based toilets were built. In this process the group went under debt. For instance, as per the guideline, of the total cost of one toilet, i.e., Rs 1,800, PHE provide Rs 1,500 as a grant and the beneficiary is supposed to provide remaining Rs 300 from his own, but in this case beneficiaries declined. As a result, group could not clear dues of all those who had supplied raw material on credit. Hence, toilet construction experiment became painful for SHG. One of the reasons for lack of cooperation from villagers in this matter is their unawareness and complete non-use of toilet facility provided by SHG. Needless to mention that village is near to the forest and there is huge open space for defecation. In the case of lack of environmental awareness as well as shortage of water for use in toilet, villagers continue the century old traditional practice to go to open space for defecation.

Firewood: Collection and Marketing

Collection of firewood from nearby forest and its marketing is an important source of income and livelihood in the life of tribals of Pathai today. This work is primarily done by women on regular basis. Needless to mention that Sahpur is a small town with having several tea-shops, hotels, offices, schools, health centre, bus stand, *thellawalla* and government employee. Besides, there are also some households of retired persons and farmers. Most of these households and shops of different types including tribal hostel depend on firewood supplied by tribal women from neighbouring villages for cooking purpose. Distance of Sahpur from Pathai is about 4 km. From two sides firewood is supplied in Sahpur town. One is from Itarsi side from across the Machna river. From this side most of the women who carry head load are from Aamdhana and Chapra Ryt villages. Women supply firewood during both morning and evening hours. In the evening they supply less in comparison to the morning. Weight of individual bundle is around 12–15 kg and the cost is also between Rs 12–15 for each bundle. Women from other side such as Pathai, Nishana, Bhaktandhana, Kalapani, Giridhana and Jamundhana supply firewood in a massive manner. They carry bigger size of bundle and weight of an individual bundle is around 30–32 kg and cost of each bundle is also between Rs 30–35. Sometimes women from these villages carry bundle upto 50 kg and they divide the main bundle into two equal bundles at community health centre at Sahpur and by doing this they try to get maximum price out of it.

Besides the traditional customers as mentioned above, since the recent past truck drivers who carry empty truck from Itarsi side to Betul, they also purchase 10–15 bundle of firewood on the road itself in the morning hour when they see women in group carrying firewood. Locals are of the view that such truck drivers generally purchase firewood for their own consumption. However, no permanent link between truck drivers and women carrying firewood was reported as it exists between them and Sahpur customers.

Collection and marketing of firewood is generally the domain of tribal women. They sell it at Sahpur and whatever income they have, they immediately spent it on meeting basic requirements such as rice, pulse, edible oil, soap, detergent powder, tobacco, bidi and so on. They return from market, prepare food, consume it and again they move to forest to collect firewood for the next day. They come back from forest in the evening and next day in the morning they again move to Sahpur for its marketing. This is their life cycle.

Perception about Head Load and Its Implications

Do tribal women know that collection of firewood from forest in such a massive manner is legal or not? Do they know consequences of this process of fuel wood collection and its impact on health status of forest? Women respondents at large are silent on the former question but local level forest officials have their observation. For instance, forest of Sahpur block is divided under seven forest circles and 32 forest beats. Pathai beat is one among these. This beat covers forest around the villages of Pathai, Nishana and Kalapani. Beat guard Bharat Lal Ingule stay at Kalapani centre.

Although, the office of this beat is located in Pathai, Bharat Lal stays in Kalapani in order to protect forest because in this area forest require more protection. Ingule observed that it is illegal to cut alive trees and plants. Tribals are allowed only to collect dried branches of trees or plant. But the way they are carrying firewood each day everybody can easily guess that how branches of tree or plants dry out all the days in such a massive manner? It is a fact that women cut plants and branches of trees which are alive. It is difficult to stop them. Even when they are caught red-handed with *Kulhari* (axe) and they are asked to come to the beat most often they run away by leaving their Kulhari. He lamented that it takes about 60 years to grow the plant into a tree but these tribal women cut it within a couple of days. If this process is not stopped immediately days are not very far when the area will be without forest.

To him high officials know the entire story but it is the lower level employees, who has to bear the cost of destruction of forest. He presented an example. Krishna Rai Aldok was a beat guard of Pathai. During his time large number of trees were logged. Also, to complete a road which was being constructed under Prime Minister Rural Road Scheme, *Muram* (specific type of soil) was illegally taken out from forest land by the contractor. High officials noticed it and the result was termination of Krishnarai from his job.

Range officer of Sahpur forest range K.S. Khairwar and Asstt. Range Officer R.K. Ledhe observed that Forest Act do not permit tribals to carry wet log/firewood from forest. They are not supposed to cut green trees or plants. Also, if a log is thicker than 15 cm it is also not supposed to be taken away by tribals. They said that huge amount of wood is supplied to Sahpur. This incident is taking place in all the forest villages of Sahpur but here it is more massive because an NGO called Sharamik Adivasi Sangathan which primarily work in Betul, Harda and Hosangabad districts instigate tribals to cut trees and in case action is taken they go against forest officials.

Everybody engaged in protection of forest know that massive logging, marketing and use of firewood and forest wood on constant basis will extend unrepairable loss to forest in both economic and environmental terms and one day forest will disappear, locals will be the immediate victim of disappearance of forest but in spite of that no concerted effort is made by all the concerned stakeholders to protect and promote the existing forest.

Needless to mention that from Pathai side on each day about 150 bundles of firewood is supplied to Sahpur. For example on 22 November, 2008 by using head count technique we observed that 146 bundles were supplied and on 23 November, 2008, 162 bundles were marketed. Usually, this work is done by adult women but on holiday especially on Sunday, even school going boys and girls are engaged in this activity. Involvement of school going boys and girls in firewood collection and marketing especially on holidays refers to (a) socialization of younger generation in this work which brings continuity in head load practice, and (b) absence of effort by school teachers in favour of environmental protection. School teachers may discourage such behaviour which damages environment by motivating students and inculcating relevant lessons in the syllabus.

So far as marketing of log is concerned it was observed that some of the villagers are engaged in this work specially during nights. They cut the tree in the night and after few days they carry it to Sahpur or either supply it to furniture shops or to others at Sahpur. One such incident took place during the night of 11 December, 2008. On the basis of an information, forest guards tried to capture 10 persons who were carrying log, 9 persons run away and one was caught red-handed. They all belonged to Pathai village. The person who was caught, is relatively weak and aged. Similarly on 10 December, 2008 two tribal youths namely Kalu and Mukesh, were caught red-handed. They also belonged to Pathai.

Public Distribution System (PDS)

PDS is working in this village since 1997. A non-tribal from local Shahpur Bazar is owner of this shop. More than 50 per cent villagers know the shopkeeper by name. More than 75 per cent villagers also know that wheat, rice, sugar, and kerosene oil is supplied by this shop. Some of the villagers (32) are aware that iodized salt is also available at PDS. Villagers obtain above items disproportionately, no matter their family size is big or small, equal amount of items are provided to them. During one month towards the fall of 2007 total quantity of items lifted by villagers was 6,575 kg which also included 798 litre of kerosene oil. Cost of all these items was Rs 42,648. Maximum quantity of wheat was lifted.

Table 9

Total Items Lifted from PDS in the Last Month (2007 fall)

Items	*Kg/Litre*	*Amount (Rs)*
Wheat	3,892	20,381
Rice	1,078	7,607
Sugar	490	3,490
Kerosene	798	10,853
Salt	317	317
Total	6,575	42,648

Data reveal that 171 households took wheat during the month immediately before study and maximum number of them (164) lifted above 10 kg. In contrary to this majority of beneficiaries lifted either or less than 10 kg of rice. This shows that villagers are more wheat centric than rice. 133 lifted sugar of which 99 had taken less than 5 kg of sugar. Maximum number of villagers (175) lifted kerosene oil but 135 lifted less than 5 litres of it. There are 200 households in Pathai but data provided by PDS shopkeeper reveals that total 231 ration cards were issued. 211 cards were issued to those who are from below the BPL and 20 to those who are from above the poverty line. There are two rates of ration, one for BPL card holders and the other for those who either do not have BPL card or those who are from above the poverty line.

Table 10

Statuswise Cost of PDS Items

Itemwise Price List	*(in Rs)*	*(Per card per month)*
Wheat (for BPL card holder)	5 per kg	15 kg
Rice (for BPL card holder)	6.5	4
Wheat (Antodaya Ann Yojana)	2	31
Rice	3	4
Wheat	7	10
Kerosene oil	10.22 per litre	5 litre
Sugar	13.50 per kg	3 kg

Of course there is difference in cost for different categories of population but all get equal amount of commodities, no matter their family size is big or small. Here joint or extended families are forced to suffer or are bound to manipulate. Logic behind providing 4 kg of rice to one card holder for one month is also not easily digestible.

In short, our finding reveal that wheat is consumed by maximum number of villagers. It seems that it is the most preferred item. But villagers of the same number consume less than 10 kg/litre of items like rice, sugar and salt.

Table 11

Materials taken in Last One Month

	Wheat	*Rice*	*Sugar*	*Kerosine*	*Salt*
Upto 5 kg/litre	2	86	99	135	102
5–10 kg/litre	5	61	34	38	8
10–15 kg/litre	69	22		1	2
Above 15 kg/litre	95	3		1	
Total	171	172	133	175	112

Quality/Quantity of Food Items

Villagers at large are satisfied with quality of rice, sugar, kerosene oil and salt but about half of those who lifted wheat (85) during last month are not satisfied with its quality. About 43 beneficiaries took step to ensure proper quality supply and the remaining were indifferent, 23 made complaint to the shopkeeper, some (8) washed wheat before use and some on complaint were told by the shopkeeper that he is distributing as it is received.

About 74 per cent respondents are not satisfied with the present quantity of items distributed. They want food grains to be supplied in huge quantity as per the individual requirements of each of the households. They are strongly opposed to the practice of equal supply of items to each of the card holders no matter wether their family size is big or small.

Respondents had mixed opinion about weight, closing and opening time of PDS shop, price of items received, behaviour of shopkeeper and so on. Almost 87 per cent were satisfied with weight and measurement, not at all satisfied with the opening of shop once in a week and behaviour of shopkeeper and his attendant. It was observed that many card holders were provided only 4 litre kerosene oil in a month although they are entitled for 5 litre. Because they were unaware therefore, they did not raise voice. Under-measurement of kerosene oil was also reported by many respondents. Many said that behaviour of shopkeeper was satisfactory but his attendant is cleaver. Some also reported practice of black marketing of food grains, late opening of shop and disproportionate price structure, i.e., relatively low price for those who have ration card and high price for those who do not have ration card but they are also from the same village. However, most of the items supposed to be provided by PDS is most often available in shop.

Strengthening PDS

Respondents expressed views to strengthen functioning of PDS. About half of them (105) opined that effort should be made to ensure proper weight, no matter one has PDS card or not, they all should be provided items at a fixed price, items supplied must be as per the rule and effort should be made to supply good quality items. Needless to mention that during the yester month 171 households lifted 3,892 kg wheat of which 89 reported about its poor quality. It was red in colour and also not tasty. Only 15 respondents strongly opined that mere on the basis of having ration card and not having ration card disproportionate cost should not be charged. Similar number of respondents suggested that instead of once in a week PDS shop should remain opened on all days and also for longer hours.

Table 12

Suggestions to Improve PDS (multiple response)

Suggestions	*F*	%
Proper weight, price, quality and quantity	105	47.94
No discrimination among beneficiaries in terms of price	15	6.84
Increase days/hours of PDS shop	15	6.84
Regular ration supply	08	3.65
Shopkeeper from same village	01	0.45
Vigilance from above	05	2.28
Ration free/on credit	03	1.37
Space/scope of shop to be increased	14	6.39
No response/unclear response	53	24.20
Total	219	100

Tribals also opined that many times ration is not made available to them. Sometimes it is infrequent and sometime insufficient. In time delivery should be made essential. Today shopkeeper is an outsider. This is one of the reasons for opening shop once in a week. He should be replaced by the person from Pathai itself. In order to deal with the problems of underweighting, improper behaviour of shopkeeper and poor quality of supply, pressure form above, viz., panchayat, BDO office, etc., should be made. In response to a question that how many of them have lodged formal/informal complaint against malpractices, some have reported informally to the shopkeeper himself and some villagers apprehend that in the case of complaint they may be denied ration. Some respondents advised that the aged should be provided ration free of cost. Also, there should be a provision to provide ration on credit. About 14 respondents opined that space in the ration shop should be increased. Also many other essential items such as common medicine should be supplied through the PDS.

Income and Expenditure

Data was collected during the months of October-February 2007–08. Wage work emerged as the most important source of income. In one month during the above period 179 villagers did wage work. Their total income from this source was Rs 2,16,939. Hence, on and average an individual wage earner earned Rs 1,212 in one month.

Marketing of firewood helped 32 households to earn Rs 25,720 in one month. Most of the other sources of income was also primary in nature. Total income of all the villagers in one month was Rs 3,08,059 of which more than 60 per cent earning was from wage work. Hence, on average each of the 200 households earned Rs 1,540 in one month from all the sources. However, this figure may not be applicable for all the 12 months. There is always possibility of variation due to seasons, availability of wage work, marketing of firewood and so on.

Table 13

One-month Income Immediately Before Study

	Households	*Total Income*	*Average Income*
Wage	179	2,16,939	1,212
Firewood sell	32	25,720	804
Job/pension	22	49,500	22,500
From relatives	2	1,000	500
Sell of food grain	8	7,500	937
Cattle sell	5	3,700	740
Shop	4	3,700	925

Villagers spent their monthly income on different items. Most of these items are related to their basic requirement. There are 28 items on which expenditure was made. Maximum number of households spent on wheat, rice, vegetable oil, kerosene oil and vegetable. Although majority of villagers are non-vegetarian but only 8 households consumed non-vegetarian during one month. In many of the households Mahua liquor is prepared. They prepare liquor mainly for their own consumption but many families had to purchase it in one month. They spent Rs 1,426, i.e., average Rs 158 per household on this head. Further average and total expenditure on each of the items reflect that on tea, medicine, clothes, sweets, toothpowder they spent less and on smoking and chewing, soap and detergent powder and Mahua liquor they spent more.

Table 14

Headwise Expenditure in One Month

	Households (N)	*Amount*	*Average Expenditure by One House out of N*
Wheat	154	27,283	177
Rice	178	19,511	110
Pulse	77	8,496	110
Vegetable oil	154	15,860	103
Hospitality	2	432	216
Mahua liquor	9	1,426	158
Kerosene oil	130	3,844	30
Maize/Jwar/Besan	14	5,900	421
Vegetable	161	30,708	191
Bath Soap/Cloth Soap/Detergent	90	3,078	34
Medicine	7	3,252	465
Clothes	8	2,138	267
House repair	8	4,012	502
Salt/Spices	234	7,578	32
Sweets/Namkeen	9	275	31
Bidi/Cigarette/Tobacco	45	4,369	97
Sugar/Gur	70	3,062	44
Flouring cost of wheat	4	179	45
Coconut oil	10	333	33
Tea	7	151	22
Copy and pen for children	6	1,350	225
Meat/Fish	8	1,120	140
Agricultural assets	2	3,000	1,500
School fee	1	100	100
Sugarcane	1	60	60
Petrol	1	600	600
Toothpowder	1	10	10
Total		1,48,127	

One tribal family had to spent Rs 50,000 on the eve of marriage during the month.

In short, during one month their total income from all sources was Rs 3,08,059 and total expenditure on all heads was Rs 1,48,127. This amount does not include expenditure of Rs 50,000 by one household on marriage. On this basis it seems that there may be about Rs 1.5 lakh saving in each month. But this is not meaningfully supplemented by data relating to saving status of respondents. If they do not have proper saving but they have surplus income this shows that they have unforeseen expenditure which they do not like to disclose or they are unable to recall. And one of the unforeseen items may be consumption of liquor. Most of the male villagers consume liquor regularly. Many of them prepare Mahua liquor but they have to obtain Mahua flower and urea fertilizer from the market. And rate of dried Mahua flower is between Rs 35–40 per kg. However, in case they have saving they spent it in obtaining household and agricultural assets occasionally.

Income

They have mixed perception about increased/decreased income of their families in comparison to the situation about 15–20 years back. 53.5 per cent believe that income has increased. To them factors responsible for increased income in order of merit are increasing cost of firewood which they sell regularly, increasing wage rate, increasing cost of cereals which some of them sell, increasing income through salary and pension and so on.

Those who perceive decreasing income their number is only 17.5 per cent. Others are indifferent on this issue. These 17.5 per cent respondents opine that due to lack of wage work regularly, decreasing crop production due to decreasing quality of soil, increasing family size, ageing and disease among earning hands, division of land among brothers, death of earning hand, increasing price and expenditure, etc., income and economic status of families have decreased.

Saving

Only 31 households (15.5%) have their account in bank/post office. Most of them have opened account during or after 2000. In most of the cases it is single handed and on the name of male head of the household. They opened account for saving purpose. There are five who are in government job where it is must to have bank account. Except three all the remaining 26 properly recalled current balance in their account. And balance amount differ from Rs 500 to either or above Rs 10,000.

However, maximum number of them have either or less than Rs 5,000 as balance.

Table 15

Balance in Passbook (in Rs)

Response	*F*
No reply	3
Upto 500	9
501–1,000	3
1,001–2,000	6
2,001–5,000	5
5,001–10,000	4
10,000+	1
Total	31

Villagers opened account due to different reasons. For salaried person and those who draw pension it was essential. And, the remaining opened account for saving to meet expenditure related to marriage, treatment, house construction and so on.

Indebtedness

About 45 villagers (22.5%) are under debt. They have taken loan during last five years from different sources. For instance, 14 took loan from bank, seven from Sahukar and remaining 24 from friends and relatives. This means informal source, i.e., both from Sahukars and relatives, is most preferred source than the institutional source.

Table 16

Households Taken Loan During Last Five Years

Amount	*Bank/Govt.*	*Sahukar*	*Friends/Relation*	*Total*
Upto Rs 1,000	2	2	7	11
1,001–5,000	9	3	13	25
5,001–10,000	1	–	4	5
10,000+	2	2	–	4
Total	14	7	24	45

It is here needless to mention that only 8 villagers have provided loan to their co-villagers and that too upto Rs 10,000 only.

Villagers take loan for various purposes, no matter from which source they take loan. However, of 45 under debt maximum (15) have taken loan for agriculture purpose. Villagers' access to both bank and Sahukar is limited in comparison to their access to relatives especially for consumption purpose loan. Most of the time they depend on relatives and friends for loan. However, they equally depend on bank and relatives especially for assets creation.

Table 17

Prime Reasons Behind Loan

Reasons	*Bank/Govt.*	*Sahukar*	*Friends/Relation*	*Total*
Agricultural work	7	1	7	15
Marriage	–	2	4	6
Treatment	1	1	5	7
Maintenance	–	1	2	3
Festivity/worship	–	1	3	4
Open shop	2	–	1	3
Motorcycle purchase	2	–	–	2
Bullock cart/goat purchase	2	1	1	4
Land purchase	–	–	1	1
Total	14	7	24	45

Interest Rate

Interest rate differ in all the three cases. If loan is taken from bank the interest rate (per month) differ from 2 to 8 per cent. However, rate of interest charged by both Sahukar and relatives is much higher. In the case of Sahukar it differs from 4 to 10 per cent and in the case of friends and relatives it is also from 3 to 10 per cent per month. In spite of having high interest rate villagers prefer informal sources to avoid complex procedure. Also, door of bank is virtually closed for consumption purpose.

Impact of Loan

Of 14 loanees from bank, four were not worried at all, six were worried, one found that his income was badly affected and remaining were doing hard labour to return loan. Loanees of Sahukar were also worried, half of them were doing hard to generate extra income to repay the debt at the earliest. More or less same techniques were followed by loanees who had taken loan from their relatives and friends.

None of them were in favour of loan amount to be waved by the respective loan provider. It is because of the thinking that of seven loanees from Sahukars, four have already repaid upto 50 per cent of the total loan amount taken. Further, of 14 loanees from bank 7 have repaid loan amount varying from 10 to 75 per cent. Of 24 loanees from relatives and friends 14 have not returned at all and the remaining have returned loan amount from 25 to 100 per cent. Since villagers dependence on loan is limited and that too on bank and Sahukar, therefore it was important to seek their views to increase dependence on bank and decrease dependence on Sahukar. Some of the respondents expressed views. To them if cooperative society is strengthened, subsidy on loan or items obtained is increased, people are made aware about negative consequences of dependence on Sahukars, paper work and other formality which take lot of time is reduced in bank, loan amount is released by bank without delay, even small amount of loan say Rs 500 is advanced by bank, bank is made available near to the village, warrant is not issued in the case of default, behaviour of bank official is made friendly, land paper is not asked by the bank because in many cases tribals have land without proper paper and credit card is made available to villagers, definitely tribals dependence on bank will increase and simultaneously their dependence on informal source will decrease.

Moneylending

Traditionally lending money on loan was a sign of prosperity and higher social status and in contrary to this those who used to take loan they were looked down and they had lower social status. We asked six related questions to all respondents. Respondents were advised to respond in three categories, i.e., agree, disagree, no reply.

In response to a question that is it difficult and tiresome to take loan from government? Almost 75.5 per cent replied in the affirmative. Only 12 per cent disagreed and remaining 12.5 per cent were indifferent.

In response to a question that Mahajans and Sahukars are better source of loan in comparison to formal source, 46.5 per cent agreed and 41.5 per cent disagreed on this question. Remaining were indifferent.

Table 18

Views about Sources of Loan

Views	*Agree*	*Disagree*	*No Reply*	*Total*
It is difficult to take loan from government	151	24	25	200
Mahajan and Sahukars are the better choice	93	83	24	200
One should not take loan	127	57	16	200
Money lending in sin	127	45	28	200
Loan is waived so better not to return	61	90	49	200
Better to take loan for farm work	116	33	51	200

Villagers at large dislike to take loan. And, therefore, to them it is sin and socially undesirable to take loan from any of the sources. Majority of villagers do not know about occasional waving of the institutional loan amount under any of the schemes. However, 116 respondents agree with the idea that it would be better if loan is taken only for agricultural activities.

Village Income: Then and Now

More or less similar perception is expressed in relation to development status of the village in comparison to the situation about 15–20 years ago. Here also to search answer of this question recalling technique was used. About 53.5 per cent and 64.5 per cent respondents opined that income of their families and village income have increased today in comparison to situation about 15–20 years ago respectively.

Table 19

Family/Village Income in Comparison to Situation 15–20 Years Ago

Response	*Family Income*	*%*	*Village Income*	*%*
Unclear	4	2.0	5	2.5
As usual	54	27.0	54	27.0
Decreased	35	17.5	12	6.0
Increased	107	53.5	129	64.5
Total	200	100	200	100

If we examine economic status of village in general and its inhabitants in particular it has definitely changed in the positive direction. They name different reasons responsible for this state of affair.

Social Implications

Improvement in economic status at the individual and village level is by and large the product of external forces, viz., government schemes and outmigration, etc., and therefore there is doubt about its stability but it is true that today the income have increased. It has affected quality and quantity of households and agricultural assets as discussed above. It has also affected management of health and disease in a positive way. For all the diseases villagers' dependence on modern medicine, doctors and hospitals have significantly increased. Parents' views about education of their sons and daughters have also positively changed. They do not hesitate to spent some money upto the level their wards complete middle level education. Their means of entertainment have completely changed. Many of them are now keeping telephone and mobile. Their attitude in favour of girl child has also positively changed. But due to near absence of formation of social capital among villagers political apathy and indifference exists among them. They take some interest at panchayat level politics because representatives are personally known but as one move towards block and higher level political matters villagers' awareness, inclination and participation drastically decreases.

III

Conclusion

In short, in spite of the fact that villagers at large perceive improvement in their economic condition and in the economic condition of village as such during last 15–20 years, but still most of the villagers are from below the poverty line. Their main source of income, i.e., farming and wage work is less profit making. Many do not have land and many of the landowners do not have assured irrigation facility. Land productivity is low. They manage land traditionally. There is no modernization in agricultural process. There is not even a single tractor in the village. As a result, villagers have mixed reaction about social status of farmers today and tomorrow. Because farming provide food security to many, therefore, they do not like to quit farm work, but at the same time they do not wish to engage children in farm activities. They wish to see them in job because government job will provide them security and social status. There is no problem of indebtedness in the village. Also land is not available for sell. Villagers do not have water problem especially for domestic consumption but for irrigation it is scarce. Lack of irrigation affect farm work negatively. However, wind is blowing in favour of cash crop. Decreasing amount of production of *Kodo* and *Kutki* and increasing production of soyabean may be taken as an example. Villagers spent most of their income to meet basic requirements. However, number of households and agricultural assets have increased over the time in the village. Most of them have obtained the modern household and agricultural assets from their own saving after 1999. Liquor consumption is rampant in the village. Role of seasonal outmigration to the neighbouring districts and marketing of firewood in the nearly market is a viable source of income. Later is women dominated activity. There is positive relationship between availability of even small amount of land, seasonal outmigration for harvesting work and food security with reference to poor tribals who constitute bulk of village population. Government schemes of different types have also benefited many of the villagers but in spite of that they have number of suggestions which needs to be taken care of. To them if (a) loan is made available for goat/cattle, (b) embroidery work is promoted, (c) students are engaged in both study and income generation work, (d) wage rate is increased and related laws are honestly enforced, (e) support for farming work is made available, (f) pump set is made available for irrigation, (g) land is made available to the landless, (h) irrigation facility is assured, (i) required agricultural assets are provided, (j) source of income other than agriculture is searched, (k) proper market is made available to them for their farm produce, (l) functioning of PDS is strengthened, (m) well construction is completed in time, (n) SHG is strengthened, (o) supply of thick log by tribals to saw mill and furniture shops at Shahpur is immediately discontinued, (p) Sahukar at Sahpur who purchase firewood and soyabean from tribals of Pathai are warned to pay properly, and (q) they are motivated to manage income properly and depend more on banks than others then only income will increase. PDS is also working as an effective institution to ensure food security. Hence, it may be said that village is at the crossroads in economic term. And as a result of economic development there is change in other aspects of life, viz., health management, food, dress and entertainment and education to children in a significant manner.

6

Indebtedness and Land Alienation among Tribals of Madhya Pradesh

Y.G. JOSHI

In spite of the fact that the alienation of land in the tribal area had been the result of a number of historical processes, indebtedness is also one of the important reasons for the loss of land from tribals, both covertly and overtly, and thus, indebtedness and land alienation are related issues. As per the document of the Tenth Plan, nearly 9.75 lakh acres of tribal land was reported as alienated in 1999 and a sizable proportion of it was in Madhya Pradesh (Nandkumar, 2004). The Parliamentary Committee expressed its stern view that welfare programmes for the tribals will have no meaning if they are deprived of the land on which their very livelihood depends. The Committee also desired that, besides revenue department, a comprehensive review must be made by a high level committee to assess the problem of alienation of tribal land in the state of Madhya Pradesh (Government of India, 2000). In the National Tribal Policy Document, drafted to address tribal issues, high priority has been given to effectively arrest, both the problems of indebtedness and land alienation (Government of India, 2006).

The present paper is based on a research project undertaken by the author in Dr Babasaheb Ambedkar National Institute of Social Sciences, Mhow during 2006–07 to bring out a comprehensive report on the incidence of indebtedness and land alienation in different tribal regions of the state, together with assessing the role of existing institutional credit mechanism in coping up with the problem.

Theoretical Context and Review of Literature

Land Alienation in Tribal Areas

Tribal people's rights, being a part of the broad human rights discourse, have acquired significance in recent times. As human beings, the people who live in the tribal lands, acquire a similar set of rights like others. Being citizens of the country they are entitled to a number of privileges, as well. From time immemorial there have been violations of their fundamental rights. In the contemporary society the state comes to their rescue to some extent. The increasing awareness towards the concept of human rights under the aegis of UNO, world media, NGOs, etc., has proved beneficial to the victims.

Ethnic communities in many countries, including India, have been treated differently with respect to rights of property and residence. It is not only the territorial reservation for the indigenous, but also a question of special measures designed to make it possible for the communities to preserve their distinctive identity. In the constitution of India, provisions have been made in the 5th and 6th Schedule to safeguard the rights of the tribals on their land. In Madhya Pradesh Land Revenue Code (1959) following provisions have been made to check the alienation of land in these areas:

1. Section 165(6) makes strict prohibition on transfer of land from tribals to non-tribals in the Scheduled areas.
2. Section 170A and 170B provides for the cancellation of previous transfers made by fraudulent means.

However, in spite of legislative measures, large-scale unlawful transfer of tribal land to non-tribal has been reported in different parts of the country. A noted Supreme Court advocate has rightly commented that law can work for the tribals only if we work for them (Upadhyay, 2007). In the 10th Plan Document it has been mentioned that, as per the information available with the Ministry of Rural Development, as many as 4.65 lakh cases involving 9.17 lakh acres of land had been officially registered in the country by January, 1999 and in four districts of Orissa, 56 per cent of tribal land was lost to non-tribals over 25–30 year period.

A majority of tribals are agriculturists. The entire life was historically built upon two major means of production, i.e., forests and land.

To understand the dynamics of land problem in totality, one has to understand the logic of the underlying forces that govern the ownership pattern. There are ample historical evidences to prove that depeasantization had been the result of the uneven structural changes that have taken place from time to time (Rout, 1999).

Alienation has acquired multiple meanings. It was Karl Marx who introduced the concept of alienation in the sociological theory. In his earlier writings, especially in his "Economic and Philosophical Manuscripts", he discussed the concept of 'estranged labour'. It basically denoted the state of man in a capitalist society, where what is proper to man, becomes alien. As per him, alienation is inherent in the exploitative relation of production and its nature varies with that of exploitation. Hence, the manifestation of alienation also differs among societies based on slavery, serfdom, capitalism, etc. The concept of alienation of tribal land may, thus, be interpreted as a specific problem where land becomes the primordial source of exploitation and results in creation of a society where exploitative production relation has been established (Rout, 1999). In India, the concept has been used by the social scientists as sociological phenomena. Since land alienation is the crux of the process of dispossession of land and depeasantization of the tribals, the concept assumes utmost importance in the analysis of tribal rights as a part of human rights discourse. The problem is, however, not just the result of the existing situation but due to various structural changes which occurred within and outside tribal system during historical periods, forcing the tribals to vacate the land traditionally owned by them. Basically, moneylenders, traders, feudal lords or the rich peasants exploited the tribals most. The phenomena was further accentuated by the emergence of new forces of production, namely, industrial houses, mining complexes, power projects, commercial forestry and major irrigation projects. In the process of denudation of forests also, tribals lost their land. Though the process of alienation of tribal land had been in operation from past many decades through manipulation, benami transfer, leasing and mortgaging, encroachment, concubine or marital alliance and fictitious adoption, etc., the problem attracted the attention of the scholars largely after independence.

Historically, the phenomenon of alienation of tribal land can be traced to the medieval periods when they were invaded by the non-tribal rulers (Vidyarthi and Rai, 1985: 33–34; Rao, 1987: 29). The tribals had a craving for land. It is for land that for years they fought and had been killed (Swamy, 1980: 20–42). It is evident from historical documents that at one time tribals controlled large parts of the country. Till the seventeenth and eighteenth century there were many tribal kingdoms in central India known as Gondwana and Bhilmal, which respectively had Gond and Bhil chieftains (Kosambi, 1970: 166–76). Similar was the case with Assam, Bihar and other parts (Banerjee, 1980: 32–33).

With the advent of British rulers, various systems devised for the collection of taxes, like, *Muttehdari, Zamindari, Malguzari* and *Ryotwari* initiated alienation of land in the tribal areas (Yonus, 1974: 140; Singh, 1986: 6; Rao, 1987: 2; Viegas 1991: 33). The system of private property and civil legal system which were alien to the tribal areas was later on introduced. These brought threat to the tribal system of land ownership and their socio-economic life. The colonial legal policy on common property held that the property which was not under legal ownership of an individual belonged to none and was the property of the state. This legal perspective derecognized group control of land based resources, especially those used for non-agricultural purposes. This also affected the traditional customary land laws of the tribals. Communal land became the common property with state claiming sovereign right over it, affecting the tribal economy and their cultural attachment to the forests (Burman, 1987: 400; Pathy, 1991: 9).

After independence, in spite of Nehru's policy statement in his famous *Panchasheel* that tribal rights over land and forests should be respected, in actual operation the state deviated from this principle in determining the historical rights of the tribal communities. Over the decades the historical rights of the tribals over the forests were converted into privileges and from privileges to concessions. The Forest Conservation Act of 1980 further treats them as trespassers (Singh, 1986; Pathy, 1991; Behura, 1993).

Studies have revealed that in the name of 'national interest' and development, thousands of tribals have been displaced due to construction of big dams, industrial complexes, large-scale mining activities, and erection of mega thermal power plants. During the first three five-year plans, more than 50,000 Scheduled Tribe's families were uprooted in Chotanagpur area, to make the land available for the construction of public sector industrial projects (Areeparampil, 1989: 20–24; Basu, 1994: 8). It is estimated, that during last four decades, dams alone have displaced between 140 to 200 lakh tribals (PRIA, 1987; Singh, 1978: 66; Fernandes, Das and Rao, 1989: 73). It is estimated that the Narmada Sardar Sarovar Project has potentially affected about two lakh people, of which one lakh seventeen thousand are tribals (Morse, 1992: 62). Added to these are the displacements caused by coal and other mining operations all over the country, of which 90 per cent of coal mines and 40 per cent of other mines are located in tribal populated regions. Fernandes (1993) writes:

> "Thus, at least 185 lakh persons have been displaced by all the development projects between 1951 and 1990. This is the lower estimate and the reality may be higher than that. This comes to more than two per cent of Indian population in 1991 and around 27 per cent of tribal population in that year. Rehabilitation has been all but non-existent. According to one study, only thirty per cent of those displaced till the 1970s have been resettled ... ."

In sum, after independence, though the state has enacted laws to curb land alienation from tribal to non-tribals, in the context of capital intensive development projects, the state itself has acted as an agent of tribal land alienation. Legally only the state can acquire tribal land under the outdated Land Acquisition Act, 1894. The Act, as amended in 1984, is indiscriminately invoked to alienate tribal lands in the name of public interest (Pathy, 1996: 486). Land alienation in recent years, mostly through displacement, continues to be a "menace to tribal economy" (Rao, 1978: 27). The root cause of tribal land alienation, therefore, cannot be pinned on to one single factor. It has been a historical process, where the tribal society, basically characterized by subsistence economy with communal control and collective management of economic resources, has been invaded by an "alien system of thought and values" centred on individualism, power and money economy.

Major part of the anthropological knowledge on tribals during British regime was basically designed for efficient governance and is overloaded with the colonial prejudices which ignored the economic and political dimensions of tribal society (Rao, 1978: 4). Except for few passing remarks, major problems among tribals which deserved to be understood were not attended to. For instance, the growing 'revolting' nature and spirit of the tribals, decay in their life standard, the continuous inflow of the intruders, the consequent discontent and ever-increasing exploitation in the tribal life, particularly in land relation, were left unstudied.

In the post-independence period, Raghavaiah (1971) in a chronological sketch of the tribal revolts in India from 1778 to 1971 has shown land alienation as the cause for many tribal revolts. The study of Patel (1974) is a pioneering effort on the land problems in Madhya Pradesh. He has also tried to establish a causal relationship between the tribal unrest and the loss of land. Kulkarni's study (1974) on Harsal tribals in Maharashtra touches upon the resource utilization, land relations, and the housing condition. The study argues for providing certain benefits to improve the existing condition but does not see the root cause that lies somewhere else, i.e., land alienation. Patnaik's study (1972) of two development blocks in Orissa attempts to show the impact of the development programmes on the political and economic condition of the tribes. He points out that the presence of caste Hindus and their dominance has resulted in the frustration of the tribals and the consequences are discontent and engendering of a rebellious outlook. He has also covered some aspects of land alienation in the study, most dominant being the illegal transfer of land to non-tribals.

The edited work of Dube and Murdia (1977) is an important contribution to the subject of land alienation and restoration. The articles by different administrative officers provide exhaustive data on different states, viz., Andhra, Maharashtra, Rajasthan, Madhya Pradesh, West Bengal, Orissa, Bihar and Gujarat. The articles contained in this book throw light on the phenomena of land alienation in respective states, in spite of protective legislations. It was observed in Andhra Pradesh by Sharma that different systems of money lending ultimately resulted in land alienation. Dube and Murdia (1977) observed that due to illegal transfer of agricultural land there had been a decrease in the number of tribals who were engaged in farming activity in Maharashtra. Roy Burman (1987) observed that legal safeguard failed to arrest the process of land alienation in the tribal areas of West Bengal. This was, according to him, due to the desperate economic condition of the tribals, their ignorance, and apathetic implementation of government schemes and policies by the personnel of the implementing agencies. He also pointed out that manipulation of settlement records, use of force and taking advantage of their poverty were the methods used to snatch away the tribal land. Yonus (1974) traced the process of land alienation among the tribals of Orissa to the land revenue system of the Mughal Empire, and later the British. He observed that in spite of the protective legislation in the state, the tribal land had been passing into the hands of the non-tribals through mortgage and sale. In Bihar, Thakur held several factors, such as, continued influx of outside elements, moneylenders and rapid industrialization of Chottanagpur area as responsible factors for land alienation. Tribal indebtedness was, according to him, the most important single factor. In the state of Gujarat it was observed by Dube that small size of holding leading to indebtedness, benami transactions, manipulation of records and coercion were the responsible factors for the alienation of tribal land.

Pareek's study (1978) on Jatapus of Andhra Pradesh deals with forms of exploitation and role of Sahukar in their economic sphere. He has pointed out that in the area the best class of agricultural land was now under the control of non-tribals and the government had failed to arrest the illegal money lending practices.

Rao's study (1987) on Koya tribes of Warangal district is a major contribution to the subject of land alienation. He has provided an insight of the problem during Nizam's period and later on when the protective laws were promulgated. He has pointed out large-scale illegal transfer of land through encroachment, mortgage, sale and by force. He ascribed these illegal transfers to pressure on land, legal structure, tactics of alien masters and ignorance. In his opinion land question still remains unresolved and the problem of land alienation is a part of the bigger problem of the existence of the unequal class relation in the society.

The study by Fernandis et al. (1988) focuses on the intimate linkage between forests and forest dwellers in Orissa. Apart from highlighting the impact of widespread and indiscriminate deforestation, the study brings out their struggle for survival in the absence of viable economic alternatives and shows land problem as single most important and crucial issue of their economy. The study establishes the close links between forest depletion and land alienation. Viegas's study (1991) looks at the alienation of tribal lands and its dynamics. It identifies the processes involved in alienation and the ways and means devised by moneylenders, middlemen and landlords. Fernandis and

Thukral's edited works (1989 and 1994) detail the processes through which tribals continue to loose land and the role of state machinery.

A survey conducted by the Tribal Research and Training Institute, Ahmedabad in Gujarat observed the phenomena of land alienation through mortgage (Masavi, 1976). It showed that the majority of land was shown to be mortgaged to the fellow tribals. Similar were the findings of Solanki (1976); Pandya et al. (1985), and Lal (1988). All of them conducted their survey in tribal Gujarat and Nagar Haveli.

Indebtedness in Tribal Areas

Indebtedness has been acknowledged as one of the most infamous stumbling block in the rural prosperity. Especially in the tribal areas due to unscrupulous methods adopted by the moneylenders, perpetual indebtedness had been the prime cause of the passing off the best quality of agricultural land from the hands of tribals to the non-tribals.

The lexicographic meaning of indebtedness is the state (of a person, family or organization) of being under obligation, more often of financial nature. Many household borrow for enterprise and repay the lender a share of gain from the enterprise. The theory of interest is based on such sharing of gain. However, in the context of rural India, and especially in the context of tribals, this wider meaning of indebtedness is not applicable because the word indebtedness does not have a positive value but is referred as a curse, a plight and a desolating experience.

Therefore, in the context of tribals, indebtedness is not the state of being under financial obligation undertaken on account of productive utilization of resources promoting economic achievement of the borrower; rather it is the state of being under the financial obligation on account of compulsion and being ensnared in the cobweb of usury. Indebtedness of a tribal household often finds its genesis in the borrowing on account of certain exigencies like accident or illness of a member of the family or a pressing need for certain social occasion like marriage, death, etc. First, because a household hardly saves enough to meet such needs and second, because there is no provision for institutional borrowing in such cases, the only source of loan is the local moneylender who charges exorbitant interest for such a loan. Now the borrower does not have enough resources or income to enable him to repay the debt, the principal multiplies rapidly to ensuare him in the cobweb of usury. More often than not, he makes a provision of repayment by either mortgaging his land or his labour captivating his sources of income to disable him pay his debt off. Very soon he is drowned in debt.

Sometimes indebtedness originates in the loan incurred for productive activities as well, as has been in the case of Maharashtra and Andhra, causing large-scale suicides by the farmers and events, like putting entire village on sale (Sharma, 2006). We know well that farming in many parts of India is to gamble with nature. Due to natural calamities like, floods, droughts, hailstorm, or untimely rain, if the crop is destroyed, a farmer who has taken big loan has now scant chance of paying off his debt. If he has succeeded in raising some production, he is forced to dispose it off to the lender. In the literature of agriculture economics the terms like 'forced surplus' and 'perverse supply of food grains' are used to denote such a condition.

The National Sample Survey figures of December, 2005 show that the incidence of indebtedness among rural household in India has increased by 4 per cent to 27 per cent during January-December 2003, as compared to 23 per cent in 1991. The survey also found that at least one-third farmers borrow funds from private lenders who charge interest up to 70 per cent per annum. The share of loan acquired for non-business purpose was found to be 76 per cent.

The tribals are easy victims of moneylenders, and due to poor repayment capacity, are easily caught in the debt-trap. Therefore, in the National Tribal Policy Draft (Government of India, 2006) it has been stressed to take special measures to improve institutional flow of credit and provide consumption loans.

In a comprehensive study conducted in the tribal areas of Tamil Nadu, Kerala and Karnataka, Nagar (2004) has noted that 63 per cent of the tribals were facing the problem of indebtedness. It was observed that many of them could not acquire loan from institutional sources due to their earlier loans, complexity of procedures, and ignorance. During a study in Kerala, Nandkumar (2004) could conclude that the benefits accrued to the tribals through programmes were not sustainable and indebtedness and alienation were still the major issues in the area. In a study conducted in Thane district of Maharashtra in 1979 (Internet source) 31 per cent of the tribal household were indebted, as compared to 12 per cent among the non-tribals. It was observed that although government had largely replaced the private players in productive loans, moneylenders were the only source for providing loan for illness, marriage and other social obligations. The repayment of loan taken for illness and for meeting out social contingencies was found to be made in the form of bonded labour.

In Madhya Pradesh the following two acts are in vogue to check mortgage of tribal land to non-tribals and waving off the loans given to the small and marginal farmers, prior to 16 August, 1984:

1. Pradesh ke Kamjor Vergon ke Liye Bhumi Dharakon ko Udhar Dene Valon Dwara Bhumi Hadapne Sambandhi Kuchakron se Paritran Tatha Mukti Adhiniyam, 1976.
2. Madhya Pradesh Gramin Rin Vimuktikaran Adhiniyam, 1982.

In spite of legal provisions, indebtedness still persists, in some or the other form, in the entire tribal belt of Madhya Pradesh. There, however, exit many regional variations. During a survey conducted in the Raisen district (Joshi, 2005) 427 bonded labour were identified, out of whom 49 per cent were tribals. A majority of them were working on wages of Rs 750 per month and had a loan burden of 10,000 to 50,000, with a rate of interest of 30 to 36 per cent per annum. In a longitudinal study conducted in the Jhabua district (Joshi and Joshi, 2004) loan burden was found to have decreased from Rs 701 per individual in 1984 to Rs 484 in 2003 at constant price level. In sum, the problems of indebtedness and land alienation still exist in most of the tribal areas of the state of Madhya Pradesh, and therefore, needs to be analysed for a timely solution.

Objectives

The objectives of the present study are to:

1. Assess the degree of indebtedness, as compared to income and repayment capacity;
2. Analyse the role of micro-credit institutions and other public sector financial organizations, as compared to private sources;
3. Assess the degree of land alienation in covert and overt form and the reasons, therein, and
4. Work out probable solutions in the light of the above study.

Methodology

To cover a cross section of the entire tribal belt of the state within a short duration of one year and within a limited budget, the study was limited to 50 villages.

To select the villages for the survey, the state was divided into 10 clusters of districts having notified tribal areas.

To decide the number of villages from each cluster, the PPS technique was used, that is, out of total 50 villages, the number to be selected from each cluster was decided in proportion to the tribal population of that cluster. The number, so decided, has been depicted in Table 1. The actual selection of sample villages from each cluster was random, keeping into view the following:

1. Villages were selected from notifies tribal blocks;
2. Tribal population in that village was not less than 20 per cent; and
3. Village population was not below 200.

Table 1

Number of Sample Villages Selected from Each Cluster

Cluster	*District*	*Tribal Population, 1991*	*No. of Sample Village*
1	Shoupur	1,20,291	2
2	Ratlam, Jhabua	15,25,266	9
3	Dhar	9,48,479	6
4	Khargone	5,42,994	3
5	Badwani. Burahanpur	7,24,565	4
6	Betul, Hoshangabad	7,13,423	4
7	Chhindwara, Seoni	10,71,013	6
8	Mandla, Dindori	8,86,074	5
9	Shahdol, Anuppur	7,01,010	4
10	Umaria, Sidhi, Balaghat	11,01,095	7
	Total	83,34,210	50

Ten per cent of the household, or a minimum of 20 in each selected village were covered in the household survey. The villages actually covered in the survey have been set out in Table 2. The selection of household was random. The interview was held in person, with a responsible member of the family. Two types of tools were used to collect primary data, namely, Structured Schedule and an Observation-cum-Group Discussion Format. Group discussion with people was held in each village, while the observation format was filled up by the respective interviewer. Besides, every interviewer was asked to record his experience and perception of the problem of indebtedness and land alienation, separately for each village and for entire survey conducted by him, in the diary provided to him. The survey was conducted in the months of November and December of 2006 by six interviewers, simultaneously in different parts of the state. Before starting the survey work, training was imparted to the interviewers and a written instruction manual was provided to each of them, to avoid any confusion in the field.

Table 2

List of Surveyed Villages

Cluster	*District Code*	*District*	*Block*	*Name and Code of Village*
1	1	Shoupur	Karahal	1. Karahal
			Karahal	2. Gram Paroda
2	2	Ratlam	Sailana	3. Dhabai Khedi
			Sailana	4. Adwaniya
	3	Jhabua	Jhabua	5. Piliyakhadan
			Jhabua	6. Devjhiri
			Alirajpur	7. Haraswat
			Alirajpur	8. Mahiyala
			Sondawa	9. Khamat
			Sondawa	10. Guneri
			Meghanagar	11. Futtalab
3	4	Dhar	Bagh	12. Gardi
			Bagh	13. Chijaba
			Kukshi	14. Talanpur
			Nalchha	15. Miyapura
			Bagh	16. Karkada
			Nalchha	17. Kagadipura
4	5	Khargone	Bhagwanpura	18. Badi Khurd
			Gogawa	19. Piparkheda
			Bhagwanpura	20. Dejala
5	6	Badwani	Sendhawa	21. Umati

Cont'd...

Cont'd...

	7	Burhanpur	Nepanagar Burhanpur Khaknar	22. Bori Bujurg 23. Bagawaniya 24. Mandawa
6	8	Betul	Shahapura Ghoda Dogari Ghoda Dogari	25. Silpati 26. Rampur 27. Chopana
	9	Hoshangabad	Kesala	28. Kesala
7	10	Chhindwara	Chhindwara Chhindwara Mohkhed Mohkhed	29. Kewlari 30. Kudwari 31. Partalai 32. Chhabdi
	11	Seoni	Seoni Kurai	33. Khamariya 34. Aalesur
8	12	Mandla	Niwas Narayanganj Narayanganj	35. Bhikhampur 36. Bawaliya (Jewra) 37. Sukharam
	13	Dindori	Sahpura Sahpura	38. Barbaspur 39. Bharothi
9	14	Shahdol	Byohari Byohari Jaisingh Nagar	40. Paparedi 41. Pasagadi 42. Lakhanwar
	15	Anuppur	Anuppur	43. Dongariya Toli
10	16	Umaria	Pali Pali	44. Marwa Tola 45. Majhgawa
	17	Sidhi	Sidhi Wara seoni Sidhi	46. Parehara Khurd 47. Dudhamaniya 48. Nimbuha
	18	Balaghat	Wara seoni Wara seoni	49. Karjhad 50. Tumadi

Profile of the Surveyed Household

As per the procedure stated before, 50 villages were selected from ten clusters of districts. In each village, schedules were canvassed among selected tribal household. In this way a total of 1,003 households were covered in the survey, representing 5,552 family members. The clusterwise detailed list of the surveyed households and surveyed population is set out at Table 3. It may be clarified that the clusterwise variation in the number of surveyed household was due to the fact that the selection of villages from clusters was made in proportion to the tribal population of that cluster, that is, more villages were covered from those clusters whose tribal population was larger.

Table 3

Number of Surveyed Household and Surveyed Population

Cluster	Districts	Surveyed Household	Surveyed Population
1	Shoupur	41	198
2	Ratlam, Jhabua	195	1,185
3	Dhar	125	704
4	Khargone	58	346
5	Badwani, Burahanpur	81	463
6	Betul, Hoshangabad	80	434
7	Chhindwara, Seoni	119	676
8	Mandla, Dindori	94	479
9	Shahdol, Anuppur	77	405
10	Umaria, Sidhi, Balaghat	133	662
	Total	1,003	5,552

Housing Condition

Table 4 lists out the housing condition of the surveyed household. Except for Shoupur where the surveyed families were uprooted from their original dwellings and were shifted to the resettlement sites,

Table 4

Housing Condition of the Surveyed Household

Cluster	District	Condition of Housing (% of household)			
		Kutchha	Semi-Pacca	Pacca	Do not Own House
1	Shoupur	70.7	–	–	29.3
2	Ratlam, Jhabua	91.8	6.7	1.5	–
3	Dhar	80.8	12.8	4.8	0.6
4	Khargone	67.2	19.0	13.8	–
5	Badwani, Burahanpur	95.1	2.5	2.4	–
6	Betul, Hoshangabad	80.0	18.8	–	1.2
7	Chhindwara, Seoni	95.0	3.4	–	1.6
8	Mandla, Dindori	72.3	22.3	5.4	–
9	Shahdol, Anuppur	94.8	5.2	–	–
10	Umaria, Sidhi, Balaghat	91.7	5.3	1.5	1.5
	Average	86.2	9.3	2.6	1.9

nearly all of the tribals were found to be the owners of their houses. However, 86 per cent of the houses were kutchha. Semi-pacca houses were more common in the Mandla-Dindori area among the converted tribals. In the Khargone cluster where agricultural land is more fertile and wood is scarce, 13.8 per cent of the houses were pacca. Elsewhere, pacca houses were rare among the surveyed tribals; the percentage being only 2.6.

Table 5 brings out that in the recent decade the availability of electric connection in the tribal areas has significantly improved. Out of the surveyed household only 16.6 per cent denied having power connection. The worst situation was found in Shoupur cluster where 83 per cent of the respondents were without electricity. In the remote hilly areas of Sidhi, Umaria and Balaghat also, 42.1 per cent of the respondents denied to have electricity. Most of the power connections were found to have been provided by the government under the single point connection scheme for the below poverty line people. Highest number of regular domestic power connections was observed in the Khargone and Hoshangabad area which are relatively more prosperous.

Table 5

Availability of Electric Connection to the Surveyed Household

Cluster	*District*	*Electric Connection (% of household)*		
		Domestic	*One Point*	*No Connection*
1	Shoupur	–	17.0	83.0
2	Ratlam, Jhabua	3.1	92.3	4.6
3	Dhar	17.6	65.6	12.8
4	Khargone	55.2	41.4	3.4
5	Badwani, Burahanpur	7.4	90.1	2.5
6	Betul, Hoshangabad	43.8	56.2	–
7	Chhindwara, Seoni	11.8	71.4	16.8
8	Mandla, Dindori	29.8	70.2	–
9	Shahdol, Anuppur	–	71.4	28.6
10	Umaria, Sidhi, Balaghat	52.6	5.3	42.1
	Average	21.2	62.2	16.6

Economy and Assets

During the survey the respondents were asked to state their first ranking source of income. Table 6 lists out these responses. The table clarifies that 76.6 per cent of the respondents considered agriculture as the first ranking source, while for 18.6 per cent of them manual labour was the main source and agriculture was secondary to it. In Shoupur, for 78 per cent of the respondents, labour was the first source. Except Betul-Hoshangabad cluster where forest was recorded by 10 per cent of the respondents as the main source of income, in rest of the area it has not been recorded as the main source of income.

Table 6

Main Source of Family Income of the Surveyed Household

Cluster	*District*	*Surveyed House-hold*	*Main Source of Household Income (%)*					
			Culti-vator	*Labour-ers*	*Forest*	*Service Trade*	*Animal/ Fishing*	*Other*
1.	Shoupur	41	22.0	78.0	–	–	–	–
2.	Ratlam, Jhabua	195	91.3	8.7	–	–	–	–
3.	Dhar	125	80.0	16.0	–	4.0	–	–
4.	Khargone	58	81.0	15.6	–	1.7	1.7	–
5.	Badwani, Burahanpur	81	66.7	32.1	–	1.2	–	–
6.	Betul, Hoshangabad	80	58.7	27.6	10.0	3.7	–	–
7.	Chhindwara, Seoni	119	73.9	19.3	–	6.8	–	–
8.	Mandla, Dindori	94	92.6	–	–	6.4	–	1.0
9.	Shahdol, Anuppur	77	96.1	3.9	–	–	–	–
10.	Umari, Shidhi, Balaghat	133	63.2	26.3	4.5	2.3	1.5	2.2
	Total	1,003	76.6	18.6	1.4	2.7	0.3	0.4

Table 7 lists out the position of land assets owned by the respondents.

It is apparent from the Table 7 that the landlessness among the tribals was relatively lower at 12.2 per cent. However, this varied from 1.7 per cent in Khargone to 51.3 per cent in the Shoupur cluster. Among the land owners more than half owned land below 2 hectares and only 3.6 per cent of them were those whose land ownership was more than 6 hectares. The average land owned per individual was 0.3 hectares, which was nearly the same throughout the area. The Table 8 brings out that merely 4.5 per cent of the household could purchase land from their resources and 3.8 per cent were provided land by the government under various land distribution programmes. Thus, 89 per cent of the surveyed households received land as ancestral property, which is getting reduced after each division in the family.

Table 7

Land Holdings of the Surveyed Household

Cluster	*District*	*Average Size (hec.)*		*% Household in Size Class*				
		Per Household	*Per Individual*	*Land less*	*Below 2 Hec.*	*2–4*	*4–6*	*6 and above*
1	Shoupur	1.29	0.26	51.3	2.4	46.3	–	–
2	Ratlam, Jhabua	2.25	0.37	6.1	47.2	30.3	9.2	7.2
3	Dhar	1.48	0.26	7.2	65.6	20.8	4.0	2.4
4	Khargone	2.26	0.38	1.7	46.6	37.9	10.3	3.5
5	Badwani, Burahanpur	1.03	0.18	39.5	42.0	13.6	2.4	2.5
6	Betul, Hoshangabad	1.74	0.32	22.5	41.3	30.0	2.5	3.7
7	Chhindwara, Seoni	2.10	0.37	14.3	40.3	31.9	9.2	4.3
8	Mandla, Dindori	2.16	0.42	–	48.9	42.6	5.3	3.2
9	Shahdol, Anuppur	1.17	0.22	3.9	76.6	13.0	6.5	–
10	Umari, Shidhi, Balaghat	1.15	0.23	6.8	76.7	13.5	-	3.0
	Average	1.72	0.31	12.2	52.2	26.6	5.4	3.6

Table 9 shows the availability of irrigation facility to the surveyed households. The table establishes the fact that irrigation facilities are still scarce in the tribal areas. For the sample as a whole, the irrigated area was 26.2 per cent, varying considerably from area to area and from individual to individual, depending upon the availability of water and the capacity of the individual. Being situated in the Narmada basin, Khargone sample showed the highest irrigated area at 42 per cent.

Table 8

Source from which the Respondents Acquired the Agricultural Land

Cluster	*District*	*Source (% of those who own land)*				
		Parental	*Purchased*	*Received in Dowry*	*Received From Govt.*	*Encroachment*
1	Shoupur	–	–	4.8	95.2	–
2	Ratlam, Jhabua	98.4	1.1	–	–	0.5
3	Dhar	94.6	4.5	0.9	–	–
4	Khargone	89.1	9.1	1.8	–	–
5	Badwani, Burahanpur	88.2	3.9	–	2.0	5.9
6	Betul, Hoshangabad	71.0	9.7	–	1.6	17.7
7	Chhindwara, Seoni	89.1	7.9	2.0	1.0	–
8	Mandla, Dindori	97.8	2.2	–	–	–
9	Shahdol, Anuppur	92.1	5.3	1.3	1.3	–
10	Umari, Shidhi, Balaghat	82.6	4.1	–	8.2	5.1
	Average	88.7	4.5	0.7	3.8	2.3

The overall asset position of the surveyed households was found to be poor. The ownership of agricultural assets and their monitory value have respectively been set out at Tables 10 and 11. In the survey it was found that merely 3 per cent of the respondents were capable to own assets, like tractor and thresher. Even the pump, which is a commonly possessed item, was available with only 21 per cent of the respondents. The position, however, was found to vary considerably from place to place and from individual to individual. The monitory value of the assets owned was also low, at less than Rs 30,000 per household and Rs 5,254 per individual. Only 4 per cent of the respondents owned assets worth Rs one lakh and above, while the asset value of 36 per cent of the respondents was below Rs 10,000. The Tables, thus, clearly depict low credit worthiness of an average tribal, as compared to other population.

Table 9

Availability of Irrigation to the Surveyed Household

Cluster	*District*	*Per cent Irrigated Area*
1	Shoupur	Nil
2	Ratlam, Jhabua	32.1
3	Dhar	28.3
4	Khargone	42.0
5	Badwani, Burahanpur	Nil
6	Betul, Hoshangabad	10.1
7	Chhindwara, Seoni	35.2
8	Mandla, Dindori	29.6
9	Shahdol, Anuppur	02.2
10	Umari, Shidhi, Balaghat	28.1
	Average	26.2

A similar position of poor economic base is depicted in the Tables 12 and 13, showing respectively the ownership of vehicles and gadgets of entertainment. The Table shows that the bicycle was still the most affordable and popular means of transport. Motorcycle is getting increasingly popular and 10.4 per cent of the respondents could acquire it through bank loan. Similarly 60 per cent of the respondents were not having any gadget of entertainment and the colour television which is so common in cities was owned by a mere 4.3 per cent of the respondents.

Table 10

Capital Assets Owned by the Surveyed Household

Cluster	*District*	*% Household Owning the Asset*											
		Bullock	*Cart*	*Unlined Well*	*Lined Well*	*Boring*	*Pump*	*Thresher*	*Tractor*	*Cow*	*Buffalo*	*Goat*	*Poultry*
1.	Shoupur	–	–	–	–	–	–	–	–	–	–	02	02
2.	Ratlam, Jhabua	74	21	17	16	02	40	01	02	63	18	87	81
3.	Dhar	75	31	22	06	10	25	05	03	59	25	62	45
4.	Khargone	83	53	38	10	03	40	07	10	48	38	66	34
5.	Badwani, Burahanpur	42	02	–	02	01	–	01	01	26	14	11	20
6.	Betul, Hoshangabad	60	29	30	–	–	16	–	–	59	15	45	78
7.	Chhindwara, Seoni	55	24	24	10	01	31	01	02	39	10	45	34
8.	Mandla, Dindori	94	03	28	16	05	12	13	01	64	39	65	54
9.	Shahdol, Anuppur	88	23	13	01	–	03	–	–	69	39	70	25
10.	Umaria, Sidhi, Balaghat	74	56	15	–	01	11	02	01	45	08	40	21
	Average	69	26	19	06	03	21	03	02	51	20	55	45

Table 11

Value of Capital Assets Owned by the Respondents

Cluster	District	Average Value of Capital Assets (Rs)		% of Household Having Capital Assets, Worth (Rs)				
		Per House-hold	Per Indivi-dual	Less than 10,000	10,000–50,000	50,000–1,00,000	1 Lakh to 5 Lakh	Above 5 lakh
1	Shoupur	473	98	98	02	–	–	–
2	Ratlam, Jhabua	39,361	6,477	26	43	27	03	01
3	Dhar	4,295	763	39	34	26	01	–
4	Khargone	81,148	13,602	28	28	33	10	01
5	Badwani, Burahanpur	12,926	2,261	72	26	–	02	–
6	Betul, Hoshangabad	28,670	5,285	41	34	24	01	–
7	Chhindwara, Seoni	42,912	7,554	46	24	18	11	01
8	Mandla, Dindori	34,963	6,861	07	73	14	06	–
9	Shahdol, Anuppur	21,537	4,095	17	78	05	–	–
10	Umaria, Sidhi, Balaghat	21,333	4,286	29	61	08	02	–
	Average	29,080	5,254	36	43	17	03	01

Table 12

Type of Conveyance Available with the Surveyed Household

Cluster	District	Type of Vehicle (% of household)			
		Cycle	Motor Cycle	Four Wheeler	No Vehicle
1	Shoupur	7.3	2.4	–	90.3
2	Ratlam, Jhabua	62.6	4.6	1.0	31.8
3	Dhar	28.8	13.6	–	57.6
4	Khargone	27.6	20.7	1.7	50.0
5	Badwani, Burahanpur	45.7	13.6	–	40.7

Cont'd...

Cont'd...

6	Betul, Hoshangabad	42.5	25.0	–	32.5
7	Chhindwara, Seoni	49.6	7.6	–	42.8
8	Mandla, Dindori	56.4	21.3	–	22.3
9	Shahdol, Anuppur	44.2	5.2	–	50.6
10	Umaria, Sidhi, Balaghat	39.1	0.8	1.5	58.6
	Average	44.5	10.4	0.5	44.6

Table 13

Availability of Gadgets of Entertainment with the Surveyed Household

Cluster	*District*	*Availability of Gadgets (% of household)*				
		Radio	*TV (Black & White)*	*TV (Coloured)*	*Tape Recorder*	*None*
1	Shoupur	2.4	2.4	2.4	–	92.8
2	Ratlam, Jhabua	25.6	7.2	1.0	2.6	63.6
3	Dhar	6.4	20.0	4.0	4.0	65.6
4	Khargone	6.9	13.8	8.6	8.6	62.1
5	Badwani, Burahanpur	33.3	2.5	7.4	8.6	48.2
6	Betul, Hoshangabad	7.5	17.5	12.5	12.5	50.0
7	Chhindwara, Seoni	10.9	9.2	1.7	5.9	72.3
8	Mandla, Dindori	33.0	23.4	7.4	20.2	16.0
9	Shahdol, Anuppur	37.7	3.9	1.3	–	57.1
10	Umaria, Sidhi, Balaghat	6.0	6.8	1.5	9.8	75.9
	Average	17.6	10.9	4.3	7.1	60.1

Profile of the Surveyed Population

The entire survey was conducted in 50 sample villages, covering 1,003 household. The total family members covered in the survey were 5,552, putting the average size of family to 5.5. The sex ratio and the age structure of the surveyed population are set out at Table 14. The table brings out that; out of 5,552 persons 53 per cent were male, putting the average sex ratio to 888. This sex ratio is lower than the expected sex ratio among the tribals.

Quite a large regional variation was apparent with regard to this parameter. While in the Umaria, Sidhi, Balaghat cluster the sex ratio was 1,012, it was lowest at 817 in Shoupur. The lowest sex ratio in Shoupur is in consonance with the regional trend of low sex ratio found in the non-tribal population of Morena and Bhind districts.

Table 14

Sex and Age Structure of the Surveyed Population

Cluster	*District*	*Sex*				*Age Structure (% of total surveyed population)*			
		No. Male	*No. Female*	*Total*	*Sex Ratio*	*Below 7 Year*	*7 to 14 Year*	*14–60 Year*	*Above 60*
1.	Shoupur	109	89	141	817	40	30	29	1
2.	Ratlam, Jhabua	636	549	1,185	863	17	20	62	1
3.	Dhar	374	330	704	882	16	16	65	3
4.	Khargone	173	173	346	1,000	20	12	66	2
5.	Badwani, Burahanpur	255	208	463	816	14	21	64	1
6.	Betul, Hoshangabad	245	189	434	771	11	20	64	5
7.	Chhindwara, Seoni	355	321	676	904	08	18	65	9
8.	Mandla, Dindori	242	237	479	979	11	20	68	1
9.	Shahdol, Anuppur	223	182	405	816	15	17	66	2
10.	Umaria, Sidhi, Balaghat	329	333	662	1,012	15	17	66	2
	Total	2,941	2,611	5,552	888	15	18	64	3

The sample depicts a younger population, in that, 64 per cent of the population was in the working age group and 18 per cent was likely to join the workforce in few years. The above 60 year population was found to be only 6 per cent, representing low longevity, due to poor medical facilities. No significant regional variation in the age structure was observable.

The level of education in the surveyed population is recorded in Table 15. The table depicts that, on an average, nearly half of the surveyed population above 7 years of age was illiterate and merely 4 per cent had acquired education above 10th standard. The data shows large regional variation, in that, in Mandla-Dindori cluster the education level was perceptibly higher with literacy level of 88 per cent and 23 per cent having education up to high school and above. The higher literacy level in this area was due to the incessant efforts of the Christian missionaries. Lowest literacy was observed in the sample from Shoupur and in the western Bhil region, ranging from 23 to 38 per cent.

Table 15

Level of Education of the Surveyed Population

Cluster	*District*	*Population above 7 years*	*Level of Literacy (% total population above seven)*					
			Illiterate	*Primary*	*Middle*	*High School*	*Inter*	*Graduate and above*
1	Shoupur	141	77	17	4	2	–	–
2	Ratlam, Jhabua	987	62	19	11	5	2	1
3	Dhar	594	48	28	16	6	1	1
4	Khargone	278	38	30	19	8	2	3
5	Badwani, Burahanpur	398	75	16	5	2	2	–
6	Betul, Hoshangabad	387	54	27	14	3	1	1
7	Chhindwara, Seoni	619	45	28	15	6	4	2
8	Mandla, Dindori	428	12	42	23	13	8	2
9	Shahdol, Anuppur	345	35	34	13	11	5	2
10	Umaria, Sidhi, Baiaghat	560	47	32	12	6	2	1
	Total	4,737	49	27	14	6	3	1

Table 16

Work Structure of the Surveyed Population of above 14 Years of Age

Cluster	District	Gainful Workers %			Type of Work %					
		Male	Female	Total	Agriculture	Labour	Agriculture and Labour	Service	Trade	Other
1	Shoupur	45.0	40.4	42.9	20	65	13	2	–	–
2	Ratlam, Jhabua	55.5	60.3	57.7	12	16	70	2	–	–
3	Dhar	52.7	54.2	53.4	45	8	45	2	–	–
4	Khargone	54.9	47.4	51.2	50	8	36	4	1	1
5	Badwani, Burahanpur	48.6	47.1	47.9	31	44	25	–	–	–
6	Betul, Hoshangabad	57.1	56.6	56.9	18	20	53	4	5	–
7	Chhindwara, Seoni	52.7	48.3	50.6	23	19	53	4	–	1
8	Mandla, Dindori	57.4	58.6	58.0	43	1	49	2	3	2
9	Shahdol, Anuppur	66.4	67.6	66.9	63	17	18	–	–	2
10	Umaria, Sidhi, Balaghat	54.4	43.2	48.8	43	11	39	3	2	2
	Total	54.8	53.4	54.1	33	17	46	2	1	1

Table 16 records the work structure of the surveyed population. The table clearly depicts near equal participation of female in the workforce. The regional variation in this parameter was also not found to be significant. Nearly one-third of the workers were cultivators, 46 per cent were doing manual labour, besides cultivation, and 17 per cent were dependent on labour alone for their livelihood. The data shows perceptible regional variation, depending upon local conditions of agricultural productivity and work availability. Due to the absence of the component of skill and low economic base, employment in the tertiary sector was negligible.

Degree of Indebtedness

It is a well-known fact that historically the condition of perpetual indebtedness in the tribal areas which resulted in passing off tribal lands to the non-tribal traders, had been due to the unscrupulous methods used by the moneylenders. Though, due to the intervention of the state, there has been a significant change in the state of affairs, the problem of indebtedness still hovers over in most of the tribal areas as an important issue, requiring serious attention and action.

In the present study the concept of indebtedness has been used not with reference to a positive value pertaining to the productive utilization of resources promoting economic upliftment of the borrower, but as a negative value pertaining to a state of living under financial obligation undertaken on account of compulsion. The degree of indebtedness in the surveyed households has been assessed with reference to average per household and per individual loan amount taken in the last five years, outstanding loan amount, including the interest, and the outstanding loan in proportion to the agricultural holding and capital assets of the household. These have respectively been set out in Tables 17, 18 and 19 respectively.

Table 17

Loan Liability of the Surveyed Household

Cluster	*District*	*Average Loan Amount During Last 5 Year Period (Rs)*		*% of Household in Loan Category*				
		Per House-hold	*Per Indivi-dual*	*No Loan*	*Below 10,000*	*10,000–50,000*	*50,000–1 Lakh*	*1 to 5 Lakh*
1	Shoupur	4,729	979	10	83	07	–	–
2	Ratlam, Jhabua	13,561	2,231	23	38	34	03	02
3	Dhar	21,340	3,784	26	18	45	09	02
4	Khargone	42,603	7,142	28	17	47	03	05
5	Badwani, Burahanpur	13,383	2,341	12	47	32	07	02
6	Betul, Hoshangabad	5,946	1,096	27	44	29	–	–

Cont'd...

Cont'd...

7	Chhindwara, Seoni	12,005	2,113	21	45	31	01	02
8	Mandla, Dindori	15,106	2,964	09	40	46	04	01
9	Shahdol, Anuppur	9,743	1,852	19	58	16	03	04
10	Umaria, Sidhi, Balaghat	1,191	239	18	43	37	01	01
	Total	13,254	2,394	20	41	34	03	02

Table 18

Outstanding Loan Against the Surveyed Household

Cluster	*District*	*Average Outstanding*		*Amount Due (% of household)*				
		Per House-hold	*Per indivi-dual*	*Nil*	*Up to 10,000*	*10,000–50,000*	*50,000–1 Lakh*	*Above one lakh*
1	Shoupur	6,790	1,408	10	78	12	–	–
2	Ratlam, Jhabua	13,035	2,145	26	37	33	3	1
3	Dhar	25,620	4,549	26	21	40	8	5
4	Khargone	44,453	7,451	29	09	52	7	3
5	Badwani, Burahanpur	17,833	3,120	10	38	46	5	1
6	Betul, Hoshangabad	4,685	863	45	39	16	–	–
7	Chhindwara, Seoni	10,272	1,808	39	34	23	3	1
8	Mandla, Dindori	12,197	2,394	10	53	33	2	2
9	Shahdol, Anuppur	6,324	1,204	42	45	10	3	–
10	Umaria, Sidhi, Balaghat	13,123	2,636	15	40	42	2	1
	Total	14,977	2,706	26	38	32	3	1

Table 19

Outstanding Loan Amount with Respect to Land and Capital Assets

Cluster	District	Amount Per Hectare of Holding	Amount per Rs 1,000 of Capital Assets
1	Shoupur	5,253	14,350
2	Ratlam, Jhabua	5,790	331
3	Dhar	17,405	5,64
4	Khargone	19,682	547
5	Badwani, Burahanpur	17,196	1,380
6	Betul, Hoshangabad	2,696	163
7	Chhindwara, Seoni	4,890	239
8	Mandla, Dindori	5,648	349
9	Shahdol, Anuppur	5,11	294
10	Umaria, Sidhi, Balaghat	11,408	615
	Average	8,703	515

Before putting forward the detailed analysis of the tables, it will be proper to clarify that during the survey it was felt that most of the respondents were hesitant to give the details of the loans taken by them or the amount outstanding against them. Therefore, the degree of reliability is relatively low. The Tables 17 and 18 bring out that the average amount of loan taken in last five years was Rs 13,254 per household and Rs 2,394 per individual. The pattern of outstanding loan was also similar to the above trend. The amount of outstanding loan was, however, higher due to the fact that the outstanding amount also includes the interest to be paid, besides the principal due. Out of total respondents 20 per cent were those who had not taken any loan. Most of these were either landless labourers, migrating workers, or were having very low credit worthiness. Firstly, due to their not having any resources they could not get any loan, especially from the institutional sources, and in case they could get some loan for meeting out contingencies, they managed to repay it by working in the fields of the lender. A majority of persons (41%) had taken loan below Rs 10,000. This category mainly comprised of those persons who had taken loan for meeting out contingencies, like illness, marriage, and to some extent for purchasing seed for the sowing operation. The major source for this category was the private source, that is, the trader or the money lender who charged exorbitant rates of interest, ranging from 60 to 100 per cent per annum. This category was found to be the worst sufferers who required urgent attention to come out of the debt trap. In the category of Rs 10,000 to 50,000 there were 34 per cent of the respondents. The majority in this category had taken loan for agricultural purposes or for purchasing motorcycle from the banks or cooperative societies, at reasonable rate of interest. Some were found to face a dual responsibility of paying off low interest bank loan, together with the payment of high interest loan taken from private sources for meeting out contingencies, like marriage and other social obligations. The above Rs 50,000 category was of those whose credit worthiness was higher, were influential, and had better personal relations with the bank authorities. This category had acquired loan from the bank for tube wells, house construction and purchasing vehicles. Few among these were also the ones who had taken bigger loans for agriculture, but due to the failure of crop, were not in a position to repay it.

Quite a large variation within the clusters is clearly visible. While, on the one hand, outstanding loan in the Khargone cluster was as high as Rs 44,453 per household and Rs 7,451 per individual, it was the lowest in Betul-Hoshangabad cluster, at Rs 4,685 per household. The reasons for this variation were partly regional and partly individual. In areas where agricultural land was more productive and the base of agriculture had turned to commercial farming, the amount of loan taken from banks, especially in the western cotton growing areas, had been much higher. Thus, commercialization and loan liability are positively correlated. This western part shares the common characteristics of Maharashtra and Vidhharbha area, where to reap higher benefits from commercial cropping; larger loans from the banks had been acquired. However, due to uncertain weather conditions and lack of control on the markets, they were facing difficulties of repayment, in spite of the fact that the rate of interest was much lower, as compared to private sources. In the Satpura-Maikal area, where the base of agriculture is mostly subsistence, the share of loan taken for investment purpose was relatively much lower. Viewing from individual point of view, the loan liability of those farmers who had more resources was comparatively higher due to their higher repayment capacity. Most of the marginal farmers and landless labourers among tribals whose loan worthiness was low, were taking less amount of loan, but most of it was not for investment purpose but for meeting out contingencies, like sickness, marriage, death and for purchasing seeds during sowing. Because most of this loan was acquired from private sources, they had to pay exorbitant rate of interest, besides agreeing to conditions, largely unfavourable to them. The real problem faced was found to be by this section that could not get loan on lower rate of interest from the banks and were under stress due to their low repayment capacity, despite the fact that the amount of loan to be paid was comparatively lower. In the forest villages of Maikal-Satpura region where forests were providing livelihood to the poor tribals, it was noticed that due to their low economic base these too had to depend on private traders for their credit requirements and were compelled to pay very high rate of interest.

Table 19 lists out the amount of outstanding loan, as compared to the land holding and the capital assets owned by them. The Table shows contrasting situation among the surveyed household. The situation in the Shoupur cluster, inhabited by the Saharia primitive tribal group, was found to be the most alarming one. The entire surveyed household comprised of families who were uprooted from their original abode and were resettled. Though the land was allotted to them, due to scanty production and lack of resources, they had fallen in the debt-trap and due to their inability to pay off their debt, the land was covertly in the possession of the lenders.

In the western tribal belt where large-scale seasonal migration takes place, the incidence of indebtedness has decreased in recent years, especially among those who used to depend on moneylenders. Only those who had better agricultural resources had taken loan from banks for agricultural purpose. For them too, despite increased loan liability due to capital investment, the repayment position had improved due to the saving made from migration and enhanced agricultural production.

In the Narmada belt of Dhar, Khargone and Barwani where the land is comparatively more fertile, the loan liability has perceptibly increased in recent years due to the trend of commercialization, which requires higher capital investment. Though in their case the loan was mostly acquired from banks and the rate of interest was lower, due to crop failures and risky market conditions, these too were facing serious problem of loan repayment. In the Umaria-Sidhi area, though the amount of loan was less, looking to their meagre resources, the burden felt was found to be on the higher side.

To sum up it may be said that although the loan liability of the tribals is lower, as compared to the developed parts of the country, due to their poor asset position and low repayment capacity, even this loan with high interest rate goes on compounding, creating a situation where their income sources, that is, land and labour are captivated.

Table 20

Purpose for which Loan was Acquired by the Surveyed Household

Cluster	*District*	*Purpose of Loan (% of respondents)*		
		Productive	*Domestic*	*Loan Repayment*
1	Shoupur	29.7	70.3	–
2	Ratlam, Jhabua	58.7	39.1	2.2
3	Dhar	64.3	29.5	6.2
4	Khargone	93.5	5.8	0.7
5	Badwani, Burahanpur	37.4	62.6	–
6	Betul, Hoshangabad	63.9	32.6	3.5
7	Chhindwara, Seoni	83.5	16.3	0.2
8	Mandla, Dindori	64.4	33.0	2.6
9	Shahdol, Anuppur	58.2	41.8	–
10	Umaria, Sidhi, Balaghat	63.0	36.7	0.3
	Average	67.2	30.7	02.1

Purpose of Taking Loan and Its Repayment

The Table 20 lists out the purpose for which the loan had been acquired by the respondents. Viewed with respect to the amount of loan, 67.2 per cent of it had been acquired for productive purpose and 30.7 per cent for domestic purpose. Only 2.1 per cent of the amount was used for the purpose of repayment of previous loan. The situation, however, varies considerably with the availability of agricultural resources. In the Khargone cluster where the agricultural resources were better, 93.5 per cent of the borrowed money was utilized for investment in agriculture for higher production.

Table 21

Manner of Repayment of Loan by the Surveyed Household

Cluster	District	% of Repayment Made Through			
		Cash	Crop	By Labour in his Field	Other
1	Shoupur	29	14	22	35
2	Ratlam, Jhabua	52	30	01	17
3	Dhar	14	59	25	02
4	Khargone	67	22	07	04
5	Badwani, Burahanpur	36	21	13	30
6	Betul, Hoshangabad	44	13	23	20
7	Chhindwara, Seoni	65	15	19	01
8	Mandla, Dindori	45	28	25	02
9	Shahdol, Anuppur	42	25	33	–
10	Umaria, Sidhi, Balaghat	65	28	07	–
	Average	46	27	16	11

On the contrary, in the Shoupur cluster where the respondents were at the bare survival level, 70.3 per cent of the loan amount was taken for meeting out contingencies, like illness, consumption expenditure and social obligations. In the Badwani-Burhanpur cluster too, the major portion of the loan received was utilized for domestic purpose. In the Chhinwada-Seoni cluster the utilization had mainly been for the purchase of capital assets.

Viewed with reference to the number of borrowers, most of the marginal farmers and landless labourers had to take loan for meeting out contingencies. This was the section that were facing greater problem. Due to their poor resource base, they had no access to institutional sources and were compelled to approach the private sources and pay exorbitant rate of interest. During study it came to light that this section was facing additional burden on their already deficit economy in three ways – payment of very high rate of interest, compulsion of selling their crop to the lender at lower than market rate and pledging their labour to him on lower wage rates.

The overall financial situation was found to have a direct bearing on the purpose of taking loan. The well-to-do farmers who had an easy access to the institutional sources, were using most of the loan amount for enhancing irrigation facilities, house construction and for purchasing motorcycles, while the priority for the poor was illness, marriage, purchase of food grain and seed.

Table 21 lists out the manner by which the loan is repaid. As per the table, 46 per cent of the respondents repaid their loan by cash, 27 per cent in terms of the crop produced by them and 16 per cent by pledging their labour. Similar to the purpose of loan, the manner of repayment also varied considerably with the economic condition of the farmer and the source from which the credit had been acquired. All those who had acquired loan from the institutional sources had to repay it by cash only. The better off farmers and those who were migrating out for work also preferred cash payment. The small and marginal farmers and landless labourers were the worst sufferers who were compelled to pledge either their crop or labour to pay off their dues. Further, a sizable number of tribals from the forest villages of Shoupur, Badwani and Betul cluster were found to pay off their debt taken from the traders through selling them the wood and other forest produce collected from the nearby forests.

Source of Credit and the Items Pledged

The Table 22 lists out the percentage of the loan amount taken from different sources by the respondents. The table brings out that 57.8

Table 22

Amount of Loan Acquired by Surveyed Household from Different Sources

Cluster	*District*	*% of Total Loan Amount taken from Different Sources*			
		Bank	*Self-Help Group*	*Trader*	*Other*
1	Shoupur	12.9	–	85.6	1.5
2	Ratlam, Jhabua	48.5	–	39.2	12.3
3	Dhar	46.4	1.6	48.8	3.2
4	Khargone	89.0	0.4	9.7	0.9
5	Badwani, Burahanpur	25.2	–	74.3	0.5
6	Betul, Hoshangabad	30.1	0.3	68.3	1.3
7	Chhindwara, Seoni	81.3	–	18.7	–
8	Mandla, Dindori	60.8	–	39.2	–
9	Shahdol, Anuppur	67.3	3.9	28.8	–
10	Umaria, Sidhi, Balaghat	51.6	–	32.3	16.1
	Average	57.8	0.6	36.9	4.7

per cent of the loan amount was taken from the banks or other institutional sources, 39.9 per cent was acquired from traders and moneylenders, while 4.7 per cent was acquired from relatives and friends. The contribution of the self-help groups was found to be negligible. Similar to the observation made in the foregoing pages, the economic condition was found to have a profound impact on the source of borrowing. It was the better off and more influential ones who had an easy access to the institutional sources and the amount of loan acquired by them was also larger.

If the situation is viewed with reference to the number of borrowers and not to the proportion of money which was borrowed, the traders and the moneylenders still dominate the tribal scenario because most of the tribals borrowing small amount of money for the purchase of seed at the time of sowing and their small requirements of cash for meeting out contingencies, like illness of a family member, death in the family, or meeting out other social obligations, have to depend on private sources, in the absence of any established micro-credit organization, like, a self-help group. The following were the difficulties listed during field survey that came in the way of acquiring loan from the banks and other institutional sources:

1. Small holdings;
2. Difficulty in getting no dues certificate;
3. Outstanding previous dues;
4. Being in the defaulter list;
5. Complicated procedure;
6. Proper information not being provided by the bank staff;
7. Corruption and ill treatment by the functionaries;
8. Lack of awareness among the people;
9. Cornering of benefits by influential persons; and
10. Less number of banks, as compared to the requirement.

During the survey it also came to light that the functioning of the government network of health services was highly unsatisfactory and the dependence of the people towards costlier private treatment has significantly increased in last five to ten years. The expenditure on medical treatment had substantially increased in last years, putting an extra pressure, on an already deficit economy. This dependence could have been easily avoided by improving the access of the government medical network in the tribal areas.

Out of the surveyed 50 villages, the only successfully running self-help group was found in Fut talab village (Jhabua). In the village

Badi Khurd (Khargone) a self-help group was in existence, however, its effectivity was negligible. In the village Pipalkheda (Khargone) a self-help group was in operation but it was related to the plantation programme and did not provide any micro-credit. In the village Kevlari (Chhindwara) an effort was made to set-up a self-help group, but due to differences between their members, it soon became non-functional. In a majority of surveyed villages people did not have any knowledge of self-help groups. Thus, in the over all situations, the role of self-help groups in providing micro-finance to the needy tribals was found to be negligible.

Table 23 enlists the help received by the grain banks and the membership of the tribals in self-help groups. The table does not depict any encouraging trend, as only 6.4 per cent of the respondents had received some assistance from the grain bank scheme at the time of their need. A high degree of variation, depending upon the interest taken at the individual or leadership level, was clearly felt during the survey. Due to some interest taken by the authorities at individual level, the grain bank scheme was found to be relatively more effective in Betul-Hoshangabad and Chhindwara-Seoni cluster. Elsewhere the scheme had in general a negligible impact on the tribal economy.

Table 23

Household Who Received Some Assistance from Grain Bank or Were Members of Some Self-Help Group

Cluster	*District*	*% of Household*	
		Receiving Help from Grain Bank	*Member of Self-Help Group*
1	Shoupur	–	–
2	Ratlam, Jhabua	–	2.1
3	Dhar	–	15.2
4	Khargone	8.6	10.3
5	Badwani, Burahanpur	9.9	–
6	Betul, Hoshangabad	22.5	28.8
7	Chhindwara, Seoni	16.8	0.8
8	Mandla, Dindori	7.4	–
9	Shahdol, Anuppur	1.3	3.9
10	Umaria, Sidhi, Balaghat	3.8	7.5
	Average	6.4	6.6

Table 24 lists out the items which were pledged against the loan taken by the respondents. There was a clear cut difference, depending upon the source of credit. It was mostly the land which was pledged for taking loan from the institutional sources. A large number of borrowers who had taken loan from the trader or the moneylender had pledged their ornaments (53%) against the loan.

Pledging of the house property, which is very common in the urban areas, was found to be totally absent. Nine per cent, belonging to the poorest, had pledged their labour, that is, they had to pay off their loan by working in the fields of the lender. There were some other conditions too which are not depicted in the table but were noted during fieldwork. Some of the borrowers had to make a hidden contract with the lender that they would sell the crop only to him at the time of harvest. In the forest villages the borrowers had a contract to sell the forest produce only to the lender. In both of the above situations, the borrower was put to double disadvantage of paying high rate of interest, together with a compulsion to sell the produce to the trader at lower than market rate.

Table 24

Items which were Pledged Against the Loan Taken by the Surveyed Household

Cluster	*District*	*Items Pledged %*					
		Land	*House*	*Ornaments*	*Labour*	*Trees and Animal*	*Other*
1	Shoupur	–	–	90	–	–	10
2	Ratlam, Jhabua	26	–	74	–	–	–
3	Dhar	23	–	71	4	2	–
4	Khargone	46	–	54	–	–	–
5	Badwani, Burahanpur	50	–	50	–	–	–
6	Betul, Hoshangabad	32	–	45	8	8	7
7	Chhindwara, Seoni	69	01	26	–	3	1
8	Mandla, Dindori	11	–	50	32	7	–
9	Shahdol, Anuppur	13	–	50	31	6	–
10	Umaria, Sidhi, Balaghat	21	–	72	7	–	–
	Average	34	–	53	09	03	01

Table 25

Respondent's Perception about the Change in the Level of Indebtedness

Cluster	District	% Respondents who think that Indebtedness had			
		Increased	Decreased	As it is	No Comment
1	Shoupur	85	-	5	10
2	Ratlam, Jhabua	52	14	10	24
3	Dhar	30	10	42	18
4	Khargone	29	19	43	09
5	Badwani, Burahanpur	86	10	-	04
6	Betul, Hoshangabad	24	29	06	41
7	Chhindwara, Seoni	34	20	04	42
8	Mandla, Dindori	22	19	59	-
9	Shahdol, Anuppur	43	23	29	05
10	Umaria, Sidhi, Balaghat	30	08	44	18
	Average	41	15	25	19

Perception about Indebtedness

During the survey the respondents were asked to express their view whether indebtedness had increased in the past years, had decreased or had been as it is. The result of this query has been tabulated in the Table 25. Nearly 41 per cent of the respondents were of the opinion that the incidence of indebtedness had increased, 15 per cent told that it has decreased, 25 per cent were of the opinion that there had not been any change in the situation, while 19 per cent were reluctant to give any opinion. In the Shoupur, Jhabua and Barwani-Burhanpur cluster a higher number of respondents were of the opinion that the incidence of indebtedness had increased. During the group discussions in the surveyed villages also it was reported that during past years the cases of non-payment of installments had increased, resulting in refusal of further loans from the banks and societies. This situation had compelled the farmers to go to the private sources for meeting out their contingent demand of cash, resulting in increased indebtedness. Lately the banks were more strict in the recovery of their dues, and therefore, were exerting high pressure on the borrowers, resulting in higher tension over them. In the Khargone area, even the better off cultivators who had taken larger loans from the banks for capital investment in agriculture, were finding difficulty in the repayment and were in stress. An enhanced medical expense due to poor delivery of government medical network was also reported to be a cause of increased indebtedness among the poorer section of the tribals.

Land Alienation

As discussed, the problem of the alienation of land in the tribal areas had historically been a major cause for the passing off tribal land to non-tribals. In the present investigation, instead of going into the past history, discussion was focused on this topic pertaining to last 10–15 year period only. Questions pertaining to the assessment of land alienation were included in the schedule. Besides, discussion on this aspect was also held during group discussions in the surveyed villages.

The result of this query is set out in Table 26. A direct question was asked to the respondents whether the patta owned by them was in their actual possession or was covertly or overtly had passed to somebody else. Out of total 1,003 respondents only 25 such cases were detected where there had been a benami transfer due to the non-payment of loan. Thus, on the whole, the problem was not found to be that serious. Most of these cases were with mutual consent and the landowners were ignorant that this was illegal on the part of the lender. In the Shoupur resettlement basti the tribals complained that they were under a huge burden of debt taken from the private sources and were under constant pressure to covertly transfer the possession of the land allotted to them by the government. In the village Kevlari (Chhindwara) and Silpati (Betul) it was reported that 10 to 12 marginal farmers, who were under debt, were under the constant pressure to leave their land and in five cases there had been a transfer, though not on papers, with mutual consent. During discussion it was reported that there were many cases, where though the land was not transferred, their crop or their labour was pledged against the loan and they were under the unwritten obligation to sell their crop to the lender or to work in his field.

A question was also asked to the respondents whether the land which they possessed at the time of survey was smaller than what it was 10–15 years back. Out of 1,003 respondents 207 (21%) reported that their holding had decreased. However, in 57 per cent of the cases this decrease had been due to division in the family. Twelve per cent of the

Table 26

Cases of Land Alienation Among the Surveyed Household

Cluster	District	Household	Reported Cases of Transfer (%)	Cases where Land Owned had Decreased	Cause of Land Reduction %								
					Division in Inheritance	Had to Sell	Mortgage	Gave away in Dowry	Illegally Taken Over in Force	Taken Away by Government	Taken Away by Forged Documents	Other	Cases Reporting Pressure to Sell Land
1	Shoupur	41	1	18 (44)	–	–	–	–	–	100	–	–	18
2	Ratlam, Jhabua	195	2	102 (52)	95	2	–	–	2	–	–	1	2
3	Dhar	125	7	15 (12)	20	13	13	–	7	33	14	–	3
4	Khargone	58	5	4 (7)	25	25	–	–	50	–	–	–	2
5	Badwani, Burahanpur	81	3	3 (4)	100	–	–	–	–	–	–	–	3
6	Betul, Hoshangabad	80	3	6 (8)	50	–	–	–	38	–	12	–	3
7	Chhindwara, Seoni	119	1	14 (12)	38	13	38	–	–	11	–	–	2
8	Mandla, Dindori	94	2	10 (11)	50	50	–	–	–	–	–	–	2
9	Shahdol, Anuppur	77	1	23 (30)	78	19	3	–	–	–	–	–	1
10	Umaria, Sidhi, Balaghat	133	–	12 (9)	20	4	8	4	48	8	–	8	2
	Total	1,003	25	207 (21)	57	8	4	2	9	12	4	4	38

respondents lost some land under the government irrigation schemes or had to part away with the surplus encroached *charnoi* land under the land distribution programme, taken up under the Dalit agenda of the government of Madhya Pradesh.

To conclude, it may be said that though the problem of land alienation was not found to be serious in the recent past, tribals, on the one hand, were largely finding their existing landholdings to be becoming increasingly uneconomic, and due to the burden of debt, were in constant pressure to give away their land.

Summary of Findings

Indebtedness

- The average amount of loan acquired in last five years prior to 2006 was Rs 13,254 per household and Rs 2,394 per individual. The trend of outstanding loan per household was similar to this, being respectively at Rs 14,977 and Rs 2,706. The outstanding loan was higher due to the fact that it included the amount of interest to be paid, along with the principal amount due.
- Out of total respondents 20 per cent were those who had not taken any loan. Most of them were either landless labourers, migrating workers, or were those having very low credit worthiness.
- The loan amount for nearly 41 per cent of the respondents was less than Rs 10,000. This category mainly comprised of those persons who had taken loan for meeting out contingencies, like illness, death and for other social obligations. The source for this loan was mostly private and the interest rates varied from 60 to 100 per cent per annum. This category was the worst sufferers of the condition of debt-trap and required immediate relief.
- Nearly 34 per cent of the respondents had taken loan of Rs 10,000 to Rs 50,000. A majority of them had acquired loan from the institutional sources on reasonable rate of interest. The purpose of this loan had been for agriculture and for purchase of motorcycle.
- The above Rs 50,000 category was of those whose credit worthiness was higher, were influential, and had better rapport with the bank authorities. This category had acquired loan from the banks for digging tube wells, house construction and purchase of a four-wheeler or a tractor. Few among them were also the ones

who had taken bigger loan for agriculture, but due to the failure of crop, were not in a position to repay it.

- Quite a large variation in the loan liability was seen, ranging from Rs 44,453 in Khargone to Rs 4,685 in the Hoshngabad cluster. The reasons for this variation were partly regional and partly individual. The loan liability was found to be positively correlated with the degree of commercialization, level of fertility, and availability of groundwater. In the Satpura-Maikal area where the base of agriculture was subsistence, loan liability was relatively lower, but due to their dependence on private sources of credit and low repayment capacity, they were an easy prey to the debt-trap.
- Most of the marginal farmers and landless labourers had a lower loan liability, but looking to the fact that they had mostly taken consumption loan from private sources with very high rate of interest and their repayment capacity was also extremely low, these were facing real problem of loan repayment. In this category many cases were reported where their crop, labour, or forest produce was captivated with the trader. These were facing dual problem of paying unreasonable rate of interest, together with a compulsion to sell their produce and labour to the lender, at less than market rate.
- The Saharia tribal area of Shoupur was found to be in the worst grip of moneylenders. Due to the extreme poverty conditions prevailing in this area, covert land transfers were also reported.
- In the western tribal belt where large-scale seasonal labour migration takes place, the incidence of indebtedness had decreased mostly amongst small and marginal farmers, especially with reference to their dependence on private traders.
- In the Narmada belt of Dhar, Khargone and Barwani where the land is comparatively more fertile, the loan liability had perceptibly increased in past years due to commercialization of agriculture. Due the risky conditions of weather and market, problems similar to infamous Vidarbh region are also creeping up in these areas.
- Thus, though the overall loan liability of the tribals is relatively low, as compared to the developed parts of the country, due to their poor asset position and low repayment capacity, even this loan with high interest rate goes on compounding, creating a situation where their income sources, that is, land, labour and

forest produce are captivated. A majority had felt that the loan liability in recent years had increased.

- Viewed with respect to the amount of loan, 67 per cent was acquired for productive purpose, 31 per cent for domestic and 2 per cent for the repayment of loan. However, if viewed with reference to the number of borrowers, most of the persons had taken loans for meeting out contingencies, like illness, death, marriage and other social obligations and the source had been the trader or the moneylender.
- The overall financial situation was directly related to the purpose and the source of loan and also the mode of payment. Most of the better off farmers had acquired loan for investment in agriculture and the source was the banks or the societies, while a majority of marginal farmers and landless labourers had taken consumption loan and the source was private. Captivation of labour, crop, and forest produce was also reported in this category only.
- If the ground situation is viewed with reference to the number of borrowers and not to the proportion of money which was borrowed, moneylenders and traders were still found to dominate the tribal scenario. The access to institutional sources was reported to be poor with reference to a large number of poor people whose credit worthiness was poor and who required small sums for contingencies.
- During survey it also came to light that due to poor access of the government medical network, the dependence on costly private facility had significantly enhanced the medical bill during illness. This was also recorded as a cause for increased indebtedness among the poorer sections of the tribals.
- The role of both the grain bank and self-help groups for providing assistance at the time of need was found to be negligible.

Land Alienation

- Though historically alienation of land had been the main cause of land transfer in tribal areas, in the present study, instead of going into the past history, discussion was focused on this topic pertaining to past 10–15 year period only.
- Out of total 1,003 respondents, 25 such cases were detected where there had been benami transfer due to the non-payment of loan.

Thus, in spite of the fact that the problem still exists, it was not found to be on a large-scale.

- This transfer had been with the mutual consent of the borrowers and they were ignorant about the fact that this was illegal on the part of the lender.
- The pressure for covert transfer was more intense in the Shoupur cluster where Saharia tribals were living in extreme poverty conditions.
- During discussion many cases came to light where though the land was not transferred, their crop, forest produce, or labour were pledged and they were under an unwritten contract to sell their crop or forest produce to the lender or had to work in his field.
- As far as the size of farm was concerned, 21 per cent reported that their size of farm had declined in last 15 year period, however, in 57 per cent of the cases this had been due to division in the family. 12 per cent of the respondents reported that they lost some of their land under irrigation works or part away with it in the programme of redistribution of *charnoi* land under programme of Dalit agenda of the government of Madhya Pradesh.
- To sum up, it may be said that though the problem of land alienation was not found to be serious in the recent past, due to decreasing livelihood source and increased burden of loan and interest, they were in constant pressure to give away their land.

Recommendations

1. Indebtedness among tribals exists as a serious problem, especially among the small and marginal farmers and landless labourers, who have taken relatively small amount of loan from private sources and are paying exorbitant rate of interest, besides captivating their sources of production. These also face a threat of loosing their land. Vigilance Committees should be formed at block level to register and monitor such cases. Special budgetary allotment should be made on family to family basis in critical cases.
2. The Employment Guarantee Scheme should specially be made more effective in the tribal areas and the critical registered families should be given priority and be provided more number of man days of labour. The unspent amount of the developed

districts where there are few takers due to relatively higher wages in the wage market, may be transferred to these needy areas.

3. Most of the problem of indebtedness is with those tribals who are resourceless and need small amount of money to meet out contingent expenditure. This problem may be addressed by establishing strong network of self-help groups and grain banks respectively for providing micro-finance and food security. The rules in the banks and cooperative societies should be suitably amended to cater to the micro-finance requirement with the least of paperwork and guarantee.
4. Unfortunately, increasing medical expenses on private treatment is also adding to the problem of indebtedness among the poorer sections. A serious lapse in access to government medical network was noted during the survey. An urgent intervention is required to ensure that the poor tribals are provided effective treatment, free of cost. Mobile medical vans should be pressed in service in inaccessible areas.

References

Areeparampil, Mathew (1989): "Industries, Mines and Dispossession of Indigenous People: The Case of Chotanagpur", in Walter Fernandes and E.G. Thukral (eds.), *Development, Displacement and Rehabilitation,* New Delhi: Indian Social Institute.

Banerjee, S. (1980): *In the Wake of Naxalbari,* Calcutta: Sowran Rekha, pp. 32–33.

Basu, Sajal (1994): *Jharkhand Movement: Ethnicity and Culture of Silence,* Simla: Indian Institute of Advanced Study.

Behura, N.K. (1993): "Tribals of India: Planned Development", *Social Change,* Vol. 23, Nos. 2 and 3, June-September, pp. 68–78.

Behura, N.K. and P. Nilakantha (2006): *Tribals and Indian Constitution: Functioning of fifth Schedule in the State of Orissa,* New Delhi, Jaipur: Rawat Publications.

Chronic Poverty Research Centre (2006): "Chronic Poverty: Key Issues", *CPRC News Updates.*

Dubey, S.L. and Ratna Murdia (eds.) (1977): *Land Alienation and Restoration in Tribal Communities in India,* Bombay: Himalaya Publishing House.

Fernandes, Walter (1993): "India's Tribals and the Search for an Indigenous Identity", *Social Change,* Vol. XXIII, Nos. 2 and 3, June-September, pp. 33–42.

Fernandes, Walter and Enakshi Ganguly Thukral (1994): Development Induced Displacement in Tribal Areas of Eastern India (Mimeo), New Delhi: Indian Social Institute.

—. (1989): *Development, Displacement and Rehabilitation,* New Delhi: Indian Social Institute.

Fernandes, Walter, Geeta Menon and Philip Viegas (1988): *Forests, Environment and Tribal Economy,* New Delhi: Indian Social Institute.

Fernandes, Walter, J.C. Das and Sam Rao (1989): "Displacement and Rehabilitation: An Estimate of Extent and Prospects", in Walter Fernandes and Enakshi Ganguly Thukral (eds.), *Development, Displacement and Rehabilitation,* New Delhi: Indian Social Institute.

Government of India (2000): Eighth Report on Madhya Pradesh, Presented by Committee on Welfare of SCs and STs (2000–01), New Delhi: Ministry of Tribal Affairs.

Government of India (2006): National Tribal Policy Draft, Issued on Internet, NEPS, July 21 2006.

Iyer, K. Gopal and M.S. Manick (2000): *Indebtedness, Impoverishment and Suicides in Rural Punjab,* Delhi: Indian Publishers.

Joshi, S. and Y.G. Joshi (2004): Processes of Socio-Economic Transformation of Tribal Areas Under Development Programmes: A Temporal Evaluation in Jhabua District, Madhya Pradesh, Unpublished Report, Ujjain: MP Institute of Social Science Research.

Joshi, Y.G. (2005): Identification of Bonded Labour in Madhya Pradesh: Technical Report on Raisen District, Unpublished Report, Mhow: BANISS.

Kulkarni, M.G. (1974): *Problems of Tribal Development: A Case Study,* Aurangabad: Parimal Prakashan.

Lal, R.B. (1988): Land Alienation among the Tribals of Gujarat, (Mimeo), Ahmedabad: Tribal Research and Training Institute.

Masavi, M. (1976): Problems of Land Alienation among the Tribals of Gujarat (Mimeo), Ahmedabad: Tribal Research and Training Institute.

Mitra, M.K., D.C. Roy and S.K. Mishra (1986): "Rural Indebtedness: Concepts, Correlates and Consequences, A Study of Four Tribal Villages in North Lakhimpur, Assam", NEHU: *Journal of Social Sciences and Humanities,* IV, 4, pp. 37–43.

Morse, Bradford (1992): *Sardar Sarovar: The Report of the Independent Review,* Ottawa: Reserve Futures International.

Murthy, N. (2006): Fight for Tribal Rights, East Godawari District, A.P., Downloaded from Internet.

Nagar, M.N. (2004): "Land Alienation and Indebtedness among Tribals in Tamil Nadu, Kerala and Karnataka", Report of Planning Commission, Government of India.

Nandkumar, V. (2004): "Agricultural Strategy for Tribal Empowerment (Kerala)", *Kerala Calling,* January.

Pandya, Gaurish, Arun Patel and Kokila Shah (1985): Land Alienation and Indebtedness among the Tribals of Dadra and Nagar Haveli (U.T.), (Mimeo), Ahmedabad: Tribal Research and Training Institute.

Pareek, R.N. (1978): *Tribal Culture in Flux,* Delhi: B.R. Publishing Corporation.

Patel, M.L. (1974): *Changing Land Problems of Tribal India,* Bhopal: Progress Publishers.

—. (1991): "Land-Rights of Scheduled Tribes in Madhya Pradesh", *IASSI Quarterly,* Vol. 10, No. 3, pp. 106–09.

Pathy, Jaganath (1984): *Tribal Peasantry: Dynamics of Development,* New Delhi: Inter-India Publication.

—. (1991): "Some Reflections on the Culture of Forest Management among the Primitive Groups", *Adibasi,* Vol. 31, No. 1.

—. (1996): "The End of Millennium: Liberalization and Accentuation of the Tribal Problematique", *The Indian Journal of Public Administration,* July-September, Vol. XLII, No. 3, pp. 485–89.

Patnaik, N. (1972): *Tribes and their Development: A Study of Two Tribal Development Blocks in Orissa,* Hyderabad: National Institute of Community Development.

PRIA (1987): *People and Dams,* New Delhi: PUDR.

Purkayastnan, Goutam (2004): *Human Development and Rural Indebtedness in North East,* New Delhi: Anmol.

Raghviavh, V. (1971): *Tribal Revolt in Nellore,* Hyderabad: Andhra Rashtra Adimjati Sevak Sangh.

Rao, Janardhan (1987): *Land Alienation in Tribal Areas,* Warangal: Kakatiya School of Public Administration.

Rout, S.P. (1999): Land Alienation and Tribal Peoples Right: A Case Study in Mayurbhaij District Orissa, Ph.D. Dissertation, New Delhi: Centre for Political Studies, JNU.

Roy Burman, B.K. (1987): "Historical Process in Respect of Communal Land System and Poverty Alleviation among Tribals", *Social Action,* Vol. 37, October-December , pp. 391–420.

Sharma, Devendra (2006): "Indian Villages for Sale", *Counter Currents News Letter,* February 13.

Singh, C. (1986): *Common Property and Common Poverty: India's Forest and Forest Dwellers and the Low,* Delhi: Oxford University Press.

Singh, D. (1988): "Singrauli: The Nightmare Continues" in Rajan Singh (ed.) Dams and other Major Projects: Impact on and Response of Indigenous People, Report of a workshop 8–12 April, HongKong: Goa CCA–URM.

Singh, K.S. (1978): "Colonial Transformation of Tribal Society in Middle India", *Economic and Political Weekly,* July 29, Vol. 13, No. 30, pp. 1221–32.

Solanki, Siddhraj (1976): A Case Study of Land Alienation in Tribal Village (Gujarati), (Mimeo), Ahmedabad: Tribal Research and Training Institute.

Swami, A.R. (1980): "And Then There was None". A report from Shrikakulam, *Economic and Political Weekly,* Vol. VIII, No. 46, November 17, pp. 2041–2042.

Upadhyay, V. (2001): 'Tribal Land Alienation", Lawyers Collective, *Law for People Magazine,* (Tribals land alienation html).

Upadhyay, V. (2007): "Their Land and Our Laws", *India Together,* March 2007.

Vidyarthi, L.P. and B.K. Rai (1985): *The Tribal Culture of India* (2nd ed.), New Delhi: Concept Publishing Co.

Viegas, Philip (1991): *Encroached and Enslaved: Alienation of Tribal Lands and Its Dynamics,* New Delhi: Indian Social Institute.

Yonus, A.S. (1974): "Orissa", in S.N. Dubey and Ratna Murdia (eds.), *Land Alienation and Restoration in Tribal Communities in India,* Bombay: Himalaya Publishing House.

7

Impact of Colonial Rule on Santhals' Economy in Jharkhand

A Historical Overview

JITENDER PRASAD

The history of tribal economy and socio-cultural life that has been portrayed by the colonial rulers suggests their being ignorant and lacking in basic trait of human life. They are termed as savage and marauders living in the hilly and dense forest that had made their lives quite difficult. What is not being recorded in the colonial report that the jungle terry districts of that time where the Santhals lived, enjoyed full autonomy. They followed a communitarian pattern and whatever regulation on land existed, the village headman was its ultimate custodian. The ownership of land by the Santhals family did not include arable land alone, it also covered waste land, pasture land roads, irrigation channels such as wells, rivers cremation and burial sites. The British regime and their imperialistic design prepared a scheme of administration on tribal land that endangered their existence. Initially, colonial rulers exploited the Santhals by asking them to clear the uncultivable tract and make it fit for cultivation and inhabitation. Thereafter, the land came under British control. The enactment of Cornwallis Act of Permanent Settlement (1793) was entrusted to Captain James Brown with the task of finalizing schemes for the administration of lands occupied by the tribals.

The proposal conceived the allotment of land to the British Sepoys on the lands cleared by the Santhals. The non-tribal zamindars were authorized to collect the rent on the land occupied by the Santhals who had earlier cleared the forest and settled there. The zamindars were authorized by the colonial rulers to collect rent on land occupied by the tribals. This meant direct confrontation of the tribals with the zamindars of non-tribal origin. Subsequently, the exploitative structure created during the colonial rule made tribals suffer on economic, social and political front. The structures of deprivation created during the colonial regime culminated into armed uprisings. Several thousands of innocent tribals mostly including the Santhals lost their lives but they remained determined to exercise their traditional right over land. The present paper proposes to discuss the British colonial policy and its impact on the Santhals by examining the protest movements launched by them.

Impact of British Rule and Tribal Movement

The tradition of tribal movement reveals signs of restlessness which was direct response to the varied challenges emanating from both internal as well as external sources. V.R. Raghavaiah (1971: 261–66) has presented a list of over 70 tribal protests in chronological order during a period of over 190 years ranging from 1778 to 1971. Out of these 70 tribal protests about 50 occurred during the British period in the 19th century and perhaps none of them could qualify to be a revolutionary movement as majority of them were quasi-movements.[1]

Describing the effects of British rule on Indian life, Kathleen Gough (1974: 1392) has pointed out the varied impact of the insurrection movements on tribals by identifying the salient features of the British rule when she writes that "it created a structure of underdevelopment in the Indian countryside which became endemic, and which has been modified but never eradicated since independence".

Two aspects on which Marx tried to base his judgement of British rule were: (a) mode of production especially the system of extraction of surplus existing in India on the eve of British conquests, and (b) the nature of British Imperialism, which was itself subject to change as British economy was transformed under the impact of the Industrial Revolution. This was also true in case of the Santhals of Santhal Pargana whose economic conditions worsened due to the imposition of rent on the land occupied by them. The imposition of land tax further aggravated the Santhal economic position. The foremost and the primary method of surplus extraction throughout India has come to be the levy of land revenue on behalf of or in the name of the sovereign ruler.[2]

What bearing the British rule had on the ethnic group relations can be investigated properly, if we had an established traditions of analysing these issues in a colonial historiography. S.C. Roy (1915), K.S. Singh (1966, 1983, 1985), B.B. Chaudhary (1984), K.K. Datta (1940), J.C. Jha (1964) and others have shown interest in investigating some of the issues involved in the historical study of ethnic group relations. Romila Thapar and M.H. Siddiqui (1979: 1119) have investigated two misconstrued generalizations about the ethnic group relations. They observe, "The first is that the Chotanagpur plateau in Eastern India was cut off from the main stream of Indian history until the last couple of centuries and the second, that the tribal institutions have remained virtually untouched since their early beginnings with history regularly superimposing layers of immigrants but leaving the autochtones relatively intact."

Impact of Colonial Policy on the Santhals' Economy

The economic system as a sub-system of the social system includes the rules and the principles designed by the state. According to the substantivists three economic activities namely; production, distribution and consumption of material goods gave us some idea of the totality of economic operation. The colonial policy substantially affected the production relations existing among the tribal groups. The nature of the production relations stifled not only the economic growth but it also had an adverse bearing on the tribals in the socio-cultural and political field. Hence, their structures of deprivation emerged in all these three fields, viz., economic, socio-cultural and political – in the economic field it accounted for tribal exploitation, in the socio-cultural, it brought about discrimination, and in the political, it caused oppression of the tribal groups.

Exploitation of the Santhals by the colonial state and non-tribals had been the perennial source of economic misery. Within the boundary of the legal code, attempt was made to institutionalise the exploitative regime of Britishers. Recommendations made by Sutherland in 1819 testify this fact:

(a) the government should declare that the hill tract occupied by the hill people was the property of government alone, (b) that the level country skirting the external ranges of hills was distinct from the adjoining zamindari estates and was also its property, (c) that measures should be taken for defining the extent of skirts of the hills and the hilly tract, (d) that the defects in the administration of justice amongst the hill people under regulation I of 1796 be removed the inhabitants of the hills amenable to the jurisdiction of the criminal courts and subject to the ordinary system of police ..., (e) that the payments of the stipends ... to Sardars, Naibs and the inferior Manjhis ... be regulated on a more sound basis (quoted in Roy Chaudhary, 1965: 71).

These recommendations which were accepted by the government in 1823 were followed by Pontent in 1837 who was placed in charge of the revenue administration. Due to Pontent's effort the number of villages increased from 427 in 1836 to 1,218 in 1855. With the increase in number of villages there was corresponding increase in the collection of land revenues. Balance for the two years, i.e., 1848–49 and 1849–50 indicated an increase of nearly Rs 3,000 from the past year (see Table 1).

Table 1

Collection of Land Revenue (for 1848–49 and 1849–50)

(in Rs, Annas, Paise)

	1848–49	*1849–50*
Demand	40,947–1–3	43,724–5–51/2
Collection	39,230–11–9	42,080–7–3
Balance	1,695–5–6	1,693–14–2–1/2

Source: Taken from the letter Nos. 1 and 30, from the Collector of Bhagalpur to G.E. Brown, Commissioner of Revenue dated 18th September, 1850.

There was an enormous increase in government revenue in about 17 to 18 years' time. It increased from Rs 6,682 in 1837–38 to Rs 38,033 in 1854–55. Judicial department letter No. 42 of 1,856 stated that the increase of revenue was not in any degree owing to over assessment but entirely due to the increased cultivation. Contrary to this, some facts relating to the collection of land rent make it clear that the Britishers could enhance their land revenue by overassessment and not due to the growth of production. In fact the constraints under which the Santhals had to work barely fetched them enough to meet the consumption needs of the family. In the presence of the greedy mahajans, traders and zamindars, it was extremely difficult for them to increase their production. Lack of irrigation facilities coupled with unpredictable weather and the recurrent famines reduced the Santhal economic situation to one of hardships and misery. In addition to all this, they were also overburdened with the increased land revenue rent.

Rent Settlement

The rent was fixed on the classification of the soil. According to McPherson's Settlement Report (1898–1907) the cultivable land was divided into Dhani and Bari land. Dhani land was subdivided into three, i.e., first class Dhani land (well protected or irrigated land); Second class Dhani land (partially protected) and the Third class Dhani land (unprotected), Bari land is also divided into first class land which is near homestead, well manured and may bear two crops; second class is dry upland which is not manured and bears only one crop.

The land rent varied depending upon the type of soil as well as the localities. The rates in Damin areas were lower than the rates in the zamindari estates. The settlement rent for the five years of settlement of zamindari estates was Rs 16,12,779 and in Damin-i-Koh area it was Rs 2,48,858 which was revised to Rs 16,87,292 and Rs 2,67,929 from the sixth year onward, in zamindari and Damin area respectively. In the second revision, i.e., during Gantzer's Settlement of 1922–35, in the zamindari estates the rate of settlement rent was enhanced substantially. The previous settlement of Rs 16,75,733 was enhanced to Rs 21,53,715. In Damin area rent in the previous settlement was Rs 2,71,880 which was enhanced to Rs 3,80,578. The increase in both the zamindari and Damin area was 28.5 per cent and 28.6 per cent respectively.

In fact, the overall policy of collecting land rent and enhancement of revenue had a similar pattern at most of the places. When around 1836, Pontent took charge of the Damin region he found that various *Banias* had located themselves in different parts of the tract and monopolized all the trade. Pontent wanted to have bazaars in different parts of the tract. The *Banias* were allowed the option of either going to the bazaars or retaining their dookhans (shops) in the jungle by paying high ground rent. They found opposition useless and gradually one after another they took abode in bazaars with the exception of few. The extent of Santhal immigration at that time in the area known as the Daman-i-Koh was quite pronounced. By 1851, as Captain Sherwill has observed, the area was studded with the Santhal villages.

The mahajans who came to the Damin region wanted to amass wealth as much as they could by exploiting the Santhals. The customary way of exploiting the Santhals was to lure them to borrow money. Having borrowed money once, they felt quite free to spend it and borrow more. Gradually the thriftless Santhals borrowed more and more and got into a vicious debt-trap from where it was difficult to extricate themselves. Narrating the Santhal's habit P.C. Roy Chaudhary (1965: 66) observes: "With their habits the Mahajan was almost a blessing to start with but the end was disastrous. It was vicious circle in which the Mahajan thrived while the Santhals declined".

The result was that the Santhals were constantly in debt. Soon after the harvest season the largest chunk of the Santhals' produced goods would go to the moneylenders in the form of interest. As the harvest season approached, the mahajans would get out on their annual tours of collection with bullock carts. In order to cheat the poor Santhals, they would pick up a stone on the way and paint it with vermillion to show the correctness of its weight. When they would arrive at the debtor's house, debtors would provide for the boarding expenses of their creditor's parties. By weighing grains with the painted stones they would take away almost the whole produce of the lands of their debtors leaving them overburdened with debts. Pakaur record also makes mention of two sets of weighing scales:

1. Kenarism or Bara bau, the capacity of which was a little more than that of the ordinary measure and which was used by them for weighing the crops that they took from the debtors.
2. Becharam or Chota bau, the value of which was below that of the standard measure and which was used for weighing articles lent to the Santhals by them.

Besides this, the rate of interest charged was exorbitant. One can find a number of instances where the interest charged used to be more than even the money lent. A Santhal saw his crops, cattle and even himself and the family and the family appropriated for a debt which ten times paid remained an incubus upon him still.

Apart from the moneylenders, the merchant class, i.e., trading groups also exploited the Santhals. Lack of knowledge about market and the prices in the market was the chief cause of this exploitation. As the tribals who produced grain on their land did not know the market value of it, they used to sell it cheap to the traders who would make three or four times more profit by selling the grain in the market. Illegal exaction of money by the merchants made the tribals' socio-economic conditions miserable. The merchants and mahajans amassed large fortunes within an incredibly short period by securing cash. Various obnoxious ways were practised by them to secure more and more cash from the poor and illiterate Santhals. Edeward Jay (1962: 289) observed: "Deteriorating economic conditions of the Santhals were made worse due to the oppressions and frauds committed on those simple minded people by the Bengali and up-country merchants and moneylenders."

Village Crime Note Books also document the extent of exploitation of the Santhals by the moneylenders. In fact a careful reading between the lines of entries provide us with the relationship between the exploiters and the exploited. In the countryside moneylenders usually extracted exorbitant rates of interest. The landlords used to harass them by exploiting them as bonded labour. The exploited, i.e., the Santhals (in the tribal village) were forced to suffer in silence. They were deprived of their occupancy rights. Village Crime Note Books of one of the tribal village described the nature of exploitation in case of a backward tribe, i.e., Paharias. While the menfolks from within Paharias were made to work as agricultural labour, the female members of the community were utilized as prostitutes (V.C.N.B. of a tribal village in West Bengal 18 February, 1917).

The Santhals were also cheated by the moneylenders in various ways. They bore the worst brunt of exploitation. Moneylenders of Muslim origin took advantage of the Santhals ignorance and innocence. They used to extract double of the normal claims. One Bhundu Santhal in Gobindpur village (in West Bengal) complained that Amir Bux Sheikh had given a pamphlet on medicine for curing ringworms assuring to be a one rupee note. He could discover the cheating only when he went to purchase Ganja from a local shop.

Irony of the situation is that the Santhals who were forced to express their anger on the moneylender's mischief was termed as lawless act. The so-called lawless act of the Santhals included their raiding the establishments of zamindars and moneylenders. They raided their exploiters' establishment on their own and sometimes they were joined by the members of the low caste people (V.C.N.B. of 19 September, 1926 and 14 June, 1935). While the village crime notebooks disapproved the violent conduct of the Santhals by declaring it as lawless act but as a matter of fact the acts of Santhals were basically an examples of dissent within deprivation.

It would be useful to compare the Santhal response of the above type with the protest politics of other subordinate social groups. The historians have especially analysed the participation of subordinate groups in movements on such issues. Sumit Sarkar (1980) while writing on Forest Satyagraha in the Non-Cooperation and Civil Disobedience movements has analysed the role of subordinate groups during colonial time. A noted British historian E.P. Thompson has also discussed the protest politics in Hanoverian England.

In other situation the incident of bil-looting by the Santhals reveal the juxtaposition of two contending notions of rights and justice. In such situations the zamindars spoke emphatically about his formal legal rights, the Santhals were harping on their age-old rights sanctified by tradition and customary usages. The advocates of subaltern approach in history, Ranajit Guha (1983) while writing on nature of peasant insurgency in colonial India has included a paper in one of his edited volume that has recorded a similar looting of hills in the neighbouring districts of Malda in West Bengal.

Land Alienation

Two factors that caused the alienation of the tribal land were: (a) imposition of zamindari system of land tenure on tribal land, and (b) introduction of cash economy. Both the factors had adverse consequences on the tribal economy and led to the erosion of traditional rights of the tribal people on land. Earlier, the communitarian pattern of land ownership of tribal land had not created any differentiation among them.

Keeping frequent transfer of land in mind, the settlement of 1873–81 and Regulation III of 1872 restored the tribal control over land. It also evolved two principles which were fixity of the rent, settlement under the regulation and derecognition of the actual cultivator. It made a pretension of recognizing for the first time definite legal rights of the tribals by encouraging sub-letting. Within ten years of the settlement in the district over 50,000 transfers had taken place. Due to the increased rates of sub-letting, lands were permanently alienated under the garb of subleases. Mahajans practically became usufructuary mortgagers and in a number of cases they had the original raiyat as Bhaolidars in their own holdings. The district, courts between 1881 and 1894 developed a case law based on two principles: (a) no rent could legally be taken in excess of the rent fixed by the settlement and this had the approval of the government, and (b) that the proceedings of Regulation II of 1886 began to operate after 1886. The idea behind these two principles was to make sub-letting precarious. The report of the Santhal Pargana Enquiry Committee (Russel, 1938) observed: "That the regulations in the matter of transfer have always been followed by a rapid growth of alienation and of exploitation."

Therefore, other ways of transferring land, viz., sale, gift or will and mortgage continued. Since women had no explicit right of inheritance, transfers could occur only through will or gift. The real demand for a right of transfer came from the mahajans, the Bengalis and some of the bigger cultivators. The tribal cultivators did not ask for it and they did not desire it. Surreptitious mortgaging took place. Since the tribals failed to pay the rent, they were liable to be evicted from the land which worsened the plight of the tribals.

The Regulation III of 1872 and II of 1886, Alienation Rules of McPherson, Allanson and Gantzer's and all the measures adopted by these officials could not succeed in controlling the practice of land transfer. The Santhal Pargana Enquiry Committee in its report in 1938 suggested that the codification of laws, ruling and executive orders should be taken up. However, it was felt that an absolute codification might result in rigidity and inflexibility of the laws and, therefore, the Deputy Commissioner and Sub-divisional officer continued to exercise administrative powers with regard to exercise of Raiyati rights, transfers of land, evictions, settlement of waste land and abandoned holdings, etc. (Prasad, 1974: 9).

In most of the cases illiterate tribals did not even know whether such rights existed for the restoration of their land. As a result of this, mortgages continued to be in possession of the tribal lands for years. The non-tribal exploiters had various ways to gain access to tribal lands. In the year 1910, an investigation had been carried out in parts of the Central Provinces where the tribals had cleared nearly 3,614 square miles of virgin soil (but they were found in possession of only 11 per cent of those land). The rest had gone into the clutches of non-tribal moneylenders, landlords and traders (Bardhan, 1973: 34).

Against the incidence of rapid land alienation some restrictions on tribal rights to land transfer were imposed. The primary objective of this imposition was to protect the cultivator against expropriation from the land. It was also stipulated that the restrictions on transfer of land would preserve the village community from fragmentation. The Settlement Report of 1938 (Russell, 1938: 47) observes that "history of the last eight years has shown that whenever restrictions on transfer were reduced expropriation and abuse increased".

Agrestic Serfdom

As a result of heavy land tax, indebtedness and alienation of land, large number of farm servants were literally reduced to slave. The farm servant were generally referred to as landless serfs, bonded servants, agrestic slaves and the like. Since the tribal's rights on land were monopolized by the outside infiltrators on their land, the local tribal population was forced to comply with terms of service which drastically restricted their freedom. Ramkrishna Mukherjee thinks that those places where tribal population existed in great numbers were more prone to servitude. His observation (as quoted by Jan Breman, 1974: 8) in this context is quite significant, "Agrestic serfdom is most prevalent in those parts of India where the lower and depressed orders are most numerous. Central India and Chotanagpur show the largest aboriginal population and it is these areas where the status of agricultural labourers verges most nearly on slavery".

Jan Breman (1974) argues that a large part of the tribal castes under the Hindu social constellation never belonged to the class of land owning peasants. Deprived of their lands by the mahajans they stayed at the lowest rungs of the caste hierarchy. Thus they were absorbed in the agrarian production policies in a relationship of dependence.[2]

Among the Santhals three types of bondage system were found. They were the traditional forms of bondage in agriculture which existed among almost all castes of Bihar. They were called Kamiauti, Harwahi and Kandh. In Kamiauti system, a Santhal borrowed money binding himself to work without pay for the moneylender. This arrangement continued until the loan was repaid. It was a form of debt-bondage. The District Collector William Le Flemming Robinson sought to abolish it in 1858. He noted that the system was prevalent in one form or other but among the Santhal it was worst. He observes: "As interest was taken in advance, the debtor could never work out his debt, the interest was never less than 25 per cent, often much more. The son, daughter or other nearest relation of the debtor used, in case of his death, to be considered liable, and if suits were brought against these bonds in the old Munsiff's execution no matter how old the debt was or who was working it out at the time. I have had a bond brought to me in which Rs 25 was originally borrowed by a man who worked through his lifetime, his son did ditto, and I released his grandson from any further necessity; it had been running on for over thirty years, if I remember rightly."

Under the Harwahi system, the borrower had (in addition to personal service) to plough their moneylender's fields whenever required till his loan was repaid. The system was common in Bhagalpur district and bordering sub-divisions as well. In this system also the obligation of serving the master continued from one generation to another. Here, he was to work for slightly lower wages (paid in kind). Describing the implications of these two forms of bondage system, Joseph Troisi (1984: 128) observes: "It was thus practically impossible for the borrower to repay the loan because his services were required during harvest time and the other busy seasons of the year and this did not leave him enough time to plough his own fields or work for wages".

The third type of bondage was Kandh. It existed in Deoghar sub-division. Under this system the labourer had to execute a bond in exchange for the debt that he took and he was under obligation to work for the creditor until the loan was returned. Describing one of the features of this type of bondage system S.P. Tiwary (1985: 192) observes, "The rate of interest is almost never specified in the Kandh contract in lieu of which an indebted labour is bound to work for a lower wage than that paid to a free labourer. Once the contract is signed the debtor becomes munish or the security for the debt. Accepting Kandh would figuratively mean accepting a yoke on one's shoulders."

Another type of dependent relations that was prevalent among the Santhals were directly related to property relations. It was found to be in existence before British arrival. These three forms of servitude were called: Bhaoli, Krishani and Palhaiti. The practice of Bhaoli system was used by the mahajans to alienate the tribals of their land.

Even the pradhans and big cultivators made use of this system to gain prescriptive rights over tribal land. In such a situation the original ryot became a tenant on his own land paying at least half of the produce and in many cases much more than half to the creditor. Over a time such creditors might become the new owners. The marked features of such a system was that it reduced an actual cultivator to little more than a bond slave.

Next to the system of Bhaoli was Krishani. It was prevalent in Dumka, Deoghar and Jamtara sub-divisions. In this form of servitude the actual cultivator was obliged to return two-thirds of the produce to the landowner. According to Gantzer Settlement Report the system was sought to be abolished in two ways firstly, by confirming the position of the cultivating tenants, and secondly, by restoring the land to the original raiyat. The Santhal Pargana Enquiry Committee of 1938 observed that the practice was quite common and bigger cultivators regarded it almost as necessity. It noted: "The practice (sub-letting – Bhaoli and Krishan) is convenient also to poorer cultivators who have lost their land through eviction of who have insufficient land of their own, but it not infrequently leads to permanent indebtedness to the recorded raiyats and in the form known as Krishani is often indistinguishable from serfdom (quoted by Tiwary, 1985: 191).

The Gantzer's Settlement Report (1922–35) mentioned yet another form of servitude called Palhaiti. In this system a labourer was allowed to own a small patch of land where, besides, planting food crops, he could construct a house for living. In lieu of this he was required to work for his master whenever needed. He was paid wages in kind and that too half of the wage that a free labourer was allowed to own. In the Settlement Report the Palhaitis who were found to be in possession of the land of the master for twelve years or more were granted the status of raiyats on such plots. In some other cases they were allowed to possess the house only and the land was restored to the master.

Thus these forms of servitude created a feeling of hostility towards those who had gained control over the tribal land. Mostly moneylenders were responsible for this. Naturally the tribals had no option but to organize themselves against their exploiters, i.e., moneylenders. Since these moneylenders were of non-tribal origin, the tribals' reaction against them was a little more hostile. It only goes to show that men rebel not only against the exploitation but also against the exploiters. The tribal peasantry revolted against the British and the Hindu caste landlord. That is, in their reckoning the exploiters were also outsiders. When the exploiters were insiders the possibility of revolt was limited. That is a combination of two factors, exploitation and the outsider quality of the exploiters, made the rebellion a feasible proposition.

The absence of Jajmani ties and the existence of communal solidarity among the tribal agricultural workers may be the reason for hostility showed against non-tribals. Under the Jajmani relationship a non-tribal peasant could depend upon his landlord for security whereas a tribal peasant did not have this security. Thus, due to the patronizing attitude of the landlords the socio-economic condition of non-tribal peasant was better than that of the tribal peasants.

The tribals were also treated like slaves. It may be useful here to trace the history of slavery a little deeper. Coupland was of the view that slavery was a universal element in the social and economic structure of all ancient civilizations. Defeat of a country meant that the people of the defeated country would be treated as slaves. Slaves were also sold in the open market. There were two kinds of slavery: domestic slavery (employed in the gardens, harems or in the houses, etc.) and the employment of slaves in groups for large-scale industry or agriculture. Coupland (1933: 14) thinks that from the inexhaustible reservoir, the system of Negro slaves began to flow northwards, a third line of export ran eastwards to the shore of the Indian Ocean. Further, by the 15th century there were thousands of African slaves in the Moslem kingdom of Bengal.

When the Britishers were having difficulties with the African slaves in the sea port area of Calcutta and tea gardens of Assam, the tribal communities were brought to substitute the African slaves. Report of the Scheduled Area and Scheduled Tribes Commission, Vol. I, 1960–61 notes that between 1840 and 1870 the overseas migration of labourers and workers, reached the figure of 55,000. It was felt that the demand for tribal labour probably arose from the disappearance of Negro slave labour for plantation work in the European farms overseas. According to the report of the Scheduled Areas and Scheduled Tribes Commission (1960–61): "When the British Parliament in 1834 abolished trade in slave labour from its colonies, there was fear that work and profits would come to an end and India was tapped as an alternative source of labour. The tribal people of Chotanagpur were sent mainly to Mauritius".[3]

Conclusion

Due to the devastating impact of British rule the Santhals needed some stimulus to reorganize their community by recalling the golden age in which they once lived. The religious idiom came very handy to them and therefore, in a state of despair, they were left with no choice but to appeal to their fellow brethren to reorganize themselves in such a fashion that they could lay strong foundations of their solidarity based on ethnic identity.

Thus the structure of deprivation created during the colonial rule continued to affect the Santhal's economic, socio-cultural, and political life in an adverse manner. Even after the Armed Uprising of 1855 the colonial policies continued to be exploitative, discriminatory and oppressive. In order to alleviate their sufferings, the tribal groups launched the Kherwar movement which, in the beginning, was peaceful, but as the Santhal situation deteriorated they intensified the movement by mobilizing the Santhals from all the corners of the Santhal Pargana district. In order to gain support for their cause they also associated themselves with the strategies of the nationalist leaders and their association widened the scope of their movement.

Notes

1. According to P.N. Mukherji, action directed explicitly towards an alteration or transformation of the structures of a system or against unexplicit threat to alteration or transformation of a system is called a movement. Movements of an explicitly transformatory character are called revolutionary but the mobilization aimed at changes within a system are called quasi movements.
2. These bondsmen are called differently at different places. They are known as Halis in Gujarat; Pandivals, Panaiyals or Charmer in Madras; Adiyars in Kerala; Huttalus, Mannalus and Jethas in Mysore; Busaliyas and Shalkaris in Madhya Pradesh; Bhagelas in Andhra Pradesh; Muliyas, Gothis, Chars and Halias in Orissa; Kamias, Baramasiyas and Janouris in Bihar; Harwahas, Hariyas and Sevaks in Uttar Pradesh; and Halis and Sepics in Punjab. This kind of servitude was found among backward or Scheduled Castes which were traditionally tied to their occupation. Tribal population

also had the same status and in some cases even lower than the backward castes.

3. By the first quarter of 19th century efforts were made to awaken the British conscience against slavery. An Anti-slavery Society was formed in 1823. The final abolition of slavery in 838 destroyed a substantial part of the old system but by no means all of it. Finally the Indian Government Act of 1843 abolished the legal status of slavery in India. Despite all this the slavery as an institution continued.

References

Bardhan, A.B. (1973): *The Unresolved Tribal Problem,* New Delhi: Communist Party Publications.

Breman, Jan (1974): *Patronage and Exploitation: Changing Agrarian Relations in South Gujarat,* London: University of California Press.

Chaudhary, B.B. (1984): "Rural Power Structure and Agricultural Productivity in Eastern India, 1757-1947", in M. Desai, S.H. Rudolph and A. Rudra (eds.), *Agrarian Power and Agricultural Productivity in South Asia,* Delhi: Oxford University Press.

Coupland, R. (1933): *The British Anti-Slavery Movement,* London: Thornton Butterworth Ltd.

Datta, K.K. (1940): *The Santhal Insurrection,* Calcutta: Calcutta University.

Gantzer, J.F. (1936): Final Report on Revision Survey in Settlement Operations in the District of Santhal Pargana, 1922–35, Patna.

Guha, Ranajit (1983): *Elementary Aspects of Peasant Insurgency in Colonial India,* Delhi: Oxford University Press.

Jay, Edward (1962): "Revitalization Movements in Tribal India", in L.P. Vidyarthi (ed.), *Aspects of Religion in Indian Society,* Meerut: Kedarnath Ramnath.

Jha, J.C. (1964): *The Kol Insurrection of Chotanagpur,* Calcutta: Thacker Spink Company.

McPherson, H. (1909): Final Report on the Survey and Settlement Operations in the District of Santhal Pargana, 1898–1907, Calcutta.

Prasad, Pradhan H. (1974): "Reactionary Role of Usurer's Capital in Rural India", *Economic and Political Weekly,* Vol. IX, pp. 32–34.

Raghavaiah, V.R. (1971): *Tribal Revolts,* Nellore: Andhra Rashtra Adim Jati Sevak Sangh.

Roy Chaudhary, P.C. (1965): Santhal Pargana District Gazetteer, Patna.

Roy, S.C. (1915): *The Oraons of Chotanagpur,* Calcutta: Brahmo Mission Press.

Russel, R.E. (1938): Report of the Santhal Pargana Inquiry Committee, Patna.

Sarkar, Sumit (1980): *Popular Movements in Middle Class Leadership in Late Colonial India: Perspectives and Problems of a History from Below,* Calcutta: K.P. Bagchi.

Singh, K.S. (1966): *The Dust-Storm and the Hanging Myth: A Study of Birsa Munda and His Movement in Chotanagpur, 1874–1901,* Calcutta: Firma K.L. Mukhopadhyay.

Singh, K.S. (1985): *Tribal Society in India: An Anthropo-Historical Perspective,* New Delhi: Manohar Publications.

Thapar, Romila and M.H. Siddiqui (1979): "Chotanagpur of the Precolonial and Colonial Situation", in UNESCO (ed.), *Trends in Ethnic Group Relations in Asia and Oceania.*

Tiwary, S.P. (1985): "Bondage in Santhal Pargana", in Utsa Patnaik and Manjari Dingwaney (eds.), *Chains of Servitude: Bondage and Slavery in India,* Madras: Sangam Books (India) Pvt. Ltd.

Troisi, Joseph (1984): "Social Movements among the Santhals", in M.S.A. Rao (ed.), *Social Movements in India,* New Delhi: Manohar Publications.

8

Socio-economic Conditions of Tribes in India

R. SHANKAR AND ANBU KAVITHA

Excessive use of firewood, as a primary source of energy for domestic purposes, is leading to severe deforestation in the north-eastern Himalayan region. Firewood consumption pattern of three tribal communities of Meghalaya, (India) – Garo, Khasi and Jaintia was studied under varying ecological, socio-economic and socio-cultural conditions. Fuelwood consumption was highest to Khasi community (5.81 kg/capita/day), followed by the Garo (5.32 kg/capita/day) and Jaintia (3.90 kg/capita/day), respectively, irrespective of their socio-economic status. The labour energy expenditure for fuel wood collection was highest for the Jaintia (88.56 MJ/capita/yr) and minimum to Garo (70.64 MJ/capita/yr). The fuelwood is burnt for various activities such as cooking, water heating, space heating, lighting and livestock rearing, etc. Among various activities, cooking required maximum energy. Commercial fuel is beyond the reach of the tribal communities due to their poor socio-economic conditions. The estimated growing stock is unable to sustain the rate of fuel consumption. This information could be utilized for developing appropriate technology for afforestation programmes in this region since 90 per cent of the total population use biomass as an important source of energy.

Tribal economy is intimately connected with the forests. For centuries the tribals have lived in or in the fringes of forests and depended entirely on forests for their livelihood. Even today, forest products continue to be the main source of income and sustenance for many tribal communities. These communities live in abject poverty having very little access to capital assets, health and educational facilities and hardly any protection against vagaries of nature.

Their dependence centres on nature. To a vast majority of the tribal people, extraction, processing and marketing of non-timber forest products (NTFPs) is a source of employment throughout the year. Without much capital investment and with little skill it provides employment opportunities to all groups of tribals and the income generated by NTFPs significantly contributes to household income in tribal areas. Though, they lived in forests, they had known cultivation for generations. Some staple food grains were raised by them in the forests themselves. They practised shifting cultivation living in the 'phodes'. This practice made them somewhat nomadic and did not attach them to a particular bit of land or dwelling. The method of living involving shifting cultivation and food gathering in the forests did not develop interest in them for permanent housing or interest for property. In view of this, much attention has been given by the government for their rehabilitation and development.

Tribal Economy and its Patterns of Transformation

The communal ownership of land, traditional methods and means of production, non-acquisitive value pattern and lack of any feudal hierarchy have become the realities of the past. The traditional occupations of the tribe has been changed to a great extent: it has become a part of the national or local economy. They are mainly settled agriculturists, owner cultivators, share-croppers and landless labourers at present. They are employed also in industries, collieries, educational institutions and tea gardens as daily workers, technical staff, teachers, and office bearer. They are impoverished now. This changed situation is the product of money economy. With greater interaction with Hinduism and its formal economy the tribals have been socially and economically absorbed, not totally into the religious beliefs and practices of the non-tribals.

Household Economy of Tribes in India

Traditional forms of agriculture, animal husbandry and collection of forest products have been the main source of income for the tribal people all over India. In the olden times for a carefree nomadic life the meagre income from these sources was enough. But, at present, they are unable to survive on these sources of income. The average tribal households in India has only one-fourth the life of an average Indian household which itself is having only one-fourth the life of an average household in a developed country. In general we can say that the life of tribal people oscillates between survival and starvation death. Under such situation no sustainability of tribal culture will be possible let alone their social and political development. The world is fast changing and the indigenous people have to strengthen their life and economy before they think of fostering their culture. This is a challenge more to the indigenous people themselves than to their sympathizers.

Ram Dayal Munda, member of the presidium of the Indian Consortium of Indigenous and Tribal Peoples while intervening in the discussion on agenda No. 4 in United Nations Working Group on Indigenous Population (UNWGIA) forum in 1993 spoke more or less in the same wavelength and observed "indigenous in the old and the new worlds are not the same". Further, he stated "indigenous and tribal peoples form a single segment when it comes to defining the peoples concerned, particularly in the Indian and Asian context" (Roy Burman, 1994: 83–84).

Examining the Concept of Tribe

It is necessary that the concept of tribe should also be examined. Among diverse approaches in conceptualizing tribe nominalistic, evolutionary, structural and normative ones would be briefly mentioned here. The nominalistic approach is found in Winik's *Dictionary of Anthropology* where tribe has been defined as a "social group, usually with definite area, dialect, cultural homogeneity and unifying social organization". There is hardly any community anywhere in the world which could be considered as tribal in terms of the foregoing criteria. Particularly the concept of cultural homogeneity requires a closer look. Sahlins (1968: VII) considers tribe to be an ethnographic heritage from neolithic times. Tribal peoples and cultures are according to him, evolutionary advances beyond the cultural capacity of hunters. While territorial domains are associated with tribes, territoriality is embedded in society, rather than territory serving as the basis for organization of society. Beteille (1986: 316) presents a composite historical structural and social ecological approach. In his words "being a tribe has been more a matter of remaining outside of state and civilization whether by choice or necessity than of attaining definite stage in the evolutionary advance from the simple to the complex".

The UN special Rapporteur Capotorti, defined minority as a "group numerically inferior to the rest of the population of a state, in a non-dominant position, whose members being nationals of the state possess ethnic, religious or linguistic characteristics different from those of the rest of the population and show, if only implicitly, a sense of solidarity directed towards preserving their culture, traditions, religions or language" (UN sales No. E 91 XIV No. 2 para 68).

National Tribal Policy

The National Tribal Policy shall have the following objectives:

Regulatory Protection

- Providing an environment conducive to the preservation of traditional and customary systems and regime of rights and concessions enjoyed by different ST communities, and reconciliation of modes of socio-economic development with these;
- Preventing alienation of land owned by STs and restoring possession of wrongfully alienated lands;
- Protection and vesting of rights of STs on forest lands and other forest rights including ownership over minor forest produce (MFP), minerals and water bodies through appropriate legislations and conversion of all forest villages into revenue villages;
- Providing a legislative frame for rehabilitation and resettlement in order to minimize displacement, ensure that affected persons are partners in the growth in the zone of influence, provide for compensation of social and opportunity cost in addition to market value of the land and rights over common property resources – the concept of net present value (NPV);
- Empowerment of tribal communities to promote self-governance and self-rule as per the provisions and spirit of the Panchayat Extension to the Scheduled Areas Act, 1996.

- Protection of political rights to ensure greater and active participation of tribals in political bodies at all levels. Socio-economic empowerment – reducing and removing the gap in the HDI of the tribal population and the general population to bring them at par by 2020;
- Reduction in the drop-out rate at primary level by a minimum of five per cent and at secondary level by a minimum of three per cent every year, to bring STs at par with the rest by the end of the Eleventh Plan;
- Ensuring access to health care services, safe drinking water and improved sanitation by the end of the Eleventh Five-Year Plan;
- Ensuring food security to all ST families below the poverty line, providing 25 kg of food grain per ST family per month, and transferring management and ownership of PDS to the community;
- Providing livelihood opportunities in addition to the guaranteed employment of at least 100 days by improving the production capacity of the natural resource base so as to reduce the number of ST persons below the poverty line by a minimum of two per cent every year and bring STs at par with the rest by 2020;
- Social, economic and political empowerment of STs, especially women to enable them to exercise effective control over their natural resource base and make informed choices;
- Creating physical and social infrastructure in scheduled/tribal areas to optimize utilization of resources and achieve the levels of growth required to bring it at par with the rest of the state by 2020;
- Realization of 50 per cent of total irrigation potential in tribal areas by the end of the Eleventh Five-Year Plan and the total potential by 2020.
- Cultural and Traditional Rights – Increase the participation of STs in sports and culture at local, district, state and national levels by encouraging their inherent talent and ensure participation at national and international events by 2020;
- Promotion and development of tribal handicrafts and organic and ethnic products through standardization, design support, branding and organized marketing and establishing niche markets for the products by 2020: Creation of awareness about and elimination of evil and anti-social practices such as addiction to alcohol and drugs, witchcraft, etc.;

- Examination of customary practices of inheritance, that exclude women, and modification of such practices; Access to privileges – arresting the increasing demand from new communities for inclusion in the list of STs by rationalizing the process of scheduling;
- Examine the need for descheduling of certain STs and sub-categorization of existing STs to ensure that benefits are evenly spread across the tribes by 2020;
- Focussing on the development of Primitive Tribal Groups (PTGs) to be renamed as Particularly Vulnerable Tribal Groups, by formulating conservation-cum-development micro plans for socio-economic and cultural development suited to the requirements of such groups and to bring them at par with other STs by 2020; and
- Development of nomadic and semi-nomadic tribes through need-based specific programmes; Intellectual Property Rights – conservation and protection of the intellectual property regime of STs and its proper utilization on a commercial format ensuring that their rights and share remain intact;

Tribal research institutes (TRIs) have been set-up in various states and are engaged in conducting research and evaluation studies, collection of data, conduct of training, seminars and workshops, documentation of customary laws, etc. The activities of the TRIs were intended to subserve tribal development objectives and help the central and state governments frame apt policies and programmes. The functioning of TRIs over the years has become routine and has been constrained by severe financial and administrative shortages. The TRIs would be strengthened and their structure and activities revamped for a more focused role in the changing scenario, more interaction among themselves, and with other academic research institutions.

Protection of the Rights

MNCs, TNCs and international agencies have emerged as major players in contemporary world techno-economic and political order leaving hardly any space for independent decision-making by many states having sizable indigenous and tribal peoples. The Draft Declaration has nothing to say about the protection of the rights of the indigenous and tribal peoples against the unscrupulous operations of such bodies. The onus is laid on the helpless states who are thus placed in a cleft-stick situation.

Recent policies and draft bills, such as the National Tribal Policy, the Scheduled Tribes (Recognition of Forest) Bill, Resettlement and Rehabilitation Policy, the Right to Work, Right to Information, Employment Guarantee Act and other provisions for tribals in the Common Minimum Programme of the present government, all promise to empower the tribals. The biggest irony, however, is that threat to life and livelihood has never been as acute in the past as it is today. Thanks to the insensitivity of the government and the industry-politician nexus facilitating the hegemony of the multinational companies over natural resources with profiteering as their common minimum agenda tragically to the cost of the tribals.

Indiscreet industrialization of the region has alienated the tribals from the forests and their lands, upsetting their pattern of livelihood. Though the forest department and the timber mafia are primarily responsible for the destruction of forests, they are now blaming the poor tribals for the same. The tribals are harassed even for firewood which is their daily need. They have been evicted from their forest land and their houses have been destroyed and burnt. False cases have been registered and they have even been sent to jail. Some of the tribal villages are existing for hundreds of years but pattas are yet to reach them. Since their villages are not registered as revenue villages, tribe and residential certificates are not issued to them. They are not included in the voters' list. No government schemes are given to these villages. Forest officials extort money, cocks, goats, alcohols from them as reported by Tintus Samaria, one of the elders of Budakata village, Sundergarh. The tribals are being deprived of natural resources, and the existence of tribals living in the forest is in complete darkness.

Tribes in India

The ancient scriptures going back to the first millennium BC (the Vedas, Brahmans and Purans) also mention names of tribes or nations of different periods. It is the consensus among scholars that in Sanskrit the term Kirata indicated the wild non-Aryan tribes living in the mountains particularly the Himalaya and north-eastern areas of India who were Mongoloid in origin. Some scholars are of the view that the name also applied to any hill people. The *Rig-Veda* shows a very keen perception of racial discrimination. At least three distinct constellations of peoples were distinguished in the earlier times, viz., Aryan, Dasa and Asura. Colour seems to have formed an important factor in the early form of gradation; but as large-scale miscegenation took place, other factors also gained in prominence. The words Jana and Vis occurring frequently in Vedic literature are variously dubbed to signify a 'tribe', 'people' 'settlers' by modern scholars.

By 1979 the politically and economically advantaged countries (so-called developed countries) managed to set aside the declaration and in its stead put on the agenda a wholly different approach dealing with "globalization, marketization and privatization". This has resulted in economic crises for most of the world, giving birth to "burning economic, social, political and even military conflicts during the last quarter of the 20th century" (Patel, 2000). The GDP ratio between the richest and poorest countries was 3:1 in 1820, 11:1 in 1931, 35:1 in 1950, 44:1 in 1973 and 72:1 in 1992 (Mayur, 2000). Globalization in unequally structured global economy reflects imperialist impulse of capitalism involving social coercion of labour and restructuring state machinery to serve large corporations. Theo Ben Guirab, President of 54th session of UN General Assembly in his opening remark observed that globalization and unrelenting powers of transnational corporations were overwhelming governments, especially in the developing world (Guirab, 1999).

UN is seen to partner with big business (ibid.). In February 2000, Kofi Annan, Secretary-General of UN and International Chambers of Commerce issued a joint statement in which they declared: "The United Nations and the business community should work jointly to expand economic opportunities especially in countries which may face marginalization". The statement called on the UN and corporations to develop 'partnership' to advance this agenda (Boli: undated).

Camdessus (2000) the chief of IMF in his last address before lying down the office admitted that whereas globalization was expected to improve the human condition throughout the world it had "operated at the whim of more or less autonomous financial and technical forces". Samir Amin however identified Bretton Woods Institutions (IMF and World Bank) led by WTO as the hegemonic apparatuses of the American supremacy in the post-war world system in the name of globalization (Anived, 1999). When Reagan came to power in USA in 1981, these institutions were harnessed to the project of "Structural Adjustment Programme" (SAP). International peoples' Tribunal of G7 in their Tokyo verdict in 1993 have identified the consequences of SAP as follows: sharp increase in unemployment, fall in remuneration of work, increase in food dependency, grave deterioration in environment, health care system, democratic system, and continued growth of external debt (Amin, 1997: 12–13). Further, globalization has led to the erosion of autocentric nation state (ibid., p. 3). An illustration of this has been provided by Indimyor (1999). In Ogoni region in Nigeria when people vehemently protested against massive ecological degradation caused by the Shell (Royal Dutch/Shell group) MNC, the federal army unleashed a reign of terror. It is alleged that there are documentary evidences that Shell directed the Nigerian army to enter Ogoni. Also Shell has admitted to have brought weapons of the Nigerian army.

After independence, the National Forest Policy enunciated in 1952 adopted measures to prevent indiscriminate use of forests by the tribal folk. According to this policy "The needs of the local population must be met to the reasonable extent, national interest should not be sacrificed because they are not directly discernible, nor should the rights and interests of future generations be subordinated to the improvidence of the present generation". Further, the National Forest Policy of 1984 envisages that the "sole object with which state forests are administered is the public benefit. The cardinal principle to be observed is that the rights and privileges of individuals must be limited, otherwise than for their own benefit, only in such degree as is absolutely necessary to secure that advantage". This concept has affected the tribal people to their freedom to live freely in the forests and have free access to forest products. In effect, the new policy abridged the rights of grazing and emphatically opposed the shifting cultivation, ostensibly through persuasive and not coercive measures, in a sort of missionary rather than authoritarian manner thus weaning away of the tribals from their traditional methods of living.

The forest conservation measures adopted in India have put an end not only to the shifting cultivation but also to the living of the tribals in and around the reserved forests. These measures have limited their scope to derive their income from forest-based activities, especially, from NTFPs. Therefore, in the NTFPs dominated tribal economy, a number of issues have emerged in the process of exploitation of NTFPs, tribal development and forest conservation. In view of the growing national and international interest in protecting and preserving biodiversity, greater restrictions are imposed on the use of a number of different plants and animals, which are very important NTFPs. This has also posed serious conflict between the forests dwellers, wild animals and the state. The conflict of interest between the forest dwellers and the state forest department with regard to exploitation of forest resources are induced by their respective roles as a consumer and a conserver. The former needs a means of livelihood while the latter is interested in the ecological sustainability and preservation of biodiversity. Therefore, preservation of biodiversity, sustainable extraction of forest products and tribal development has become the major issues facing the government. In order to conserve the biodiversity, government intervention by way of legislation and other programmes have alienated the forest dwellers from management of the forests for sustainable development. Thus it is evident that extraction of NTFPs, tribal economy and sustainability has very strong inter-linkages. However, the exact nature of linkages and its impact on the income and quality of life of people engaged in this occupation are not known.

Tribal Peoples in the Constitution of India

The Constitution of India enshrines the political intent to constitute the country into a sovereign, socialist, secular and democratic republic and to secure to all its citizens justice, liberty, equality and fraternity. As a purported follow-up of the foregoing over-arching objectives the Constitution provides for protection and promotion of the interests of the Scheduled Tribes (STs). These include affirmative action for promotion of social and economic interests of the communities notified as STs under the Constitution; reservation in legislatures, enabling clause for reservation in educational institutions and services, protection and promotion of languages and culture and so on. There are also two important instruments for administration of the areas of tribal concentration. Before discussing them some the implications of the basic structure of the Constitution would be briefly mentioned. While in the long run social justice, liberty, equality and fraternity may be inter-related, in the short run they may not be so. Besides the rights of individuals within communities and the collective rights of communities in the overall social-political milieu may not always coincide. Such issues were not seriously considered at the conceptual level (Mahajan, 1998: 4). While liberalism encompasses both the approaches, each affects differently collectives and individuals depending on the social structure and cultural ecology of the collectivities and personal and family histories of individuals. In India tribes do not constitute a homogenous entity; hence apparently a uniform approach is not possible. But in spite of diversities of life conditions, there is also an emerging sense of oneness rooted in the feeling of being dispossessed from traditional command over respective life support systems and consequently collective marginalization (Roy Burman, 1996: 2).

Panchayat Raj for the Tribes

Panchayats at the appropriate levels shall be endowed with ownership of minor forest produce.

The Gram Sabha or the panchayat at the appropriate level shall be consulted for granting prospecting licences or mining lease for minor minerals and their prior recommendation obtained for acquisition of land in the scheduled areas for development projects or for resettlement of project affected members of the Scheduled Tribes.

Panchayats at the appropriate level and the Gram Sabha shall have the power to prevent alienation of tribal lands and to take appropriate action to restore any unlawfully alienated land of a Scheduled Tribe, have powers to regulate money lending to the members of the Scheduled Tribes, to manage village markets and to enforce prohibition or to regulate or restrict sale and consumption of any intoxicant.

State legislations shall endow the panchayats at the appropriate levels with specific powers and provide safeguards to prevent panchayats at the higher level from assuming the powers and authority of panchayats at the lower level or of the Gram Sabha.

The offices of the chairpersons in the panchayats at all levels shall be reserved for the Scheduled Tribes.

The reservation of seats at every panchayat for the Scheduled Tribes shall not be less than one-half of the total number of seats.

Several adivasi communities or indigenous people are spread over the western ghats across the southern and eastern region of the Indian subcontinent. It is the most tragical ironies of development that these adivasi communities are at their vulnerable worst at the end of this millennium. Our experience having worked with the tribal/adivasi people of Nilgiris and Sirumalai hills especially Todas, Padagas, Irulas for over a decade has been a struggle for a right to human life with dignity, a struggle to fight the severest of odds in the face of "sustainable development" theories of the state. The macro-economic and political policies of the state with their active promotion of globalization, have driven the adivasi people to the brink of survival. The effects of globalization have had far-reaching consequences in the eastern ghats, and some of the crucial issues with respect to this region.

Food Problem of the Tribes

The economic and nutrition problems of the tribes in India and elsewhere is largely linked with ecological factors and conditions. The cultural aspects of human nutritional problems gained much importance in recent times. The nutritional problems can be derived from inborn errors of metabolism or from cultural and environmental factors. Nutritional practices are largely determined by basic customs which are interrelated with other aspects of the social organization, such as basic economy (Whiting, 1958). Problem of malnutrition is associated with the scarcity of food resources in many tribal ecological zones including eastern ghats (Subramanyam, 2001). Food crisis very much prevails in most of the tribal settlements in the eastern ghats due to food material shortage and practices.

The natural resources in an ecosystem are the basic energy base for the human beings and they exploit these resources with the help of suitable technology. Technology is a means to explore and exploit the resources. All societies have technology and control it by diverse means and with the aid of diverse social and political institutions. The technological stage of development of a society is the sole basic determinant of its social and political structures. Indigenous science and technology developed early in the history of our civilization along with the development of our society. It was very much a part of our social growth and cultural growth (Sarkar, 1989).

The hill tribes' habitats are scattered homesteads. Each habitat is surrounded by fruit bearing trees, agricultural fields and forest. The economy of these tribes is agro-forest based and considered to be subsistence economy. They regularly interact with their physical environment of forests and hills. In general forests and tribals are inseparable and existence and development of one depends on the other. Therefore, it is said that "the tribal communities in India largely occupy forested regions where for a long period in their history, they have lived in isolation but in harmony with nature. They draw their subsistence largely from the forest. They have had symbiotic relationship with forest which continues undisturbed in the interior even now" (Government of India, 1987: 19). The hill tribes in the eastern ghat region practice both shifting and settled cultivation, and also collect the minor forest produce items. Forests constitute the second most important natural resources of Andhra Pradesh after minerals.

Current Situation

The traditional tribal habitats are generally forest-clad uplands. It is of particular significance for the tribals that satellite data show that India is loosing 1.3 million hectares of forest a year. Though the tribal peoples are blamed for this, even a Government Committee report holds the unscientific and incongruous forestry practices at least partially responsible. Apart from displacement because of environmental degradation, the tribal peoples are also affected by reservation of forests, displacement caused by industrial and hydel projects and urbanization without viable overall land use panning. While it is estimated that more than 10 million tribal populations have been displaced, a national rehabilitation policy is yet to be formulated. As a result, the rehabilitation measures are of very uneven quality in different parts of the country. Besides the social ecology of the tribes is affected by large-scale immigration of non-tribal population as a sequel to opening up of tribal areas for commercial exploitation of resources and ancillary activities. Change in physical and social ecology has also affected the nutritional status of the tribes.

With the advent of liberalization, the Eastern Ghats witnessed a sudden invasion of macro-economic forces for the exploitation of its rich natural resources. Virgin forests, with their enormous wealth of timber, mineral and non-timber resources have been ruthlessly, unscientifically and irresponsibly tapped first by the public sector industries and from the eighties onwards, by the private and multinational industries. Of these the mining industry has been the most extensive in its spread and destruction. Mining as the single largest industry has caused severe imbalances in the social, political, cultural and legal status of tribals. As a result, a distinct shift can be perceived in:

- Constitutional changes of the state the protective legislations of the Fifth Scheduled (tribal) areas to safeguard the lands and resources of the tribals are under severe pressure of amendment for creating easy access to industries. So powerful are the lobbies that the state itself violates the laws for granting leases in tribal areas to private industries.
- This has further led to loss of control over resources, decision-making, social and cultural identity, displacement, loss of livelihoods and all the related evils of involuntary displacement and forced migration.
- This coercive migration has made tribals minority communities in their own regions and deeply entrenched the non-tribals and commercial groups within the tribal belt.
- Development interventions by the government and non-governmental agencies with the tribal people have been very skewed, shortsighted, welfarist and far from aimed at empowerment of people. Literacy levels continue to show extremely shocking results so much so that there is very poor awareness or

accessibility to political, legal and economic systems among the tribals.

Land, water and biodiversity – the very basis of survival and the source of livelihoods of the two-thirds majority – are being privatised, corporatised and eroded. Dams, highways, mines and industrial agriculture are leading to a takeover of the lands on which tribal and peasants have sustained themselves over millennia. Fifty million people have been displaced in India because of development projects over the past sixty years. This figure dwarfs into significance in light of two mega projects linked to globalization – one to divert India's rivers, the other to build superhighways for 'connectivity' to global markets.

Basic to globalization is employment reduction. Because of mechanization, very few jobs will be created. So those who are deprived of their livelihood will not even have a job to take its place. Impoverishment is bound to follow as studies in other parts of India have shown. Women are always the worst affected. In other words, the first thrust of globalization is massive land acquisition purely for private profit. The second is impoverishment of those who lose their livelihood in order to ensure the profit of a few private companies. Such privatization is both of land and of water. So a large number of tribal and riverine communities will be affected. These processes need to be monitored.

Equity cannot depend either on keeping tribal traditions intact or on processes that bring about impoverishment. That is where one needs to question the thinking behind globalization that is presented as the market directed economy. Basic to it is consumerism with its individualism. It is resource intensive and the attack will be on the region's land, water and biodiversity that are the people's livelihood.

Significance of Traditional Knowledge

The term 'traditional knowledge' refers to knowledge, possessed by indigenous people, in one or more societies and in one or more forms, including, but not limited to, art, dance and music, medicines and folk remedies, folk culture, biodiversity, knowledge and protection of plant varieties, handicrafts, designs, literature. There are several definitions for the term 'indigenous people', but essentially the term refers to people who characteristically exist under conditions of severe disadvantage relative to others within the states constructed around them. Essentially, these people are disadvantaged and have been crippled economically and socially. Their cohesiveness as communities has been damaged or threatened, and the integrity of their cultures has been undermined, (Raghaviah, 1971).

Review of literature shows that the following objectives have been taken into account for the research purpose of tribal studies:

- To study the general knowledge, general attitude and general practice among the selected subjects on the use of medicinal plants for general health care in the study area.
- To ascertain the level of knowledge, attitude and practice of the selected tribals in their health care through medicinal plants in the study area.
- To assess the inter-relationship among knowledge, attitude and practice in health care through medicinal plants among selected respondents in the study area.

Eco-friendly tribals collect their food, fuel, fodder, housing material and herbal medicine from the forests where they live. Health care, which was a part of the traditional culture of the tribals, has become a protection in the modern industrial world. India has one of the richest ethno-botanical traditions of the world. There are about 7,500 plants out of the total of 17,000 plants which are used to treat various diseases by 4,369 ethnic communities of India, (Loganathan, 2001).

The World Health Organization (WHO) lists over 21,000 plant species that reportedly have medicinal uses around the world, (Krishnamoorthy, 2001). India has a rich heritage of more than 10,000 medicinal plants of which 1,800 medicinal plants are used in Ayurveda, 4,700 in traditional medicinal practice, 1,100 in Siddha medicinal system, 750 in Unani, 300 in homeopathy, 300 in Chinese system of medicine and finally 100 in the allopathic system, (Jaganathan, 2001).

The rural poor and tribals living in and around these locations depend on medicinal plants for their health. Ethnobotanical survey conducted among the tribals and forest inhabitants of Dindugal district in Tamil Nadu state has brought to light a number of wild plant species used by them as medicine. The various parts of the plants, viz., roots, tubers, stems, leaves, fruits and seeds are used individually or combined in some medicinal formularies (Karuppuswamy, 2001).

Medicinal Plants in India

India, at present, exports herbal materials and medicines to the tune of Rs 446 crores only while it has been estimated that this can be raised to

Figure 1

Comparative Figures on Export of Herbal Products in China and India

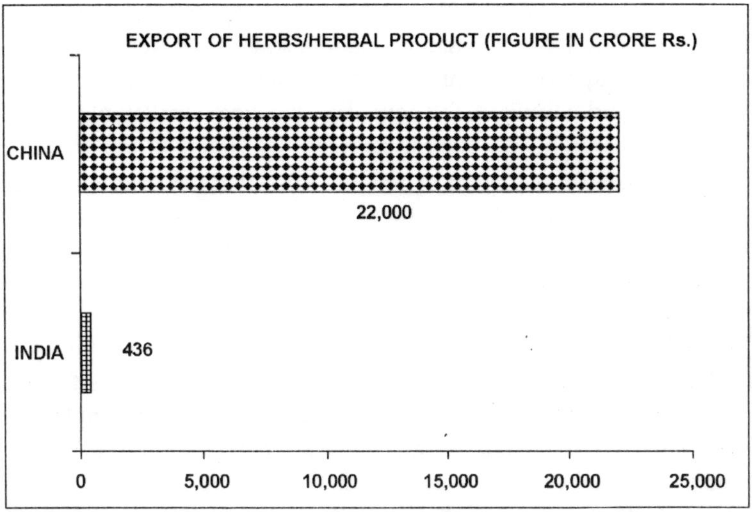

Source: Souvenir of International Seminar on Medicinal Plants, April–2002.

be US$ 62 billion poised to grow to US$ 5 trillion by the year 2050, World Health Organisation (2001). India's share in the global export market of medicinal plants related trade is just 0.5 per cent . The Chinese export based on plants including raw drugs, therapeutics and other is estimated to be around Rs 18,000 to Rs 22,000 crore. In view of the innate Indian strengths which interlace include diverse ecosystems, technical and farming capacity and a strong manufacturing sector, the medicinal plants area can become a huge export opportunity after fulfilling domestic needs.

Medicinal Plants in Tamil Nadu

Tamil Nadu is under strategic geographical location and possesses an invaluable treasure of medicinal plants holding a major share in cultivation and export of more than fifty medicinal species. Hundreds of other species, available under the natural ecosystem are gathered and exported to many countries. The state now is a potential supplier of herbal raw material, photo-chemicals, herbal medicines, essential oils, floral concrete, plant-based natural insecticides, etc. Considering the export market, a few species having the commercial significance are cultivated in large area.

Medicinal plants in Tamil Nadu are cultivated in isolated patches each being grown in its favourable soil and agro-climatic conditions. For example, Senna and Periwinkle are cultivated in the southern districts of Tamil Nadu in sandy alkaline soils while the cultivation of Glorious a superba is confined to red and black soils of Erode, Namakkal and Dindigul districts. The existing market network for medicinal plants in this state is generally confined to the traditional area of cultivation of that particular species. Whenever a new species is introduced into a non-traditional area, the farmers are constrained to market their material and are often exploited by traders and middlemen (Rajamani, 2001).

Medicinal Plants in Kolli Hills

The people of the Kolli hills use varieties of plant species for fibre, green manure, house construction, traditional agriculture implements, veterinary medicine and primary health care. A number of trees species and wild tubers are also used. Women are more familiar with plant species that are useful in primary health care and in veterinary medicine. M.S. Swaminathan Research Foundation, (2001) reported that 83 varieties of trees, 21 varieties of herbs, 18 shrubs, 10 varieties of grasses, and 11 varieties of climber are practising for medicinal purposes among the tribal people.

Indigenous of Traditional Knowledge

Maximum number of plant species used in home remedies fall in the category of herbs. It is very clear from the analysis and report that most health issues are taken care of by the households themselves. They are not only cost-effective but the knowledge of the traditional treatment of the ailments makes them self-reliant too. To quote a housewife, "We spend on an average of say Rs 300 per month on medical expenses. If we are in the know of the home remedies, we can easily save Rs 100 per month". Strengthening of household health practices could therefore contribute substantially to reducing expenditure particularly in resource poor household.

This health care system, in which the knowledge is passed on by word of mouth, is catering to the health care needs of millions of people world over. It appears that, in Indian context two 'parallels streams' are carrying on this tradition. One is at the household level, in the safe hands of Grandmas (gender bias regretted). The other is through informal clinical practices carried out by local folk healers known as 'Natuvaidyas' or 'Nadivaidyas'. Both the streams have been nurtured by the millions of knowledgeable households and thousands of folk healers specialized in various areas related to the health management. These two streams are presented in the following Table.

All India Picture of Traditional Healers

Traditional Carriers	*Subject*	*Numbers*
Housewives	Home remedies food and nutrition	Several hundred millions
Traditional birth attendants	Normal deliveries	7 lakhs
Herbal healers	Common ailments	3 lakhs
Bonesetters	Orthopaedics	60,000
Visha vaidyas (snake, scorpion, dog) specialties	Natural poisons eyes, skin, respiratory ailments dental, arthritis, mantas diseases liver, GIT, wounds	60,000 Available in every state

Source: Amruth, February, 2001.

Different reviews experienced in confronting macro-political and development issues for tribal justice has taught that an isolated movement would be ruthlessly suppressed. A strong lobby and representation of tribes concerns needs to be urgently built up at the regional level. This group takes up advocacy of tribal issues from the local to national level, brings the attention of international media and concerned groups on the impact of liberalization and globalization. The lobby group will take up legal and media advocacy, network with other tribal groups and make a collective effort to influence policy on tribals and development.

Building up literacy and awareness among tribals of their rights, laws, political and economic systems, strive towards infusing a sense of identity and voice to tribes as a community and mobilise a collective movement for achieving the same by organizing local tribal communities, networking with groups working with tribals at the regional level and extending support to small struggles.

Building up the leadership capacities among the tribal so as to represent their issues and concerns, develop a strong political identity and campaign for control over their resources and right to decision-making on their lives. Encouraging the tribal community to actively participate in reviving their customary social, legal and cultural practices and also acquire skills in facing the outside societies and environment without losing their unique identities.

Suggestions for the Future

- Tribal medicinal systems should be preserved and the tribal people should be motivated for practising their medicinal system. Tribals cure various diseases in a simple way that causes only less medical expenditure. The traditional healers should be recognized by the government and their knowledge should be used for alleviating the suffering of the poor who do not have the resources to meet the huge medical expenses caused by the western system of medicine.
- The traditional healer present in the villages and their traditional medicinal systems should be protected. Their process of curing of many diseases through medicinal plants should be exposed and brought out so that the beneficiaries could become larger in number. The traditional healers, who are socio-economically backward, may be helped by the government and the NGOs so that their traditional medical systems will survive.
- Annual conferences may be conducted in order that the system is preserved and promoted.
- Traditional tribal medicinal system may be brought closer to Ayurveda and Siddha medicine variances.
- The government and the NGOs may undertake research investigation on tribal traditional into tribal medicine and medicinal plants with a view to protecting and preserving them.
- A law may be enacted for tribal women's health education. Tribal medicine and medicinal plants should be taught to the tribal children while importing education to them and for an integrative approach to the socio-economic, cultural and medicinal aspects of tribal life.
- Awareness creation programmes may be conducted for raising tribal consciousness with regard to their medical system.
- Tribal medicinal plants may be cultivated through the Tamil Nadu Government Waste Land Development Scheme.
- The President of India, Hon'ble Dr A.P.J. Abdul Kalam has announced in Sarva Shikshan Scheme, that essential education

would be given to children and youth. In this scheme if the utility of medicinal plants is taught, it would benefit the health of the society.

- In the mid-day meals scheme of the government, nutritious medicinal plants (leafy vegetables) may be given to children as a part of their regular diet.
- In the present Nationwide Non-Formal Education Scheme of Continuing Education, adults should be given functional literacy with regard to the medicinal plants.

Suggested Topics for Further Research

- The knowledge, attitude and practice on medicinal plants among non-tribal people can be studied.
- Study on knowledge, attitude and practice of health care through medicinal plants among the tribals and non-tribals in different area may be compared.
- Factor influencing the traditional medicinal practice of tribals in hill area.
- Health education needs of medicinal plants practice of tribal people may be assessed.
- Role of tribal women on medicinal plants practice may be studied.
- Knowledge, attitude and practice of medicinal plants on taking and non-taking tribals may be done.
- Tribal attitude towards natural food and medicine and its impact on health care status may be studied.
- Knowledge, attitude and practice on medicinal plants taking few diseases and more medicinal plants among the tribals may be attempted.
- "Health Service and Their Medicinal Plants Utilization in the Tribal Area – A Case Study" may be attempted.
- An assessment of medicinal plants practice among selected tribals communities, may be attempted.
- Assessment of traditional medicine growth profile among the tribals of Tamil Nadu may be taken up.
- Causes of decrease: traditional medicinal practice among the tribals.
- Indigenous health practices related to medicinal plants among the tribals.

Hence the government of India and other state governments should take initiatives to bring the tribal to the mainstream and provide the recognition and economic returns to improve their living conditions.

References

Amin, Samir. (1997): *Capitalism in the Age of Globalization,* Delhi: Madhyam Books.

Anived, S.N. (1999): *Indian Express,* December 8.

Barthes, Roland (1975): *The Pleasure of the Text,* New York: Hill and Wang.

Beteille, Andre (1986): "The Concept of Tribe with Special Reference to India", *Journal of European Sociology.*

Burger, Julian (1987): *Report from the Frontier,* London and New Jersey: Zed Book Ltd.

Canby, W.C. (1998): *American Indian Law,* St. Paul, MN: West Publishing Co.

Coe, Paul (1994): "The Struggle for Aboriginal Sovereignty", *Social Alternative,* 13(1).

Comdessus (2000): "Message to UN Trade Talk", *Indian Express,* February 14.

Darhendorf, R. (1968): *Homo Sociologicus,* London: Routledge and Kegan Paul.

Denhez, Marc (1983): "Folk Law, National Self-Image and their Impact on Sovereignty of Countries", in H.N. Frankler (ed.), *Papers Contributed to Symposia on Folk Law and Legal Pluralism,* IUAES: Vancouver Canada, August 19–25.

Folk, Richard (1988): "The Right of People", in James Crawford (ed.), *Rights of Peoples,* Oxford: Clarendon Press.

Gareia, Alix Lola (1999): The Adhoc Working Group on the Establishment of Permanent Forum for Indigenous Peoples in the UN System, Indigenous World 1998–99, Copenhagen: IWGIA.

Gilbert, Kelvin (1994): "Aboriginal Sovereignty Position", *Social Alternatives,* 13 (1).

Government of India (1987): Report of the Study Group on Land Holding System in Tribal Area as presented in Lok Sabha vide Planning Commission O.M. No Pc/Bc/16–1(7) dt. 1988 in fulfilment of assurance in respect of Lok Sabha USA No. 675 dt. 15 April, 1987.

Godelier, Maurice (1977): *Perspective in Marxist Anthropology,* Cambridge: Cambridge University Press.

Gray, Andrew (1999): *The UN Declaration on Rights of Indigenous People is Still Intact,* Indigenous World 1998–99, Copenhagen: IWGIA.

Griggs, R.R.A. (1993): *Role of World Nations,* Washington: Centre for World Indigenous Studies.

Gros, Espiel (1980): "The Right to Self-determination", quoted by Netheim Grath (1998) in *Peoples and Population,* James Crawford (ed.), Supra.

Guirab, Theo Ben (1999): Opening Remark UN General Assembly: *UN Newsletters* 54(37), New Delhi.

Hidayatullah, M. (1983): *Right to Property and the Indian Constitution,* New Delhi: Arnold Heinman Publishers.

Hindustan Times (1995): "NAM must Redefine Goal", October 18.

ICIHI (1987): *Indigenous Peoples: A Report for the Independent Commission of International Humanitarian Issues,* London and New York: Zed Book Ltd.

Indimyor, Vincent (1999): "The Role of Multinational Oil Companies in Nigerian Federation: The Continuing Ogoni Crisis as an Example", *Indigenous Affairs,* No. 1, April-June, IWGIA.

ILO (1994): *Indigenous and Tribal Peoples and the ILO,* Geneva: The International Labour Office.

Jaganathan. C. (2001): "Revitalization of Home Remedies", Paper Presented in the National Seminar on Medicinal Plants (NSMP) held at Tiruchirappalli on October 20–21.

Jogdand, P.G. (ed.) (2000): *New Economic Policy,* New Delhi, Jaipur: Rawat Publications.

Karuppuswamy (2001): "Evaluation of Medical Plants Resources in Dindigul of Tamilnadu: Diversity, Domestic Trends Cultiration, Conservation and Uses", Paper presented in the NSMP held at Tiruchirappalli on October 20–21.

Krishnamoorthy. K.V. (2001): "Problems and Prospects of Exploiting Medicinal Plants of Indigenous Medicinal system of India", Paper presented in the NSMP held at Tiruchirappalli on October 20–21.

Lamb, Alstair (1968): *Asian Frontiers,* New York: Frederick A. Praeger Publisher.

Loganathan, N. (2001): "Ophthalmic Conditions by the Traditional Ophthalmologists", Paper presented in the NSMP held at Tiruchirappalli, October 20–21.

Mahajan, Gurpreet (1998): *Identities and Rights,* Delhi: Oxford University Press.

Mayur, Rashmi (2000): "Challenges of New Millennium", *The Hindu,* January 1.

Patel, S.G. (2000): "Conflict Ahead for the 21st Century", *Mainstream,* March 11, 4.

Raghaviah, V. (1971): *Tribal Revolts,* Nellore: Andhra Rastra Adimjati Seval Sangh.

Rajamani, K. (2001): "Medicinal Plants Scenario in Tamil Nadu", Paper presented in the (NSMP), National Seminar on Medicinal Plants held at Tiruchirappalli. October 20–21.

Rehman, Javaid (1998): "Indigenous Rights at Risk", in B.K. Roy Burman and B.G. Verghese (eds.), *Aspiring to be Indigenous and Tribal Conditions,* Delhi: Konark Publisher Pvt. Ltd.

Resurgence (1995): "WTO should not Negotiate Investment Treaty", *NGO Third World Resurgence,* No. 64.

Roy Burman, B.K. (1996): Demographic and Social Profile of the Hills of N.E. India, Monograph Series, New Delhi: Census of India.

Sahilns, M.D. (1968): *Tribesma,* Englewood Cliffs: Prentice Hall.

Sanders, Douglas (1993): "Indigenous Peoples on the International Stage", in Walter Fernandes (ed.), *The Indigenous Question: Search for an Identity,* Delhi: Indian Social Institute.

Sanders, Douglas (1998): "The UN Working Group on Indigenous Population", *Human Rights Quarterly* II, John Hopkins University Press.

Sarkar, B. (ed.) (1989): *Social Perspective of Generation and Utilization of Indigenous Science and Technology,* Allahabad: Indian Academy of Social Sciences.

Saugestad, Sidset (1999): "Contested Images: Indigenous Peoples in Africa", *Indigenous Affairs,* 1999/2, April-June, IWGIA.

Saxena, Ranjana (2003): "Globalization and Culture", *Culture Studies (Themes and Perspectives),* Chandan Kumar Sharma (ed.), p. 85.

Shendge, Malati (1977): *The Civilized Demons,* New Delhi: Abhinav Publications.

Stegeborn, Wiveka (1998): "Sri Lanka Indigenous Peoples and Self-determination", B.K. Roy Burman and B.G. Verghese (eds.), Supra.

Subramanyam, V. (2001) "Tribes and Ecology of Andhra Pradesh: An Anthropological Study", in the *Science of Man in Service of Man,* M.K. Bhasin and S.L. Malik (ed.), Department of Anthropology, University of Delhi, Delhi, pp. 49–61.

Swepston, Lee (1990): *A New Step in International Law on Indigenous and Tribal Peoples,* Oklahoma City University Law Review.

Thant, U. (1970): "Statement on UN and Self-determination", quoted by L. Macfarlane (1985), *The Theory and Practice of Human Rights, Menace,* London: Temple Smith.

Vasquez, John A. (1998): *The Power of Power Politics: From Classical Realism to Neo-traditionalism,* Cambridge: Cambridge University Press.

Whiting (1958): A Cross-Cultural Nutrition survey of 118 Societies, Ph.D. Dissertation, School of Public Health, Harvard University, Cambridge, Massachusetts.

9

Globalization and the Plight of Displaced Tribes in India

S.N. TRIPATHY

Globalization is considered the sharper and continuing integration of the world economy, while economic liberalization refers to deregulation and decontrols in the national economy – an economic process inextricably linked with globalization. The protagonists of the globalization (Bhagwati, 2004; Wolf, 2004) regard it as a wholly benign process, heralding the long awaited deliverance of humanity from economic backwardness, underdevelopment and misery. For them, allowing market forces to work largely unhindered by the state and its politics will make possible higher economic growth and therefore, human welfare. Globalization is a "process of trans-nationalization of production and capital, and standardization of consumer tastes and their legitimization with the help of international institutions like World Bank, IMF and WTO. Obviously the process is a move towards a borderless regime of free trade and transactions based on competition" (Oommen, 2001). On the contrary, the critics of globalization have mounted a powerful attack against globalization, holding it to be a malign force. Pravat Patnaik (2003: 42, 63, 102) of JNU in a wide ranging attack uses the terms globalization and imperialism and claims that:

> "The net result, taking the world as a whole, of surrounding to the process of 'globalization' in this sense is: relative economic stagnation, increased economic inequalities leading to a worsening poverty, a loss of economic and political sovereignty, an implicit attenuation of democracy ... a loss of control over domestic assets and natural resources to metropolitarian capital, the loss of food security, and an exposure to the prospects of shortly fluctuating fortunes owing to the vicissitudes of the world market, and the caprices of the international speculators ... . The current phase of imperialism entails a tendency towards stagnation, not only genuinely but in particular in the third world".

In July 1991, in wake of foreign exchange liquidity crisis, declining GDP growth rate and a near stagnating economy India adopted the reform process of globalizing the economy. Soon all the political parties across the spectrum accepted it as an 'inevitable' and 'irreversible' process. The reforms have continued since then irrespective of changes in the government at centre. The ruling argument has often been that someone will have to bear the price of 'development' in the larger interest of 'nation'. But the people have started challenging and asking, why should only the poor suffer? Why the rights of poor already at the margins of development should always suffer? Why cannot the gains of the process be distributed equitably? It is these issues which are now beginning to gather momentum for evolving effective policy of inclusive growth. The resistance has grown since then and the neo-liberal economic policy has drawn flak from various quarters. The protests have been stringent especially because of its predatory effects on the poor and marginalized communities, now pushed further along paths of impoverishment and disempowerment. These protests emanate from the enhanced understanding of the globalization process among people who are beginning to see the linkages between the government's policies, wider economic processes and the impact on their livelihood.

Of the numerous ways the globalization has impacted upon the Indian economy, livelihood security to the working class has assumed paramount importance. A large number of occupations and livelihoods are imposing insecurities and vulnerability due to lack of rights and statuary protection. There is widespread concern that the acceleration in GDP growth in the post-reforms period has not been accompanied by a commensurate expansion in employment. Because of withdrawals from the public sector, there will be slow expansion of employment leading to a rise in unemployment rates. In the era of globalization, labour is disempowered in several dimensions. There has been numerical decline of organic workforce and weakening trade unions. There has been also the shrinking of organized sector, increase of informal labour in which, labour eke out a living unprotected by a regular salary and job security and inadequacy of social security nets. Workers in the informal economy can be persons working at home, or on premises of his/her choice other than the employer's, to produce goods or services on a contract or order for a specific employer or contractor, independent wage workers not attached to only one employer, and providing services to individuals, households and enterprises, e.g., servants and watchmen working for households. Globalization unleashes the forces of competitions and marginalizes those who are unable to compete, thus, making the market forces the supreme arbiter of success or failures. Globalization of the economy also supposes an unregulated labour regime, which not only keeps labour costs at a minimum, but also statuary protection and union activities are discouraged. Globalization has promises of rapid economic growth, unhindered flow of goods, resources and capital, across and countries based on market efficiency and optimum utilization of world resources. Unfortunately, globalization has caused some disquieting trends and consequences in the labour market. It has excluded the disadvantaged areas like rural, less developed and marginalized social groups like tribes and women. Thus, the high hopes of globalization causing benefits to the poverty-stricken labour surplus could not be fructified (Papola and Sharma, 2003).

Several studies have revealed the adverse consequences of new development paradigm in terms of rising urban and rural unemployment, fall in the share of employment due to destruction of traditional arts and crafts, increasing migration and human trafficking due to deepening agrarian crisis, increasing non-availability of employment in agriculture, fall in per capita agricultural output and dangerous level of erosion of food security (Tripathy and Das, 1991; Chowdhury, 2004). It has been apprehended that the good deal of vulnerable groups like the tribes and women may have to bear the cost of globalization on livelihoods, employment and human development unless measures are taken to prevent deterioration in their socio-economic in the short-run, and improve their capabilities in the long-run to derive benefit in the long-run (Sharma, 2004).

Impact of Globalization on Tribes and Marginalized Communities

If the years of the 1990s were known for the start of economic reforms marked by increased liberalization, privatization and globalization then it was also the time which saw consolidation of resistance to attack on natural resources, and the evolution of new perspectives on development, democracy, assertion of rights. The period saw birth of consolidation of series of popular struggles such as Narmada Bachao Andolan, and many others, leading the right to information campaign, in rural and urban areas which aligned with the movements and provided resources of all kinds in their struggles. What perceptible the difference between pre- and post-90s was the abrupt surge in people's struggles over the question of livelihood, 'control' of natural resources, accountability and transparency in governance. This change can be seen in the light of general crisis of government's legitimacy on account of its failure to develop and implement a model of development catering to needs of all the sections of society. It needs to be noted that economic reforms have made situation worse in rural areas indirectly and livelihood more difficult by destroying sources of non-farm employment, increased informalization of labour, migration, etc.

In the liberalized economy syndrome since early 1990s the government machinery is increasingly becoming insensitive to the interest of poor and the powerless and also to the basic humanitarian values. For over a decade and half the government is pushing the agenda of corporate sector resulting in unprecedented trauma to the peasantry and other marginalized people who are depending on land and natural resources including forest and water for survival. The liberal grant of mining leases to the international and national corporate giants in the mineral rich states of Orissa, Jharkhand and Chhattisgarh together constitute 145 memorandums of understandings (MoUs). Similarly, in the agricultural advance regions of the country such as West Bengal, Punjab, Haryana, and western Uttar Pradesh a large number of special economic zones (SEZs) are being created misinterpreting the 'public purpose' provision in the Land Acquisition Act. The aggressive growth is being pursued violating fundamental legal obligations of the state regarding non-transferability of tribal land for the benefit of corporate sector. Women are the worst sufferers of this aggressive growth model. Projects varying from mining, industry, power, information technology (IT) or any other projects are causing total disruption of their livelihood, cultures and the physical environment. They have already been facing extreme hardships since early 1950s when the planned development was introduced with greater emphasis on infrastructure development such as: dams, industries and power uprooting their houses and hearths. While the ad hoc rehabilitation resettlement policy has been enforced from time to time, most of them were virtually neglecting women's issues and concerns.

In this backdrop, we can enumerate some of the dam, mining project which have adversely impacted the tribes leading to involuntary displacement and as such, necessitating the imperative need for policy paradigms for their inclusion in the growth process.

According to the 2001 Census, Scheduled Tribes (STs, or adivasis) numbered 84.3 million, or 8.2 per cent of the country's total population. Almost nine out of 10 adivasis depend on agriculture for their livelihood; this is more than any other social section. However, not only is the quality of their land poor, but part of it is suspended in a legal limbo, rendering them vulnerable to various types of exploitation. Driven to moneylenders for consumption loans in order to survive, they frequently are forced to part with their lands: In the words of the draft National Tribal Policy (NTP), "Land is the most important source of livelihood for STs. However, and in spite of state enactments to prevent alienation of tribal land, wrongful alienation of tribal land is the single most important cause of pauperization of tribals … ." Further, they are prevented from exercising their traditional rights over the forests, even as the forests have been opened up to all sorts of plunder and destruction by the process of so-called development. Suggesting that the "deep sense of exclusion and alienation" among tribals was responsible for unrest in certain tribal areas, the NTP states candidly: "A situation is thus developing where the STs view the state as their exploiter and enemy, and the preachers of violent actions as their protector and friend. Tribal people tend to support these violent movements as they feel that it would help them get their rights, protect them from exploitation and redress their grievances."

The World Commission on Dams Report (November 2000) estimates the total number of the displaced people by 4,500 large dams in India to be 30–40 million while Walter Fernandes et al. (1995) have estimated that 30 million people were affected by these projects till 1994. The figure quoted by Arundhati Roy (1999) in her essay "The Greater Common Good: The Human Cost of Big Dams" reflects the same.

Causes or categories of development-induced displacement include the following: water supply (dams, reservoirs, irrigation); urban infrastructure; transportation (roads, highways, canals); energy (mining, power plants, oil exploration and extraction, pipelines); agricultural expansion; parks and forest reserves; and population redistribution schemes. Construction of roads, establishment of industries, and mining activities disrupted the settled tribal properties leading to landlessness, homelessness, joblessness, food insecurity, loss of access to common property resources and social disruption. Thousands of families have been involuntarily displaced from their age-old traditional habitat, and tribes constitute about 40 per cent of the total project displaced population (Fernandes, 1994).

The Problems of Tribal Displacement and Deprivation

The process of industrialization in India since the advent of 20th century, the Tata Iron and Steel Company, Jamshedpur (Bihar), The Bokaro Steel Plant (Bihar), The Rourkella Steel Plant (Orissa), have detrimental impact on the tribals resulting in alienation of land, displacement and deprivation of this poverty-stricken community. Though the development activities in Orissa surged as early as 1950s, there were about 8,117 displaced families from 1,446 villages because of development projects during the period 1950 to 1993. The UNDP estimates that till date more than one lakh people in Orissa have been displaced while 20 lakhs have been effected by development projects. Industrial projects like Rourkella Steel Plant (RSP), The Hindustan Aeronautics (HAL) and National Aluminum Company (NALCO) have displaced people mainly the tribals (Fernandes, 1994; Tripathy, 2003). Number of tribals facing displacement in different states are as under.

Table 1

Dams and the Displacement of Tribal People

Name of Project	*State*	*Population Facing Displacement*	*Tribal People as Percentage of Displaced*
Karjan	Gujarat	11,600	100
Sardar Sarovar	Gujarat	200,000	57.6
Maheshwar	Madhya Pradesh	20,000	60
Bodhghat	Madhya Pradesh	12,700	73.91
Icha	Bihar	30,800	80
Chandil	Bihar	37,600	87.92
Koel Karo	Bihar	66,000	88
Mahi Bajaj Sagar	Rajasthan	38,400	76.28
Polavaram	Andhra Pradesh	1,50,000	52.90
Maithon and Panchet	Bihar	93,874	56.46
Upper Indravati	Orissa	18,500	89.20
Pong	Himachal Pradesh	80,000	56.25
Inchampalli	Andhra Pradesh-Maharashtra	38,100	76.28
Tultuli	Maharashtra	13,600	51.61
Daman Ganga	Gujarat	8,700	48.70
Bhakra	Himachal Pradesh	36,000	34.76
Masan Reservoir	Bihar	3,700	31.00

Sources: Satyajit Singh, *Taming the Waters*, New Delhi: OUP, 1997, and government figures.

When people are aware that displacement leads to loss of habitat, unemployment and distressed migration and culminating a situation of vicious circle of poverty, they are reluctant to accept compensation. Police forcing the adivasis into accepting the compensation have resorted to lathi-charges, tear-gassing, impoverishment, torture and the shooting deaths of three adivasis near Maikanch village (Kashipur, Rayagada block, Orissa) on 16 December, 2000. This happening repeated on 2 January, 2006 when 12 adivasis were shot dead by police in Kalinga Nagar massacre to make way for Tata Steel Corporation (Goodland, 2007). The clash between tribals and police at Kalinga Nagar Steel Complex in Jajpur district (2 January, 2006) resulted in 13 deaths, has cast a shadow on Orissa's efforts towards industrialization. Tata Steel, which had signed an MoU to establish a six million tonne capacity plant at Kalinga Nagar at a cost of Rs 15,400 crore in two modules. The incident occurred when the company took up earth work at the project site triggering a clash between tribals opposed to the project with the police. The Orissa government had already signed 43 MoUs for establishment of steel plants in the state with a proposed investment of over Rs 1,18,000 crore with the South Korean Pohang Steel Company (POSCO) interested to set up a project at Paradip at a cost of Rs 51,000 crore. The thickly forested and riverine region of Lanjigarh in Kalahandi is under sever pressure from mining development for bauxite deposits and aluminum processing by the London-based Vedanta group, which has initiated its Rs 3,500 crore alumina plant in collaboration with Government of Orissa (Press Trust of India, 16 January, 2008)

According to the official estimate the total number of families displaced due to river dam projects and other development projects in Orissa between 1950–93, was 81,176 of which 80 per cent families have been displaced only due to irrigation projects (Pandey, 1998). The picture pertaining to displaced families because of various development projects in Orissa can be seen in the Table 2.

Table 2

Displaced Families in the Development Projects in Orissa

Name of the Project	*Displaced Families*	*ST/SC Families*
Balimela Multipurpose dam project on Sileru river at Chitrakonda.	2,000	-
Salandi Lrrigation project	589	552 tribal families.
Rangali multipurpose river valley project on the Brahmani river in Angul district.	10,897	1,710 SC families, 1,172 ST-families
Upper Kolab multipurpose dam project on the river Kolab in Koraput district.	3,179	442 SC families, 1,421ST families
Upper Indravati Multipurpose project.	5,301	2,223 tribal families, 796 families SC
Rourkela Steel Plant.	4,251	-
Talcher coal belt region in Angul district.	23 villages affected by underground mines due to open cast mining project 38 villages.	-
IB velly area in Jharsuguda district.	17 villages affected and 130 families displaced due to five opencast mining.	-

Source: Pandey, Balaji (1998), *Depriving the Underprivileged by Development,* Bhubaneswar.

The unreplenishable mineral wealth has been looted leaving behind the barren land and poverty-stricken people. Tribals evicted by industrial houses had been pushed to starvation in Koraput district and other parts of the state, promoting the multinational corporations and big houses will destroy the livelihood of the tribals and poor people. The Vedanta alumina project in Langigarh area would benefit only 250 persons as they would get permanent employment with an investment of Rs 4,500 crores. The livelihood of around 300 villages would be affected by this project, while Bansadhara and Nagabali rivers would dry up. The tribals living in the forests should be adequately compensated in the shape of insurance coverage, educational guarantee and future loan facilities in case of sickness before they are displaced from their age-old habitation for industrialization.

In the tribal tracks of Andhra Pradesh, the Polavaram project threatens to displace more than 1.75 lakhs people mostly the adivasis and will submerge 300 villages. The adivasis in their present habitat, i.e., the schedule areas, enjoy a unique set of constitutional rights and privileges, which would no longer be available after they are uprooted. This project has been designed to impound water from Godavari and, apart from irrigating the coastal districts; it would also divert a portion of the stored water to the Krishna.

Displacement of Tribals in the Bargi Dam of Madhya Pradesh

Narmada is the fifth largest river in India and largest west flowing river of the Indian peninsula with its annual flow approximates to the combined flow of the rivers of Sutlej and Ravi. Originating from the Maikala ranges at Amarkantak in Madhya Pradesh, it flows westwards over a length of about 1,312 km of which it covers 1,072 km in Madhya Pradesh, finally falling in the Arabian Sea. The Bargi dam has been one of the first completed dams among the chain of 30 major dams in the finalization of their completion on river Narmada. The proposal of this dam construction was conceptualized by the Central Water and Power Commission in 1968 envisaging irrigation in 2.98 lakh ha and hydropower generation capacity of 105 MW (Tripathy and Samantary, 2008, p. 81). Later, the Bargi diversion scheme was planned, increasing the total irrigation potential to 4.37 lakh ha. The total cost estimates initially conceived were Rs 64 crore, escalated to 566.31 crore in 1989, excluding the cost of canal construction which estimated to be about 1,660.80 crore (Samagra Narmada Ghati Vikas, Madhya Pradesh, 1997).

The submergence area of the Bargi dam once had prosperous farmers, tilling the fertile lands of the Narmada Kacchar, producing abundant food grains of all varieties without any sort of irrigation or chemical fertilizers. There was availability of vegetables and seasonal fruits in abundance along with healthy and sufficient livestock. There was no dearth of milk and milk products and the region was prosperous and people enjoyed good mutual cooperation in times of marriages and deaths, festivals and all other occasions. All their needs were met from the local markets nearby and thus, hardly any contact with cities.

The Bargi dam affected 162 villages and uprooted about 7,000 families without the estimation of population indirectly affected. The oustees were forced to live in the slums of Jabalpur (Madhya Pradesh) and eke out their living through pulling rickshaws or work as construction labourers or migrate to the supposedly command areas of the Bargi dam. The Sardar Sarovar Reservoir level at 455 ft would affect 193 villages in the middle of the Satpura hills. A village has been considered affected even when the water level touches the farm/hut at lowest level. It may be noted that only 4 villages (3 villages in Gujarat and 1 village in Madhya Pradesh) were getting submerged fully and the rest 241 villages were getting affected partially.

Table 3

Different Projects and the Extent of Benefits as well as Submergence

Name of Project	*State*	*Benefit Area (in ha)*	*Submergence Area (in ha)*	*Irrigation Benefit per ha. Submergence*	*Percentage of Area Submerged to Area Irrigated*
Hirakud	Orissa	2,51,150	73,892	3.40	29.42
Shriramsagar	Andhra Pradesh	2,30,679	44,517	5.24	19.14
Gandhisagar	Madhya Pradesh	5,03,200	66,186	7.60	13.15
Paithan	Maharashtra	2,78,000	35,000	7.94	15.29
Tungbhadra	Karnataka	3,72,000	37,814	9.84	10.16
Pench	Maharashtra	94,000	7,750	12.13	8.24
Nagarjunsagar	Andhra Pradesh	8,95,000	28,500	31.40	3.18
Bhakhra	Himachal Pradesh	6,76,000	16,800	40.24	2.48
Sardar Sarovar	Gujarat	19,03,800	37,533	50.17	1.97

Source: Data compiled from various sources.

The statewise land coming under submergence (categorywise) has been presented in the Table 3, which shows that as much as 11,279 hectares of agricultural land and 13,385 hectares of forest land have been submerged in three states of India due to the dam projects built on the river Narmada. When compared to other similar major projects, the Sardar Sarovar Project has the least ratio of submergence to the area benefited (1.97% only). The ratio of some of the existing schemes has been as much as 25 per cent as can be seen from the Table 3.

Countering the assertion that the construction of the dam would result in large-scale relocation and uprooting of tribals, the factual position seems to be that the tribals constitute bulk of project affected families (PAFs) in Gujarat and Maharashtra, namely, 97 per cent and 100 per cent respectively. In the case of Madhya Pradesh, the tribal PAFs were only 30 per cent while 70 per cent were non-tribals. The affected tribals have been deprived of modern fruits of development such as tap water, education, road, electricity, convenient medical facilities, etc. The majority of the project affected families were involved in rainfed agricultural activities for their own sustenance. There is partial employment in forestry sector. Since the area is hilly with difficult terrain, they are wholly dependent on vagaries of monsoon and normally only a single crop is raised by them. Out of the PAFs of Madhya Pradesh who have resettled in Gujarat, more than 70 per cent are tribal families. Majority of the total tribal PAFs are stated to have already been resettled in Gujarat after having exercised their option. It is the contention of the state of Gujarat that the tribals in large number have responded positively to the resettlement package offered by that state.

The schedule areas in Orissa as well as Madhya Pradesh are populated by small, scattered tribal settlements. The plight and the socio-cultural trauma of women whose livelihood is solely food-based is worse when they are evicted from their familiar social networks. Unfortunately, the tribal people and other marginalized ethnic communities make up a disproportionately large percentage of these displaced by development activities

Michael Cernea (1988, 2000), a sociologist based at the World Bank, points out that being forcibly ousted from one's land and habitat carries with it the risk of becoming poorer than before displacement. Those displaced "are supposed to receive compensation of their lost assets, and effective assistance to re-establish them productively; yet this does not happen for a large portion of oustees". Cernea's impoverishment risk and reconstruction model proposes that "the onset of impoverishment can be represented through a model of eight interlinked potential risks intrinsic to displacement". These are: (i) Landlessness, (ii) Joblessness, (iii) Homelessness, (iv) Marginalization, (v) Food Insecurity, (vi) Increased Morbidity and Mortality, (vii) Loss of Access to Common Property, (viii) Social Disintegration, (ix) Loss of Access to Community, and (x) Violation of Human Rights.

The Land Acquisition Act, 1894 has the provision that the government is not bound to provide a displaced person anything but cash compensation if the concerned person can show the evidence of his land title, unfortunately, the tribals could not produce the same and as a result of which, are usually deprived of the compensation. The elite have therefore; through such pseudo-developmental activities impoverished the earth of its natural resources. The earth's impoverishment has meant that communities who depend upon the natural base for sustenance have been deprived of their resources. This alienation cannot be described in terms of loss of material livelihood only; it is most profoundly the loss of culture autonomy, knowledge and power (Baviskar, 1995).

However, the voices of the displaced are no longer extraordinary. Echoed in virtually every displacement situations be it Tehri, Narmada, Singrauli or Keol Karo, only to name a few they reveal what it means to be a 'displaced lot': loss of livelihood and traditional lands; demolition of homes; loss of social networks; severance from an ecosystem that sustained them earlier and, above all, a feeling of powerlessness and insecurity for the future.

The Special Economic Zones and the Tribals

There is no doubt that these anti-people legislations have been brought forth under the pressure and for the benefit of big corporations and private industrial and capitalists interests. The Government of Andhra Pradesh has acquired 340 acres of village common land, 70 acres of temple land from the endowments department and 500 acres from the local gram panchayat – China Mambattu of the Tada Mandal in Nellore district – to set-up a special economic zone (SEZ). Some private industrialists have purchased another 100 acres of agricultural land in the vicinity and 400 acres of the SEZ are being given to Apache to set-up a shoe factory. Three hamlets of the panchayat, N.M. Kandrika, China Mambattu and Peda Mambattu, are being affected by the SEZ. These villages are inhabited by weavers, shepherds, barbers, washermen and women and Yanadi tribals. The most vulnerable among these are the Yanadis, because they do not own land and are thus ineligible to receive any sort of compensation for the displacement caused by the SEZ. For projects like these, the question of these communities whose livelihoods do not depend on farms but on natural resources and community property resources is very crucial.

Displacement is a multidimensional phenomenon not confined to physical relocation; it reduces the 'quality of life' of the communities into sub-human conditions. This understanding of displacement highlights (i) the alienation of the individual and community legal and customary rights and dislocation of the social and economic organization, and (ii) the politics of legal and policy instruments that sanctions such disenfranchisement.

In this context displacement refers not only to those who are forced to physically relocate in order to make way for the project and its related aspects but also includes those who are displaced from their resource base and livelihoods. Ironically, the existing definition of project affected people (PAP) did not include the landless, the non-asset class, the seasonal farmers, the fishermen, boatmen, those engaged in work of art, culture and handicraft, and small shopkeepers in the affected village; also it did not recognize those affected by the canals, colonies, sanctuaries, catchments area treatment, secondary displacement and displacement through subsidiary and ancillary projects as 'oustees', making the whole process as class biased and only in terms of cash economy. Ideally, it is to be expected that those likely to be negatively affected by the projects would be consulted and kept informed in such a way as to enable them to best rebuild their ravaged lives. However, it is not the case, rather, from the inception of planning of most projects, through various stages of displacement and resettlement, there is bewilderment and confusion among the resettlers in virtually every large project about the extent and intensity of the damage (Hemadri, http://www.dams.org).

Women not only suffered in terms of health and nutrition, they also lost the capacity to provide a secure future for their children. By resorting to seasonal migration they have unwittingly denied their children access to school, health care, child welfare, and other welfare services. Further, considering widow, deserted and unmarried adult daughters as dependents ceases their right to claim separate or independent rehabilitation package with no land allotment in their names. The Uttar Pradesh policy is even more gender biased. If a couple holds property separately, they will be considered one unit and will receive one package. In this situation, a woman will have to forego her right to the package as it will be given to the head of the family, the man.

The displaced persons be resettled in a safe habitat wherein they can start their life afresh. However, this would require more than mere allocation of certain piece of land for resettlement or mere construction of make shift camps for temporary settlement. What is needed is the 'rehabilitation' of the persons affected by the projects; rehabilitation means to 'restore to the former condition', and thus, all that was lost by displacement, the emotional, cultural, social, political and economic losses must be restored at a priority basis than to the project itself, which is the cause of the impoverishment.

Conclusion

Thus, on the whole, we can conclude that one of the fundamental reasons of dismal record of resettlement and rehabilitation is the biases and prejudices of those who design the projects, for them it is the responsibility of the local authorities and something that is outside the ambit of the project, in other words, an 'external cost' to the project. Most of the time the matter is dealt on an ad hoc basis, virtually with no practical information rather based on guesswork. Delay in work, involvement of middlemen, corruption and red-tapism further aggravate the miseries of the poor and vulnerable victims.

For the government and its agents of development, cash compensation seems to be the only panacea for the problems induced by displacement and only policy for rehabilitation, whereas, in practice it is the most inadequate means for rehabilitation. No procedure and principles are laid down to estimate the costs, showing the arbitrariness of compensation. Apart from loss of land, the villager suffers loss from common property resources forest produce, village grazing land, community centre, social security, and so on. The problem is more acute with the artisans, some of them may own land, but their major income is from their profession within the known community. There seems no provision with regard to their rehabilitation. Besides, the landless and the tribals are probably the worst sufferers.

The situation of the tribal people is all the more thorny, since the compensation is paid on the basis of land owned, the tribals who have no inclination to own land but use it as a common property fail to claim compensation on the basis of the lost common land. It is hard to believe that how land, natural resources, means of livelihood, social and cultural loss resulting from displacement can be quantified and compensated in monetary terms? And, the non-quantifiable nature of numerous human and ecological costs is not even acknowledged? The government acknowledges the problem that in tribal areas, where the displaced persons are given only cash compensation, the tendencies to spend the compensation amount by buying consumer goods and becoming destitute are common.

Development means the development of the 'people'. Why care for the people? Because the aim of development is to provide ultimately benefits to the people and as such, if they are left out, if they are pushed around by self-experts and high-handed planners, then nothing can ever yield fruit.

The empirical perspective on the worldwide and most definitely in the Indian context, as has been told earlier, reveals a bias in the development discourse; one which has posited the individual and the investor at its helm and on account of which development as we know it, is inherently ill suited to promote human and social development, as was and is being envisaged. Thus, we face a paradox wherein endeavours to promote the one human right (development) furnishes to the violation (displacement) of another. "Development-induced displacement is the forcing of communities and individuals out of their homes, often also their homelands, for the ostensible purpose of social and human development, but which is actually nothing more than 'economic growth' and the benefits accruing from such almost never if ever percolate down to the one's that bear its costs."

The first goal should be to find alternatives that cause minimal displacement, in those instances where displacement is inevitable, it is imperative that the full costs of rehabilitation be internalized into the project cost.

Development, which has entailed many large-scale forced evictions of vulnerable populations, without the countervailing presence of policies to assist them to rebuild their lives, has only accentuated the negative aspects of displacement, such as lack of information, failure to prepare in advance a comprehensive plan for rehabilitation, the undervaluation of compensation and its payment in cash, failure to restore lost assets or livelihoods, traumatic and delayed relocation, problems at relocation sites, multiple displacement, and neglect of the special vulnerabilities of the most disadvantaged groups. It is incumbent upon the operators of the wheel of development to seek the participation of those displaced or to be displaced. It can be done directly or through their formal and informal leaders, representatives and even the non-governmental organizations.

It would help in understanding the needs and preferences, prevent costly mistakes and reduces the sense of insecurity among the displaced lot. We have already waited too long to challenge the development model that is biased to certain perceptions and class of society; alternatives for power generation, irrigation, means of production, etc., that do not exert such an enormous toll on human suffering, are now available and which might well be followed to reduce forced displacement.

To achieve the goals of sustainable development and for the development itself to sustain, it must come from the bottom; which is possible only when the third tier of the governance (is functional in its real sense) has determinative rights of participation in policy framing and decision-making when it proposes to affect their interests. Though the structural arrangements in this regard are ensured through 73rd and 74th Amendments of the Constitution and numerous Panchayat Acts in the states, the irony (all too common place now) is that the provisions are seldom upheld in practice. A functional grass roots democracy and people's participation in decision-making that benefits and harmonizes all interests, is probably the best possible way to complete the projects on time and keep the costs from escalating and minimizing the miseries of affected. "Development which cannot provide the basic necessities of life should be shunned" and attempts be made for an alternate mode of development which should aim at providing roads in villages instead of flyovers in cities, schools in all places instead of five star hotels." Protagonists of development should understand that it is not possible for the multinational companies to ameliorate the plight of the starving millions in the country.

For greater equity in development, we need to forge a development strategy that takes into account the immense social, ecological diversity benefiting the tribals who are in the grip of unemployment accompanied by acute distress and poverty (Sundaram and Tendulkar, 2003; Mukhopadhay and Raja Raman, 2007).

It has been observed that non-recognition of tribes over resources and restrictions on their use, alienation tribes from the means of production, denial of due entitlement of labour, distressed payment of wages, and misappropriation of funds have kept the tribal labour in the web of misery and starvation. In tribal dominated states in India, the life support system of the local tribes has been snatched away by non-tribals and state institutions. As a result, tribal movement originated in fierce struggle of their rights (Tripathy, 2000).

Article 244 and 244A read with Fifth and Sixth Schedules of the Constitution outline in detail the powers, privileges, rights and responsibilities of the President, Union Government and the Governors regarding the scheduled areas. In addition to Article 46 (of Part IV Directive Principles of State Policy) of the Constitution which states that 'The State shall promote with special care the educational and economic interests of the weaker sections of the people and in particular of the Scheduled Castes and the Scheduled Tribes, and shall protect them from social injustice and all forms of exploitation". There are about 20 other Articles which prescribe the whole framework for regulatory and development functions of the state relating to the Scheduled Tribe population of the country. In addition to the above, special provisions for Scheduled Tribes have also been made through certain acts and orders which are protective and ameliorative in nature. Laws protecting land rights of the tribal communities have recognized their traditional rights over it and restricting its alienation to non-tribals.

The Panchayat Extension to Scheduled Areas (PESA) Act, 1996 has made it mandatory for the states having scheduled areas to make specific provisions for providing wide range of powers to the tribals for their development. The Act recognizes traditional customary rights over local natural resources. It accepts the validity of customary law, social and religious practices of community resources. Under PESA, the protective aspects have aimed at the preservation of their unique cultural traits, their rights on land and forests and safeguarding against the inhuman exploitation. It empowered villages to protect community resources, control social sector functionaries, own minor forest produce, manage water bodies, give recommendations for mining leases, be consulted for land acquisition, identify beneficiaries for poverty alleviation and other government programmes and have a decisive say in all development projects in the villages. It empowered villages to protect community resources, control social sector functionaries, own minor forest produce, manage water bodies, give recommendations for mining leases, be consulted for land acquisition, identify beneficiaries for poverty alleviation and other government programmes and have a decisive say in all development projects in the villages. Section 4 (M) of PESA authorizes the Gram Sabha to act in all areas where the tribals face threat to their survival and welfare because of their continued exploitation. The PESA creates legal space for direct community action, and therefore, PESA directly confers ownership to the Gram Sabha on minor forest produce (MFP) which has been a support for their survival. But it has been observed that this right has been neglected or violated rather than adhered to. The commercial value of MFP has been appreciated resulting in the nationalization of MFP and thereby optimizing the state's revenue.

Thus, despite PESA, as well as several other protective legislations in the tribal regions of our country, there has been extensive violation of fundamental rights and human rights of the tribal people. The second hindrance lies in the inability of the poor peasants to make their voice heard in the face of elite domination of the traditional power structures. The ingrained problem of elite domination can hardly be resolved, unless the poor themselves can exercise enough bargaining power and be organized so that their collective voice can be audible to the irrigation executives and bureaucrats. It is lamentable fact that the purpose of the PESA Act has not been completely understood either by the political leaders or by the bureaucracy. People at large are also not aware of the provisions of PESA Act except in those areas where the NGOs are seriously working with the people.

Thus, PESA aims at ensuring significant protection against any arbitrary, discriminatory and motivated action of the state relating to land acquisition and resettlement and rehabilitation (R&R) in tribal regions. It has been revealed that the local administration in league with the company officials was indulging in deliberate falsehood. In the consultation of 'Gram Sabha' the method adopted is dubious as the consent was obtained through coercion and brutal force (Das, 2003, 2005).

All projects in tribal areas were considered 'public purpose' even for private mining industries. This is the biggest fallacy of our development paradigms in tribal areas. The Land Acquisition Act should be amended in consonance with the PESA Act so that rights of the people are protected in fifth schedule areas. No act of force should be used when there is conflict over resources and as per the recommendation of the 28th report of the Scheduled Castes and Scheduled Tribes commissioner, law should be passed prohibiting use of force in case of disputes over resources in the tribal areas.

Adequate safeguards need to be provided in the SEZ policy to ensure that irrigated and agriculturally fertile land is not used by the SEZs. The SEZ proposals should be supported by certification of the agricultural quality of land by the local revenue authority and the format of assessment for building on prime agricultural land should be made clear. It is high time that the government must review the Land Acquisition Act in light of the SEZ rules, 2006 and the SEZ Act, 2005. State governments must prescribe minimum prices for land in various areas, which will be valid both for registration of sales deeds as well as payment of compensation. The prices should be high enough to reflect the opportunity prices of land. In addition to suitable financial compensation, the displaced farm labour and tribal workers should be given preference in employment either by the SEZ developer or in the business units in the SEZ. Every SEZ developer should be required to set-up a training institution where appropriate training is provided for these workers who have been displaced from their traditional employment. The government has drafted a National Policy on Relief and Rehabilitation stating that all projects leading to 'involuntary displacement' can be challenged in court, if violated. The policy, which also underlines that farmers be effectively compensated for their land and rehabilitated fairly, comes in the face of mounting pressure from farmers and political parties who consider that the development of business interests, took precedent over the interests of India's farmers. There should be a policy of Social Impact Assessment (SIA) along with the current norm of Environmental Impact Assessment. The SIA would also involve public hearings on displacement related issues such as loss of livelihood; compensation; and effects on family and for tribal/agricultural workers, at least one person in the family shall be given employment or a one time rehabilitation grant.

The Arjun Sen Gupta Committee has reported government's policy on SEZ, rehabilitation due to dams, urban planning by displacing millions of urban-slum dwellers as 'major areas of concern'. For 'backward' states (normally with high concentration of Dalits and tribals), the minimum land requirement has been eased to 200 hectares and 50 hectares respectively for multi-product and sector specific SEZs. The Land Acquisition Bill allows land to be vigorously acquired in favour of private companies and investors, thus including private purpose in the definition of 'public purpose'. It is more regressive and anti-people than even the original Colonial Act! While the government talks of protecting the rights of those whose lands are acquired, it is mere lip service. The R & R Bill does not even guarantee basics like land for land and alternative livelihood-based rehabilitation. The demand of people's struggle across the country is one – a decentralized development planning process which ensures 'development' that is truly people centric and bases itself firmly on the principles of democracy, social justice and equity. Since concerns regarding development planning, land acquisition and resettlement and rehabilitation are intrinsically linked with one another and cannot be addressed in isolation, people's movements and organizations have, for several years now, been demanding the enactment of a comprehensive legislation on development planning.

The crux of the issue has been displacement of people – agricultural labourers, landless tribal labourers whose livelihood support and employment has been at a stake. The farm labourers who earn their livelihood on land are deprived of their livelihood support because of the fact that the MNCs or the industrialists, along with the administration snatch away their land even; apply cohesive methods for land acquisition. Massive corruption and bribery are the hall mark of SEZ land and other benefits sanctioned to the industrialists. Considered from the social justice and inclusive growth point of view, the benefit must percolate to the deprived sections through guaranteed provision of livelihood strategy before adoption of SEZ and its outcome to the vulnerable community.

Thus, if the government is really welfare-oriented or people friendly, it must ensure social security measures extensively to the deprived people who are victimized by development projects or SEZ, and the MNCs or the industrialists who are to gain from such SEZ should guarantee sustainable employment or livelihood support as a part of their social accountability.

References

Baviskar, Amita (1995): *In the Belly of the River,* New Delhi: Oxford University Press, p. 36.

Bhagwati, Jagdish (2004): *In Defense of Globalization,* New York: Oxford Press.

Cernea, Michael M. (1988): "Involuntary Resettlement in Development Projects: Policy Guidelines in World Bank Financed Projects", World Bank Technical Paper No. 80, World Bank, Washington, D.C.

Cernea, Michael M. (2000): "Risks, Safeguards and Reconstruction: A Model for Population Displacement and Resettlement", *Economic and Political Weekly,* October 7, p. 3659.

Chowdhury, Supriya Roy (2004): "Globalization and Labour", *Economic Political Weekly,* January 3–9.

Das, Vidya (2003): "Kasipur Politics of Underdevelopment", *Economic Political Weekly,* January 4.

Das, Vidya (2005): "PESA: A Reality", National Consultation on PESA Act, AGRAGAMEE, Kashipur, Rayagada, Orissa.

Fernades, Walter (1994): Development Induced Displacement in Tribal Areas of Eastern India, (Mimeo), New Delhi: Indian Social Institute.

Fernandes, Walter, et al. (1995): "Tribal Displacement: Struggles and Implications for Resettlement", *Lokayan Bulletin,* 11:4.

Goodland, Robert J.A. (2007): "Utkal Bauxite and Alumina Project: Human Rights and Environmental Impacts", India: Orissa, Kashipur, Washington D.C. (report).

Mukhopadhay, A. and I. Raja Raman (2007): "Rural Unemployment 1999–2005: Who Gained Who Lost?", *Economic and Political Weekly,* July 28.

Oommen, M.A. (2001): "Globalization and Poverty: The Indian Case", *Malayala Manorama Year Book,* p. 563.

Pandey, Balaji (1998): *Depriving the Underprivileged by Development,* Bhubaneswar: Institute for Socio-economic Development, Bhubaneswar.

Papola, T.S. and Alakh N. Sharma (2003): "Globalization and Social Exclusion: Evolving an Inclusionary Policy Framework". Paper prepared for World Commission on the Social Dimensions of Globalization, Geneva: International Labour Office, February.

Patnaik, Pravat (2003): *The Retreat to Unfreedom: Essays on the Emerging World Order,* New Delhi: Tulika.

Roy, Arundhati (1999): "The Greater Common Good: The Human Costs of Big Dams", *Frontline,* June 4.

Sharma, Alakh N. (2004): "Globalization, Labour Markets and Poverty: Emerging Perspectives in India", D.T. Lakdawala memorial lecture at the 87th conference of the Indian Economic Association, Banaras Hindu University, Varanasi, December 21, 2004.

Sundaram, K. and Suresh D. Tendulkar (2003): "Poverty among Social and Economic Groups in India in 1990s", *Economic and Political Weekly,* December 13.

Tripathy, S.N and Soudamini Das (1991): *Informal Women Labour in India,* New Delhi: Discovery Publishing House.

Tripathy, S.N. (2000): *Glimpses on Tribal Development,* New Delhi: Discovery Publishing House.

Tripathy, S.N. (ed.) (2003): *Economic Development and Problem of Displacement,* New Delhi: Anmol Publication.

Tripathy, S.N and P.C. Samantary (2008): *Tribal Cooperatives and Rural Development: Searching New Paradigms,* Delhi: Mangalam Publications.

Wolf, Martin (2004): *Why Globalization Works,* New Haven: Yale University Press.

10

Perspective Scooping of Development of Tribal Economy and Strategic Planning in India in Decentralized Planning Framework

R.D. SINGH

Vicious circle of regional development and core-periphery situation and dependency theories have dominated during 1950s and 60s resulting from the modernizational approach to development in colonial and post-colonial periods. Though modernizational approach to industrial development has resulted in increase in industrial capacities, it has resulted in serious socio-economic and environmental conflicts.

The global concerns of environmental and ecological degradation drew the attention to the sustainable development policy of the United Nations, sustainability defined in terms of social sustainability particularly the poor and environmental sustainability emphasizing conservation of resources while continuing with the modernizational policies.

Despite of continuation of sustainable development and modernizational policies in decentralized planning framework, the tribal economies continue to face problems due to predominance of poverty, unemployment, livelihood insecurities, inefficiencies of resource use, infrastructural scarcity and inaccessibility and immobility of tribes to modern economies.

The problems may be identified in anthropogenic exogenous political economic dominance and succession and social-economic constraints to adaptation of tribes to the modern activities. This has resulted in serious political economic conflicts in the form of ethnic and naxal problems in majority of tribal areas.

The problems have generated due to the failure of tribal regional plan which either emphasize on conservation of resources or social welfare and development and lack of development of tribal economies. The majority of the tribes are dependent on subsistent agriculture with lack of diversification – both horizontal and vertical diversification of the tribal economies. Horizontal diversification is induced either by use of the resources in allied activities like horticulture, animal husbandry and forestry and through vertical integration of the tribes through social development and occupational mobility in non-form modern activities like mining, industries and services.

Tribal communities are facing serious problems of unemployment, poverty and livelihood insecurities due to environmental conflicts, population pressure and lack of infrastructure for social and economic growth.

The problems of tribal economy may be analysed at the level of tribal communities or the changes observed in the tribal habitat in terms of environmental problems identified by the indicators of fluctuation of rainfall and recurrence of drought resulting in increase in fallow lands and wastelands and landuse changes resulting due to deforestation due to internal and external anthropogenic forces.

Since the majority of the tribal communities are dependent upon subsistent agriculture, population changes is leading to marginalization of landholding and employment leading to poverty, underdevelopment and migration. The lack of horizontal and vertical diversification of tribal economy and occupational immobility has created vicious circle of underdevelopment to majority of the families.

Conceptual and Theoretical Premises

The concept of human ecology and occupational base was first introduced by geographers in explaining relationship of human communities with the natural resources and their occupational base. Later, regional economic base enlarged its scope in terms of level of production and productivity in regional framework.

Nevertheless, these theories did not get importance in political economic dominance of modernizational concepts resulting in colonization of resources for industrial and market demands leading to vicious circle of underdevelopment of resource regions (Myrdal) and core-periphery situation in which peripheral resource regions are exploited for the benefits of industrializing core-regions (Friedman). The problem led to serious environmental conflicts in majority of the resource regions and socio-economic conflicts in the developing countries. Sustainable development concept largely focused on socio-economic sustainability, particularly the poor and long-term strategy of environmental conservation programmes along with the modernizational approach through globalization, privatization and decentralization programmes. These programmes have further increased the market access to the common property resources with increasing unaccess to the tribal communities leading to serious socio-economic and socio-political conflicts and deterioration of tribal resource, economic and occupational base.

Increasing vertical integration of forest and other products and constrained vertical occupational mobility of labour in the production cycle has resulted in market orientation of the products, without supply-based planning of the tribal economy. This has led to decreasing access to and the stakes of tribes to the common property resources in the political economic restructuring policies in the privatization policies. This would require not only the conservation of resources, but development of community-based resource and economic development in different landuse and economic zones in geographic landscape framework. Experiencing the problems in Europe of early environmental, social and economic conflicts Geddes (1949) proposed for restoring synergic balance between the three important components of functional regions – people, activities and space to achieve organismic balance. Geddes identified forestry, mining, horticulture, animal husbandry, agriculture and urban-industrial activity zones in geographic landscape starting from hilly, plains and basin regions.

The tribal conflicts may be identified in their demand for their political independence from the colonial dominance and for socio-economic access to development for inclusive development. Sen identified the issue of entitlement and capability building as the prerequisite of socio-economic development of any community.

The above conceptual and theoretical premises indicate to the regional integration of social, sectoral and regional development programmes to evolve socio-economic equity, faster economic development and regional balance in geographic landscape framework. It is necessary to evolve tribal regions' development plans in view of socio-economic, environmental and ecological and sectoral development with their integration in regional and functional framework.

Objectives

The paper identifies the following objectives for investigation:

1. Pattern diversities in community and regional development with a set of indicators and variables.
2. Selection of key instrumental indicators of development and strategic indicators for planning.
3. Developing criteria and approach to strategic planning.

Methodology

1. For identification of the pattern diversities and status of development, regional framework is identified identifying the regional systems at macro-regional, tahsils, economic zones and micro-systems as sample villages. Agricultural, animal husbandry and forestry zones are identified as economic zones to indicate to micro-regional pattern identification.
2. Selecting a set of indicators for micro- and macro-system changes. The macro-system changes and their factorization has been made with the help of demographic, infrastructural, agricultural and industrial indicators. For micro-system analysis at activity zones and village levels, representative sample analysis is made selecting sample villages taking from different activity zones and geographical landscape framework.
3. With a set of indicators at sample village levels in different activity zones, it is checked how the sectoral developments have impacted them to establish sectoral development linkages with the community development.
4. With the sample community development analysis, the priorities of community development have been identified.
5. With the help of sectoral development, inter-sectoral linkages and impacts have been analysed in regional and temporal framework to select a set of community, sectoral and regional development indicators to be used as policy indicators for growth, regulations and development.

Techniques Used for the Study

1. The composite index analysis was used to identify the levels of development in the district during 1990–91 and 2001–02 with the help of a set of indicators and variables.
2. Factor analysis techniques was used for selecting the factors to identify the instrumental indicators of growth and development, indicating to regional and inter-sectoral imbalances and constraining factors to growth to development in the region.
3. Method and techniques of priority setting for community development used interpretive structural modeling (ISM) on the basis of peoples' perceptions and opinion of the community and public representatives.

Techniques of Analysis

1. For identification of community development, priorities setting analysis is made using interpretive structural modeling and scaling methods suggested by Warfield and Waller and Modak respectively.
2. The technique of composite index analysis is used for comparative regional analysis of pattern and pattern diversities.
3. Factor analysis technique is used to select instrumental indicators affecting growth as positive indicators and constraining indicators as negative indicators.

Results and Discussion

Levels of Regional Development

Demographic, agricultural, industrial and infrastructural indicators were used for composite index analysis for indicating to the levels of regional development during 1992–93 and 2001–02 with a set of variables. The demographic indicator comprised of 11 variables relating to population, decadal growth rate of population, literacy level, etc. The agricultural indicator used 9 variables including agricultural infrastructure, modern technology transfer, commercialization of agriculture and animal husbandry in the region. The industrial indicators used number of industries, fixed capital and per unit capital used in industries. The infrastructural indicators included 20 variables relating to different social services in terms of areas and population served health services, patients and educational services, etc.

It was found that region is relatively backward in terms of demographic, infrastructural and economic development and growth is also constrained in socio-demographic and agricultural development particularly. It was found that Betul tahsil experienced relatively higher growth rate in regional development as compared to other tahsils primarily due to mining and industrial activity and the administrative centre of the district located in the tahsil leading to centrality and agglomeration. Bhainsdehi tahsil is relatively most backward region. Betul tahsil was taken as prospective region and Bhainsdehi tahsil as problematic one for detailed sample analysis in representative activity zones.

Table 1

Composite Indices of Agriculture Sector in Betul Tahsil (1992–93)

Tahsil	$X_{1,1}$	$X_{1,2}$	$X_{1,3}$	$X_{1,4}$	$X_{1,5}$	$X_{1,6}$	$X_{1,7}$	$X_{1,8}$	$X_{1,9}$	Total Tahsil
Betul	1.17	1.29	-2.47	2.61	-9.03	-4.19	2.36	7.36	6.06	5.16
Bhainsdehi	0.54	1.19	-1.51	1.22	-10.04	-4.30	2.23	9.74	8.27	7.34
Shahpur	0.53	1.12	-2.32	0.61	-9.54	-5.40	0.91	13.85	13.46	13.23
Multai	0.82	1.09	-1.62	1.74	-8.11	-2.97	3.83	4.85	3.17	2.79
Amla	1.57	1.05	-1.74	2.27	-8.84	-5.11	2.78	7.78	7.04	6.79
Total	4.64	5.73	-9.67	8.45	-45.56	-21.98	12.11	43.58	38.00	35.32

Source: Primary Level Sample Survey, district Betul.

Table 2

Composite Indices of Agriculture Sector in Betul Tahsil (2001–02)

Tahsil	$X_{1,1}$	$X_{1,2}$	$X_{1,3}$	$X_{1,4}$	$X_{1,5}$	$X_{1,6}$	$X_{1,7}$	$X_{1,8}$	$X_{1,9}$	Total Tahsil
Betul	0.53	4.19	2.11	3.46	-2.39	5.59	-2.31	-1.27	1.05	10.96
Bhainsdehi	0.26	3.29	0.56	1.55	-2.85	5.54	-2.18	-1.00	1.49	6.65
Shahpur	0.40	5.34	1.53	3.71	-3.18	7.22	-0.89	-0.29	1.22	15.06
Multai	0.38	2.80	1.22	2.01	-3.37	4.36	-3.74	-1.18	0.75	3.22
Amla	0.57	2.80	1.34	1.91	-3.34	5.64	-2.72	-0.38	0.24	6.05
Total	2.13	18.42	6.76	12.64	-15.13	28.34	-11.84	-4.12	4.74	41.94

Source: Primary Level Sample Survey, district Betul.

Table 3

Composite Indices of Infrastructure Sector in Betul Tahsil (1992–93)

Tahsil	$X_{3,1}$	$X_{3,2}$	$X_{3,3}$	$X_{3,4}$	$X_{3,5}$	$X_{3,6}$	$X_{3,7}$	$X_{3,8}$	$X_{3,9}$	$X_{3,10}$	$X_{3,11}$	$X_{3,12}$	$X_{3,13}$	$X_{3,14}$	$X_{3,15}$	$X_{3,16}$	$X_{3,17}$	$X_{3,18}$	$X_{3,19}$	$X_{3,20}$	*Total Tah.*
Betul	6.05	0.42	1.38	1.42	2.73	-1.44	0.17	2.52	-0.07	-0.11	3.08	-1.64	-2.97	3.19	3.25	-0.54	-1.48	3.04	-1.03	5.24	23.20
Bhainsdehi	5.97	0.24	0.89	1.02	2.65	-1.67	0.11	0.38	-0.54	-0.47	1.57	-3.61	-3.67	1.36	2.44	-0.46	-2.21	2.59	-1.35	3.89	9.11
Shahpur	5.83	0.28	0.29	0.17	0.64	-1.57	0.13	0.08	-0.61	-0.67	0.33	-3.95	-4.97	0.48	3.28	-0.39	-1.51	0.75	-1.14	3.79	1.23
Multai	5.20	0.23	1.59	1.55	1.36	-2.33	0.19	0.08	-1.93	-2.07	1.05	-3.90	-4.82	1.06	1.63	-0.60	-2.39	1.98	-1.81	4.46	0.53
Amla	4.40	0.53	0.41	0.22	0.88	-1.44	0.17	0.08	-0.77	-1.20	0.52	-3.12	-5.57	0.59	3.33	-0.69	-1.91	1.06	-1.02	4.80	1.26
Total	27.45	1.70	4.57	4.38	8.26	-8.45	0.76	3.13	-3.92	-4.53	6.55	-16.23	-22.00	6.68	13.93	-2.67	-9.50	9.42	-6.36	22.16	35.33

Source: Primary Level Sample Survey, district Betul.

Table 4

Composite Indices of Infrastructure Sector in Betul Tahsil (2001–02)

Tahsil	$X_{3,1}$	$X_{3,2}$	$X_{3,3}$	$X_{3,4}$	$X_{3,5}$	$X_{3,6}$	$X_{3,7}$	$X_{3,8}$	$X_{3,9}$	$X_{3,10}$	$X_{3,11}$	$X_{3,12}$	$X_{3,13}$	$X_{3,14}$	$X_{3,15}$	$X_{3,16}$	$X_{3,17}$	$X_{3,18}$	$X_{3,19}$	$X_{3,20}$	*Total Tah.*
Betul	5.45	-0.29	0.83	0.44	2.71	-2.93	-1.00	2.77	-0.42	-0.97	2.98	-1.66	-4.04	3.23	2.87	-0.80	-1.14	3.23	-0.76	0.96	11.45
Bhainsdehi	5.72	-0.15	0.51	0.47	2.76	-3.23	-0.61	1.18	-1.11	-1.41	2.22	-2.52	-3.34	2.04	2.30	-0.62	-1.61	2.65	-1.04	0.72	4.93
Shahpur	3.65	-0.28	0.16	0.09	0.75	-2.70	-0.64	0.37	-0.81	-1.31	0.51	-2.48	-4.19	13.34	0.77	-0.53	-1.10	0.85	-0.79	0.65	6.28
Multai	4.16	-0.16	1.02	0.75	1.52	-4.20	-0.88	0.44	-2.13	-3.02	1.11	-3.62	-5.36	19.29	1.53	-0.74	-1.74	1.71	-1.65	0.89	8.92
Amla	4.57	-0.30	0.27	0.12	0.70	-3.66	-1.16	0.37	-1.02	-2.20	0.68	-2.36	-5.29	24.05	0.38	-1.80	-2.78	1.03	-0.83	0.90	11.67
Total	23.54	-1.19	2.79	1.87	8.44	-16.72	-4.30	5.13	-5.49	-8.91	7.50	-12.64	-22.22	61.94	7.85	-4.49	-8.36	9.48	-5.07	4.11	43.25

Source: Primary Level Sample Survey, district Betul.

Table 5

Composite Indices of Industrial Sector in Betul Tahsil (1992–93)

Tahsil	$X_{2,1}$	$X_{2,2}$	$X_{2,3}$	*Total Tahsil*
Betul	3.02	2.58	2.34	7.93
Bhainsdehi	2.42	0.11	0.12	2.65
Shahpur	0.71	0.04	0.17	0.92
Multai	1.59	0.28	0.49	2.36
Amla	0.99	0.11	0.29	1.39
Total	8.72	3.12	3.41	15.26

Source: Primary Level Sample Survey, district Betul.

Table 6

Composite Indices of Industrial Sector in Betul Tahsil (2001–02)

Tahsil	$X_{2,1}$	$X_{2,2}$	$X_{2,3}$	*Total Tahsil*
Betul	3.18	2.63	2.38	8.18
Bhainsdehi	0.79	0.05	0.17	1.01
Shahpur	0.92	0.09	0.28	1.28
Multai	1.51	0.44	0.83	2.78
Amla	0.39	0.09	0.63	1.11
Total	6.79	3.29	4.29	14.36

Source: Primary Level Sample Survey, district Betul.

Table 7

Composite Indices of Demographic Sector in Betul Tahsil (1991)

Tahsil	$W_{1,1}$	$W_{1,2}$	$W_{1,3}$	$W_{3,1}$	$W_{3,2}$	$W_{3,3}$	$W_{5,1}$	$W_{5,2}$	$W_{5,3}$	$W_{5,4}$	$W_{5,5}$	*Total Tahsil*
Betul	2.51	2.17	1.75	-2.00	0.15	2.07	4.78	5.34	3.96	2.31	3.64	29.57
Bhain-sdehi	1.59	2.03	0.16	-1.72	0.12	1.29	3.01	3.67	2.14	2.00	2.99	20.54
Shahpur	0.45	0.60	0.00	-1.99	0.11	0.00	2.98	3.86	1.84	0.00	3.14	11.96
Multai	1.39	1.72	0.22	-0.84	0.06	0.88	4.82	5.54	3.83	2.37	4.70	27.54
Amla	0.80	0.86	0.31	-1.32	0.11	0.50	4.78	5.47	3.82	2.44	4.28	25.42
Total	6.74	7.38	2.44	-7.87	0.55	4.74	20.38	23.88	15.59	9.13	18.77	115.03

Source: Primary Level Sample Survey, district Betul.

Table 8

Composite Indices of Demographic Sector in Betul Tahsil (2001)

Tahsil	$W_{1,1}$	$W_{1,2}$	$W_{1,3}$	$W_{3,1}$	$W_{3,2}$	$W_{3,3}$	$W_{5,1}$	$W_{5,2}$	$W_{5,3}$	$W_{5,4}$	$W_{5,5}$	*Total Tahsil*
Betul	2.52	2.54	1.45	-2.22	-0.33	2.20	6.88	9.18	5.07	-18.05	5.44	14.69
Bhains-dehi	1.55	2.29	0.12	-1.92	-0.27	1.37	5.87	8.21	4.06	-17.31	5.24	9.22
Shahpur	0.45	0.67	0.03	-2.21	-0.24	0.00	5.87	7.54	3.10	-19.19	4.41	0.42
Multai	1.24	1.78	0.17	-0.94	-0.13	0.94	7.60	10.02	5.71	-18.08	6.84	15.15
Amla	0.76	0.96	0.23	-1.47	-0.24	0.53	6.94	9.32	5.08	-18.63	5.93	9.40
Total	6.52	8.23	2.00	-8.76	-1.21	5.04	33.16	44.27	23.02	-91.27	27.87	48.04

Source: Primary Level Sample Survey, district Betul.

Table 9

Sectoral Composite Indices of Betul Tahsil (1991–2001)

	Demo (W_1)		*Agri* (I_1)		*Infra* (I_2)		*Indus* (I_3)	
	1991	*2001*	*1991*	*2001*	*1991*	*2001*	*1991*	*2001*
Betul	29.57	14.69	5.16	10.96	23.20	11.45	7.93	8.18
Bhainsdehi	20.54	9.22	7.34	6.65	9.11	4.93	2.65	1.01
Shahpur	11.96	0.42	13.23	15.06	1.23	6.28	0.92	1.28
Multai	27.54	15.15	2.79	3.22	0.53	8.92	2.36	2.78
Amla	25.42	9.40	6.79	6.05	1.26	11.67	1.39	1.11
Dist. Total	115.03	48.04	35.32	41.94	35.33	43.25	15.26	14.36
Average	23.01	9.78	7.06	8.39	7.07	8.65	3.05	2.87
S.D.	6.29	5.61	3.46	4.16	9.39	8.82	2.52	2.73
Gini Coef.	53.33	24.88	17.59	20.93	24.99	20.26	8.85	8.86

Source: Primary Level Sample Survey, district Betul.

Table 10

Total Composite Indices of Betul District (1991–2001)

Name of Tahsil	1991		2001	
	Index	Rank	Index	Rank
Betul	65.86	1	45.29	1
Bhainsdehi	39.65	2	21.81	5
Shahpur	27.33	5	23.05	4
Multai	33.23	4	30.06	2
Amla	34.86	3	28.24	3

Identification of the Factors of Sectoral Development

The factor analysis technique has been used to identify the contribution of factors in the development pattern in the region. It was found that total number of animals, area under non-food grains, number of tractors and irrigated area contributed the highest in agricultural development in the study area during 1991.

In the infrastructural sector, the contribution of the variables like number of cooperative societies, doctors, family welfare centre have contributed the highest in the region during the study periods. In the industrial sector, installed capital has contributed the highest in the region. In the demographic sector which represents the level of community development, the literacy level contributed the highest in the study area.

It may be inferred that there is low level of sectoral development in the region. The poor infrastructure has led to the backwardness conditions. The welfare and living conditions of the communities was regressed with the indicators of economic development in the region, which indicated that level of agriculture development has contributed to the welfare in living condition of the people in the region, followed by infrastructural sector and industrial sector respectively. It is observed that during the study period, 1991 and 2001, the regression coefficient have improved related to agricultural sector as they have declined to those of infrastructural and industrial significantly.

Table 11

Principal Component Analysis of Agriculture Sector (1991)

	Contribution of the Variables (%)			
	F_1	F_2	F_3	F_4
$X_{1,1}$	4.53	7.67	26.91	15.40
$X_{1,2}$	0.21	28.65	7.81	3.20
$X_{1,3}$	4.35	1.68	28.52	33.52
$X_{1,4}$	14.88	0.08	24.60	3.48
$X_{1,5}$	12.30	12.83	0.78	23.30
$X_{1,6}$	20.74	0.78	7.32	15.10
$X_{1,7}$	25.63	2.82	1.64	0.11
$X_{1,8}$	14.55	15.83	2.10	0.34
$X_{1,9}$	2.80	29.66	0.31	5.56

Source: Calculated from the sectoral indicators data.

Table 12

Principal Component Analysis of Agriculture Sector (1991)

	Contribution of the Observations (%)			
	F_1	F_2	F_3	F_4
Betul	6.03	22.11	46.67	5.20
Bhainsdehi	0.13	30.04	23.65	26.17
Shahpur	63.31	1.19	0.38	15.13
Multai	30.42	8.51	19.74	21.33
Amla	0.12	38.15	9.56	32.17

Source: Calculated from the sectoral indicators data.

Table 13

Principal Component Analysis of Agriculture Sector (2001)

	Contribution of the Variables (%)			
	F_1	F_2	F_3	F_4
$X_{1,1}$	0.30	38.96	0.30	11.57
$X_{1,2}$	22.87	0.43	0.08	8.91

Cont'd...

Cont'd...

$X_{1,3}$	6.08	22.19	9.77	4.30
$X_{1,4}$	18.67	3.46	3.06	18.69
$X_{1,5}$	3.29	0.79	33.24	40.28
$X_{1,6}$	19.89	0.22	7.27	4.86
$X_{1,7}$	20.42	2.63	2.79	7.47
$X_{1,8}$	4.07	1.56	38.42	3.55
$X_{1,9}$	4.41	29.76	5.09	0.38

Source: Calculated from the sectoral indicators data.

Table 14

Principal Component Analysis of Agriculture Sector (2001)

	Contribution of the Observations (%)			
	F_1	F_2	F_3	F_4
Betul	7.65	9.11	59.86	3.38
Bhainsdehi	3.50	60.34	0.03	16.13
Shahpur	51.58	1.04	15.50	11.88
Multai	30.94	0.12	0.84	48.10
Amla	6.32	29.39	23.78	20.51

Source: Calculated from the sectoral indicators data.

Table 15

Principal Component Analysis of Infrastructure Sector (1991)

	Contribution of the Variables (%)			
	F_1	F_2	F_3	F_4
$X_{3,1}$	4.12	0.01	13.47	7.43
$X_{3,2}$	0.14	4.97	16.78	2.66
$X_{3,3}$	2.81	12.47	0.32	1.82
$X_{3,4}$	3.63	11.59	0.00	0.26
$X_{3,5}$	8.19	0.95	1.20	14.57
$X_{3,6}$	1.17	14.97	0.36	3.06
$X_{3,7}$	0.01	3.96	16.28	12.83
$X_{3,8}$	9.72	0.14	0.90	4.89

Cont'd...

Cont'd...

$X_{3,9}$	4.08	10.45	0.33	1.30
$X_{3,10}$	4.94	7.66	2.39	0.53
$X_{3,11}$	10.32	0.48	0.10	0.00
$X_{3,12}$	7.77	0.83	5.46	0.23
$X_{3,13}$	9.49	0.22	2.36	0.12
$X_{3,14}$	10.22	0.25	0.39	1.18
$X_{3,15}$	9.60	1.22	0.41	1.54
$X_{3,16}$	0.12	1.16	20.48	10.25
$X_{3,17}$	1.42	10.45	0.14	30.45
$X_{3,18}$	8.13	3.07	0.22	6.02
$X_{3,19}$	0.94	15.05	1.40	0.25
$X_{3,20}$	3.19	0.09	16.99	0.61

Source: Calculated from the sectoral indicators data.

Contribution of the Observations (%)				
	F_1	F_2	F_3	F_4
Betul	66.62	0.74	5.70	6.95
Bhainsdehi	2.10	0.40	33.67	43.83
Shahpur	12.11	20.85	17.22	29.81
Multai	6.97	66.65	1.13	5.24
Amla	12.19	11.36	42.29	14.17

Table 16

Principal Component Analysis of Infrastructure Sector (2001)

Contribution of the Variables (%)				
	F_1	F_2	F_3	F_4
$X_{3,1}$	6.89	0.46	1.87	24.23
$X_{3,2}$	0.05	9.68	6.74	11.86
$X_{3,3}$	1.21	12.51	0.99	7.40
$X_{3,4}$	0.68	15.17	0.09	0.63
$X_{3,5}$	9.22	2.30	0.02	3.77
$X_{3,6}$	3.25	9.90	2.17	1.93

Cont'd...

Cont'd...

$X_{3,7}$	0.51	0.00	24.36	1.38
$X_{3,8}$	9.72	0.00	2.80	2.85
$X_{3,9}$	3.65	10.38	1.03	0.21
$X_{3,10}$	6.17	7.13	0.49	0.01
$X_{3,11}$	10.23	0.88	1.04	0.35
$X_{3,12}$	4.48	7.63	3.57	0.02
$X_{3,13}$	6.84	1.28	6.03	7.12
$X_{3,14}$	9.81	1.22	1.13	1.42
$X_{3,15}$	9.71	2.33	0.00	0.12
$X_{3,16}$	2.40	0.69	16.82	8.09
$X_{3,17}$	4.17	0.04	8.79	24.10
$X_{3,18}$	9.60	1.96	0.69	0.57
$X_{3,19}$	1.24	13.77	1.15	0.29
$X_{3,20}$	0.16	2.65	20.23	3.66

Contribution of the Observations (%)

	F_1	F_2	F_3	F_4
Betul	47.22	0.28	17.17	15.33
Bhainsdehi	12.72	1.56	14.68	51.04
Shahpur	4.50	30.48	30.90	14.12
Multai	11.97	59.28	0.64	8.11
Amla	23.58	8.41	36.61	11.40

Source: Calculated from the sectoral indicators data.

Table 17

Principal Component Analysis of Industrial Sector (1991)

Contribution of the Variables (%)

	F_1	F_2	F_3
$X_{2,1}$	28.36	71.32	0.32
$X_{2,2}$	36.27	10.94	52.79
$X_{2,3}$	35.38	17.74	46.88

Source: Calculated from the sectoral indicators data.

Table 18

Principal Component Analysis of Industrial Sector (1991)

Contribution of the Observations (%)			
	F_1	F_2	F_3
Betul	75.39	3.56	1.00
Bhainsdehi	0.67	70.80	8.06
Shahpur	14.00	17.73	29.29
Multai	1.47	0.21	59.23
Amla	8.46	7.70	2.42

Source: Calculated from the sectoral indicators data.

Table 19

Principal Component Analysis of Industrial Sector (2001)

Contribution of the Variables (%)			
	F_1	F_2	F_3
$X_{2,1}$	32.87	57.19	9.94
$X_{2,2}$	33.96	1.12	64.92
$X_{2,3}$	33.17	41.69	25.14

Source: Calculated from the sectoral indicators data.

Table 20

Principal Component Analysis of Industrial Sector (2001)

Contribution of the Observations (%)			
	F_1	F_2	F_3
Betul	75.57	0.33	4.07
Bhainsdehi	9.67	9.42	23.15
Shahpur	7.00	10.65	3.44
Multai	0.02	7.48	69.21
Amla	7.73	72.12	0.13

Source: Calculated from the sectoral indicators data.

Table 21

Principal Component Analysis of Demographic Sector (1991)

Contribution of the Variables (%)				
	F_1	F_2	F_3	F_4
$W_{1,1}$	8.83	11.23	3.47	6.62
$W_{1,2}$	6.39	8.25	27.60	3.34
$W_{1,3}$	7.97	9.95	11.90	8.76
$W_{3,1}$	3.20	16.91	13.94	0.44
$W_{3,2}$	0.00	20.04	12.33	26.14
$W_{3,3}$	8.42	12.18	3.90	0.30
$W_{5,1}$	14.57	2.49	6.79	0.04
$W_{5,2}$	13.13	4.00	8.64	0.72

Source: Calculated from the sectoral indicators data.

Table 22

Principal Component Analysis of Demographic Sector (1991)

Contribution of the Observations (%)				
	F_1	F_2	F_3	F_4
Betul	25.38	38.13	11.20	5.28
Bhainsdehi	6.57	14.95	43.68	14.81
Shahpur	54.05	0.24	11.61	14.11
Multai	12.00	30.17	17.35	20.48
Amla	1.99	16.51	16.17	45.32

Source: Calculated from the sectoral indicators data.

Table 23

Principal Component Analysis of Demographic Sector (2001)

Contribution of the Variables (%)				
	F_1	F_2	F_3	F_4
$W_{1,1}$	9.19	11.24	0.01	8.80
$W_{1,2}$	9.53	8.18	10.49	8.50

Cont'd...

Cont'd...

$W_{1,3}$	5.02	10.86	24.46	5.51
$W_{3,1}$	4.30	17.55	2.34	0.29
$W_{3,2}$	0.08	20.45	4.11	58.89
$W_{3,3}$	10.02	10.38	0.25	0.58
$W_{5,1}$	14.54	3.30	4.07	2.43
$W_{5,2}$	13.65	4.42	4.61	0.71
$W_{5,3}$	15.08	2.64	3.51	4.22
$W_{5,4}$	7.09	2.52	46.08	9.94
$W_{5,5}$	11.50	8.47	0.06	0.13

Source: Calculated from the sectoral indicators data.

Table 24

Principal Component Analysis of Demographic Sector (2001)

	Contribution of the Observations (%)			
	F_1	F_2	F_3	F_4
Betul	16.43	41.96	19.23	2.38
Bhainsdehi	0.10	9.71	63.99	6.21
Shahpur	63.94	0.00	2.71	13.34
Multai	19.51	35.76	2.19	22.55
Amla	0.03	12.57	11.88	55.52

Source: Calculated from the sectoral indicators data.

The following results of regression analysis have been found:
Regression Equation of the Model (1991):
$W=28.60+0.85*I_1+0.74*I_2+0.47*I_3+e$
Regression Equation of the Model (2001):
$W=15.21+0.94*I_1+0.64*I_2+0.41*I_3+e$
W=Welfare and Living Condition of the Communities
I_1=Composite Indices of Level of Agricultural Development
I_2=Composite Indices of Level of Infrastructural Development
I_2=Composite Indices of Level of Industrial Development

Table 25

Values of Regression Coefficients Representing Level of Community Development

Year	*Constant*	b_1	b_2	b_3	*e*	R^2
1991	28.6	0.85	0.74	0.47	0.001	0.93
2001	15.21	0.94	0.64	0.41	12.26	1.00

Priority Setting for Community Development

The priority setting for community development at the micro-level (village) and macro-level (tahsil and district) were undertaken with the help of public opinion and their priorities with a set of opinions related to economic, social, ecological and environmental development. For this, the models suggested by Modak and Patkar (1983) and interpretive structural modeling method (ISM) developed by Warfield and Waller were used for identifying the priorities of community development. By taking representative samples from the communities and public representatives, the priorities were identified. The respondents (65) in prospective region (Betul tahsil) identified the lack of educational infrastructure as the main impediment to the economic growth, the other factors were identified as health, lack of employment opportunities, transportation, etc. On the contrary, in the problematic region (Bhainsdehi tahsil), lack of employment opportunities, education, irrigation and health were the main priorities for economic growth.

There was variation in the perception of the economic problems in the activity zones in the study area. The respondents in the agricultural zone of Betul tahsil identified electricity as the main priority followed by employment opportunities, education and health. In the animal husbandry zone of the tahsil, transportation, education and health were identified as of equal importance followed by irrigation and employment opportunities. In the forestry zone, education, health and employment were identified as the main priorities followed by irrigation and others.

In Bhainsdehi tahsil, the respondents (52) identified lack of employment opportunities, irrigation, electricity and education of equal importance as priorities. In the animal husbandry zone of the tahsil, the respondents identified lack of employment opportunities and health infrastructure as the topmost priorities followed by education and irrigation. In the forestry zone, the respondents had difficulties in identifying the priorities due to the serious backwardness and indicated to lack of employment opportunities, irrigation, electricity, education and other problems in the zone.

Public Opinion and Priorities of Social Development

The schedule covered the questions like social superstitious beliefs, lack of education, traditional occupation, lack of social infrastructure, social tension, problems in the plans, lack of local and regional levels plans, lack of social and economic information and others. In Betul tahsil, the respondents identified lack of education, traditional occupation, lack of local regional level plan and lack of social and regional level information as the main factors constraining socio-economic development. In Bhainsdehi tahsil, along with lack of education, traditional occupation, lack of social and economic information and superstitious beliefs were identified as the main factors of social backwardness.

Public Opinion and Priorities of Ecological Development

The opinions on the ecological issues covering questions related to the land conservation and development, water conservation and development, animal husbandry and milk production, gardening, forestry, agro-industry, skill-based industries, drinking water facility, forest-based industries, housing facilities, food products and others. In the district, the respondents identified agricultural development as the topmost priorities followed by animal husbandry and milk production, agro-industry and drinking water facility as priorities for rural ecological development.

Public Opinion and Priorities of Environmental Development

Relating to the environmental problems, the respondents identified drought as the main environmental problem followed by deforestation and soil erosion.

Table 26

Public Opinion and Priorities of Economic Development in Betul Tahsil

	Villages/ Tahsils	*NOR*	*LOEO*	*LOEUR*	*SOSL*	*Shortage of Infrastructure*					*Others*	
						Irr.	*Ele.*	*Tra.*	*Edu.*	*Hl.*	*Name*	*No*
	Betul Tahsil											
1.	Surgaon	9	8			9	9		5	4	(1) LOGS	1
											(2) LOF	1
2.	Malkapur	11	10	2			11	11	11	11		
3.	Mandhai	11	10	4		10	11	11	11	11		
4.	Sihari	13	8	2	1	2			8	7	(1) LOI	1
											(2) LODW	1
5.	Gyarspur	11	8	4		10		11	11	11		
6.	Dharakhoh	10	7	6		10	10	10	10	10		
	Bhains											
1.	Matka	8	8	0	1	8	8	7	8	6	Road	8
2.	Ghogama	9	9	1		9	9	9	9	9		
3.	Jamjhiri	9	9			9	9	8	9	8		
4.	Junapani	8	8			8	8	7	8	7	(1) Road	8
											(2) Bridge	2
5.	Majarwani	8	8	1		5		3	6	8	Road	6
6.	Pipariya	10	10			10	10	10	10	10	Firewood	10
	Total	117	103	20	2	90	75	87	106	102		38

Source: Primary Level Sample Survey, district Betul.

NOR=No. of respondent, LOEO= Lack of employment opportunity,

LOGS=Lack of government support, LOEUR=Lack of efficient utilization of resources,

LOI=Lack of industries, SOSL=Shortage of skilled labour.

LOF=Lack of finance for seed and technique,

LODW=Lack of drinking water, Irri=irrigation.

Ele.=electricity, Tra.=transport, Edu.=education, Hl=health.

Table 27

Lack of Resources in Betul District

	LOEO	*LOEUR*	*SOSL*	*IRRI*	*ELE*	*TRA*	*EDU*	*HL*	*OTH*
LOEO	0	0	0	0	0	0	1	0	0
LOEUR	1	0	0	1	1	1	1	1	1
SOSL	1	1	0	1	1	1	1	1	1
IRRI	1	0	0	0	0	0	1	1	0
ELE	1	0	0	1	0	1	1	1	0
TRA	1	0	0	1	0	0	1	1	0
EDU	0	0	0	0	0	0	0	0	0
HL	1	0	0	0	0	0	1	0	0
OTH	1	0	0	1	1	1	1	1	0
Total	7	1	0	5	3	4	8	6	2

Status of Resources in Betul District

Type	*Opinion*
LOEO	103
LOEUR	20
SOSL	2
IRRI	90
ELE	75
TRA	87
EDU	106
HL	102
OTH	38

Source: Primary Level Sample Survey, district Betul.
LOEO=Lack of employment opportunities, ELE=Electricity, TRA=Transport.
LOEUR=Lack of effective utilization of resources, EDU=Education, HL=Health.
SOSL= Shortage of skilled labour, IRRI=Irrigation, OTH=Others.

Table 28

Availability of Resources in Betul District

	LOEO	*LOEUR*	*SOSL*	*IRRI*	*ELE*	*TRA*	*EDU*	*HL*	*OTH*
LOEO	0	0	0	0	0	0	1	0	0
LOEUR	1	0	0	1	1	1	1	1	1
SOSL	1	1	0	1	1	1	1	1	1
IRRI	1	0	0	0	0	0	1	1	0
ELE	1	0	0	1	0	1	1	1	0
TRA	1	0	0	1	0	0	1	1	0
EDU	0	0	0	0	0	0	0	0	0
HL	1	0	0	0	0	0	1	0	0
OTH	1	0	0	1	1	1	1	1	0
TOTAL	7	1	0	5	3	4	8	6	2

Table 29

Public Opinion and Priorities of Social Development in Betul Tahsil

Villages/ Tahsils	*SSB*	*LOE*	*TO*	*LOSIS*	*ST*	*PIP*	*LOLRLP*	*LOSEI*	*OTH*
Betul Tahsil									
1. Surgaon		9	6	3			5	1	
2. Malkapur	2	9	11	3			7	6	
3. Mandhai	2	11	11	2			7	6	
4. Sihari	3	11	11	2		1	10	3	
5. Gyarspur	2	11	11	4			9	8	
6. Dharakhoh		10	10	2		1	10	5	
Bhains									
1. Matka	3	8	8	1				5	
2. Ghogama	4	9	6					3	
3. Jamjhiri	3	9	7	1				5	
4. Junapani	2	8	7					4	
5. Majarwani	3	8	6	1			1	3	
6. Pipariya	5	10	9	3		1	1	4	

Source: Primary Level Sample Survey, district Betul.
SSB=Social Superstitious Believe, LOE= Lack of education, TO= Traditional occupation.
LOSIS=Lack of social infrastructural and system, ST= Social tension.
PIP=Problem in implementation in plan, LOLRLP=Lack of local regional level plan.
LOSEI= Lack of social and economic information, OTH=Others.

Table 30

Public Opinion and Priorities of Ecological Development in Betul Tahsil

	Villages/Tahsils	*LCD*	*WCD*	*FCD*	*AD*	*AHMP*	*Gard.*	*For.*	*AI*	*EBI*	*DBI*	*DWF*	*FBI*	*HF*	*FP*	*OTH*
	Betul Tahsil															
1.	Surgaon	1	9		6	4			6	3		7		1		
2.	Malkapur		2		8	8	2		11	4						
3.	Mandhai	3	11		10	10			11	4	2					
4.	Sihari		4	10	6	7	2	1	6	3	1		10	1		
5.	Gyarspur	1	11		8	5			8	3		7				
6.	Dharakhoh		9	10	6	7	4	10	6				10			
	Bhains															
1.	Matka		8	4	7	7	1		1			8				
2.	Ghogama	5	9		6	6	1		9	6	4	9	2	1		
3.	Jamjhiri	3	9	1	8	8	4		9	5	5	9	1	2		
4.	Junapani		8	8	8	6	4	1	7	2			6			
5.	Majarwani	2	8		8	8	2		2							
6.	Pipariya	4	5		9	10	1		10	6	4					

Source: Primary Level Sample Survey, district Betul.
LCD= Land conservation and development.
WCD= Water conservation and development.
FCD= Forest conservation and development, AD= Agriculture development.
AHMP= Animal husbandry and milk production, Gard.= gardening, For.= Forestry, AI= Agro industry.
EBI= Efficiency based industry, DBI= demand based industry, DWF= Drinking water facilities.
FBI= Forest-based industry, HF= Housing facilities, FP= Food product, OTH= Others.

Table 31

Public Opinion and Priorities of Environmental Development in Betul Tahsil

	Villages/ Tahsils	Drought	Deforestation	Soil Erosion	Barren Land	Pr. by Outer Po.	Im. Lu	OTH
	Betul Tahsil							
1.	Surgaon	9						
2.	Malkapur						1	
3.	Mandhai	11						
4.	Sihari		13					
5.	Gyarspur	11						
6.	Dharakhoh	7	10					
	Bhains.							
1.	Matka	6	7	2		1	2	
2.	Ghogama	9		4	1		2	
3.	Jamjhiri	9	6	4	1			
4.	Junapani	8	7	3				
5.	Majarwani	8		3				
6.	Pipariya	10		3			6	
	Total	88	43	19	2	1	11	

Source: Primary Level Sample Survey, district Betul.

Pr. by Outer Po= Problem by outer population, Im. Lu= Imbalanced landuse, OTH=others.

Table 32

Status of Resources

	DRT	DEFO	SE	BL	PBOP	ILU	OTH
DRT	0	0	0	0	0	0	0
DEFO	1	0	0	0	0	0	0
SE	1	1	0	0	0	0	0
BL	1	1	1	0	0	1	0
PBOP	1	1	1	1	0	1	0
ILU	1	1	1	0	0	0	0
OTH	1	1	1	1	1	1	0
	6	5	4	2	1	3	0

Cont'd...

Cont'd...

Type	*Opinion*
DRT	88
DEFO	43
SE	19
BL	2
PBOP	1
ILU	11
OTH	0

Source: Primary Level Sample Survey, district Betul.

Identification of Strategic Instrumental Indicators of Tribal Economic Development

The present level strategy of planning is being approached for social, sectoral and area development in decentralized planning framework in Panchayati Raj system. The strategy aimed at empowerment and capacity building has failed to generate economic empowerment and capacity building because of the lack of sectoral integration in regional, functional and social framework.

The grass roots approach to planning of the tribal economy would require regenerative resource base planning to develop the tribal economic capacities by maximizing production in agriculture, animal husbandry, forestry and horticulture, etc., to generate employment and resource base for the communities and generating surplus for the market. Once, the socio-economic capacities of the tribes is created, they can integrate to the secondary and tertiary activities like industrial processing, marketing, transportation, services, etc., in an evolutionary growth process to ensure communities' competitiveness to the anthropogenic forces.

This would require identification of the structural and developmental indicators of the communities in regional framework. An integrative regional system analysis for identifying the levels of regional development may be used for indicating to the communities' socio-economic development status, levels and conflicts, sectoral development of both economic and infrastructural sectors during the decentralized planning period in Panchayati Raj system.

It is generally found that tribal communities' economic base is constrained due to environmental conflicts and lack of infrastructural facilities for conservation and development of the resources. The modernizational model of agricultural development through technology transfer and agriculture credit financing has failed due to serious infrastructural constraints and environmental risks. The increasing indebtedness among tribes is resulting due to the increasing market impacts.

It is found that there is increasing marginalization of employment due to the increasing population pressure leading to fragmentation and marginalization of holdings, environmental risks leading to increase in culturable wastelands and fallow lands and increasing deforestation and change in landuse by increasing anthropogenic pressure on forest and grazing lands for extensive agriculture.

The structural indicators in space economies in tribal areas may be identified as demographic, infrastructural and sectoral development of the economies in the region. The traditional accounting of the economic sectors are for agriculture and allied activities and the contribution of allied activities like animal husbandry, horticulture and forestry which may provide and expand occupational base, resource base and economic base to the tribal communities through horizontal mobility have been ignored in economic analysis. The demographic indicators indicate to the socio-economic conditions and level of development and the problems at the community and population ecological levels. The sectoral developmental indicators indicate to the level of agricultural development which provide economic base to the tribes in majority, mining and forestry which is controlled by the government do not have access to the tribes, because of the social and institutional constraints. The infrastructural sectors are poorly developed in tribal regions due to geographical constraints and lack of the effective demand by the society and the economy in backward conditions.

The institutional structural changes in Panchayati Raj system are not effective because of the centralized control of higher level of institutions and local communities not able to create effective demand in political institutional framework. The increasing socio-political conscietation of the tribal communities though is resulting in increasing demands and adaptation and development, it is generating conflicts for entitlement, autonomy and capability development in the region under the condition of historical anthropogenic dominance and succession. The planning process has to be responsive for initiating organismic development model for tribal economic development to restore the environmental and ecological conflicts resulting due to colonial exploitation of resources in industrialization policy in centralized planning process resulting in vicious circle and core-periphery situation in tribal resource regions.

Identification of Community and Regional Development Priorities

It is now being recognized that much of the tribal economic problems have resulted due to the anthropogenic impacts leading to environmental and ecological conflicts in the tribal areas. The planning process as yet has not properly been initiated in tribal areas and the development programmes have failed to identify the priorities of community and regional development in which community development programmes do not lead to sectoral integration in terms of occupational and social mobility of tribes in vertically organizing regional sectoral development. On the other hand, the infrastructural and economic sectoral development strategies do not recognize the community and regional development priorities in terms of the geographically determined functional zones in landscape framework.

The community development programmes are narrowly related to the community level services and utilities such as road connectivity, health, education, communication and drinking water and electrification, etc. They ignore the infrastructural services such as irrigation and water conservation, which could regenerate ecological-economic development through conservation of land, forest, animal resources.

The regional economic development though is taking place through forestry and mining, access to the tribes is constrained due to the lack of social development for vertical integration. The lack of development of environment and economic forestry, horticulture and animal husbandry in tribal regions has confined the tribes in the subsistent agriculture in the tribal regions and forcing them to migrate to other regions for livelihood security.

It is generally found that education and irrigation are identified as most important priorities for development in the tribal regions.

Conclusion

The problems of tribal economies have resulted due to the unbalanced growth strategy in centralized planning system through mining and forestry. It has resulted in cumulative causation of environmental and ecological degradation and vicious circle of socio-economic conflicts. Due to the centralized controlled of forests, the tribes in majority have been forced to depend upon subsistent agriculture without proper infrastructure facility and environmental risks and uncertainties. The high level of poverty and economic constraints has restricted the social development of the community and vertical mobility of the tribes to non-farm modern economy and service activities.

It in necessary to strengthen the resource base through conservation and development programmes in different activity zones including water conservation and development, agricultural development, animal husbandry and milk processing, horticulture and forestry programmes. This will ensure faster employment and income generation in the rural sector and generate higher level of production and productivity at the primary production levels. The increased production surpluses would provide material basis for secondary and tertiary level growth and the income generation would lead to social mobility through education and employment generation as vertical integration and labour mobility in secondary and tertiary activity. Since the rural products are vertically integrating to the urban industrial and trade markets, the planning should focus on regenerative grass-roots level planning for increasing resource and economic base for meeting the increasing demands of the primary products through community participation in different specialized activity zones to develop specialized regional production cycle and production complexes.

References

Conkling, Edgar C. and Maurice Yates (1976): *Man's Economic Environment,* New York: Mcgraw-Hill Book Company.

Geddes, Sir P. (1949): *Cities in Evolution,* London: Williams and Norgate.

Mishra, R.P., K.V. Sundrum and V.L.S. Prakasha Rao (1976): *Regional Planning in India,* Delhi: Vikas Publishing House (P) Ltd.

Mishra, S.K. and S.B. Gaikwad (1979): "Impact of Economic Development on Welfare and Living Condition of People of MP", *Indian Journal of Regional Science,* Vol. XI, No. 1.

Modak, S.K. and V.N. Patkar (1983): "Priority-Setting in Planning Rural Development Programmes", *Indian Journal of Regional Science,* Vol. XV, No. 2.

Sen, Amartya (2003): *Commodities and Capabilities,* New Delhi: Oxford University Press.

Singh, R.D. (2000): "Community Based Information System for Urban and Regional Planning", in proceeding of annual conference at Calcutta.

—. (2004): "Pattern Diversities in Community Development in Tribal Regions: A Case Study of Madhya Pradesh, India", *Journal of Social Anthropology,* New Delhi: Serials Publications, Vol. 1, No. 2, December.

—. (2007): "Agricultural Development and Regional Carrying Capacity Measurement of Agro-ecosystem in Jhabua Tribal District in Madhya Pradesh", *Indian Journal of Development Research and Social Action,* 3(1), pp. 85–92.

11

Hinduization of Tribes and Development

J.J. ROY BURMAN

The term 'tribal economy' in the context of India is a misnomer. Majority of the anthropologists in the country almost invariably consider tribals to be forest dwellers who thrive on forest produce, leading a subsistence economy. This is not very surprising considering the fact that the emergence of anthropology has a colonial legacy and tribes by and large are considered to be primitives who need to be civilized. But the matter of fact is that tribes in India are extremely diverse. While there are the hunting, gathering and fishing tribes like Onge and Jarwas of Andamans on the one the side, there are the extremely westernized and educated Mizos of Mizoram on the other hand. Mizoram has almost 50 per cent urban population and majority of them are employed in the tertiary sector. The Minas of Rajasthan are similarly quite educated and dominant, with many of them occupying very senior ranks in the civil services. It is a vertibale fact that in the central tribal belts of the country there has been large-scale denudation of the forests and tribals in large number have been forced to eke out their living as labourers either in the mines and industries which have sprouted in their domains or in the adjoining urban areas and sugarcane and cotton growing regions. Seasonal migration in these areas is a common phenomenon.

Aerthayil (2008) provides a very clear picture of the present tribal economy, particularly in the context of Kerala through a study conducted in three tribal inhabited districts of the state. Almost three-fifth of the respondents are coolies and a good proportion is small farmers (16%). On the other hand, the proportion reported to be unemployed is also sizeable (15%). The proportion of respondents in the other occupational categories is negligible. However, a small proportion is either semi-government or government employees. Normally the tribal groups are supposed to gather forest products besides their routine work, but the study shows that only a negligible proportion of them is engaged in such work (1%). Unlike in olden times, today forest is no longer a source of livelihood for tribals in India, particularly Kerala. The study also shows how land, which was the main source of livelihood for the tribals in Kerala, was lost to them and how it ceased to be a means of livelihood. When the tribals lost their land, the next means available for them was wage labour in farmlands – mostly of non-tribals and even of upper caste people. They worked in plantations of cash crops and paddy fields as coolie workers. There is a huge flock of migrant adivasi labourers working in the tea gardens of North Bengal, Assam and Tripura.

Christianity is considered to be one of the main agents of social change in the tribal areas on central India, eastern India and the north-east. No doubt, Christianity has been mainly responsible for introducing western education and western medicine, however, it has barely led to any economic revolution among the tribals. The tribals in these areas still by and large lead a poor standard of living. Shifting cultivation yet prevails widely in many of the tribal regions. No zamindari or capitalist class to be seen among the Christian tribals or any other tribal for that matter anywhere in the country.

In the recent years the proselytization of tribes into Christianity has been hotly debated. Not only has it attracted the attention of Indian mass media, it has also initiated the process of legislation in some states. But what has been relatively unnoticed is another kind of proselytization, equally real and concrete, that is the conversion of faiths of tribal masses by Hindu proselytizers. This process is being justified by the statement that it is not a part of conversion but a matter of 'Ghar Vapsi' – home coming. A matter of concern is that it is leading to religious bigotry and violence in the form of attacks on the minority tribal society.

According to Xaxa (2009) the tribes in India were viewed in opposition to civilization or out of the pail of caste system. Since the British time and after, the tribes are being viewed as being brought within the fold of civilization through the process of assimilation. Kosambi has referred to tribal elements being fused into the general society. N.K. Bose mentioned about the tribes being gradually absorbed into the Hindu society, "A large number of anthropological work in the post-independence era still points to the phenomena such as tribes being absorbed or assimilated into the Hindu society or tribes becoming castes". The process has not been uniform and different tribes are located at different stages of assimilation. The processes of acculturation, assimilation or absorption are variously termed as Sanskritization or Hinduization.

One school of thought tried to project that prior to British colonization, tribes and castes cohabited peacefully without any friction. Bose was more in favour of this portrayal. According to him, the process of tribal absorption is based on the system of the organization on production based on caste. The system is based on mutual reciprocity, hence its characteristic feature has been cooperation and not conflict. Under the caste system, production activities of the various castes were protected against competition from the other castes. It is this that the tribes found attractive in the system, although it entailed low status for them within the caste hierarchy. According to Surjit Sinha, it is the system of state formation that resulted in the socio-political framework of the tribal system into the regional caste system. Xaxa argues that the matter of tribal transformation into the larger society is due to politico-economic factors.

The politico-economic factors relate to a slow, gradual and spontaneous process which ultimately refers to the process of Sanskritization. It is a process whereby a group lower down the hierarchy tries to adopt the lifestyle of the group above its hierarchy. In the context of tribes, the term has been used to understand the process of acculturation to the value and customs of the dominant society. In this process outside intermediaries is not present. But Xaxa argues that quite frequently the state and the dominant castes did adopt aggressive postures and coercion when dealing with lower castes or tribes. Tagore through his eloquent poetry narrated the poigant tale of a girl – the cruelty meted out to her by the Hindu king on embracing Buddhism.

Xaxa points out the important difference between the process of Sanskritization and proselytization to Christianity. The Christian missionaries did not convert the tribes in mass, rather a few individuals embraced the new religion and retained many of their traditional cultural elements. The common thing in such conversion was the desire to keep and maintain social bonds of a group or families. The more common method adopted by the missionaries was developmental and social oriented works. These comprised mainly, to begin with, education, health and medicine, legal laid, agricultural-credit, etc. In the recent years they have diversified to other fields as well. These range from agricultural development and harnessing of water resources to increasing articulation of the issues of the tribal people's aspiration such as autonomy, as well as those that have been drastically affecting their life, such as displacement and rehabilitation.

Xaxa argues that the new converts were willing to pay the price and withstand the ostracism and punishment meted out by the tribes following the traditional faith. They were also debarred from food, shelter and inheritance of property. The converts weighed all these while embracing the new religion.

According to Xaxa, conversion to Hinduism is more of a process than an event. It is slow, gradual and staggered over many years. It almost takes the forms of a natural process. Conversion to Christianity has never been all encompassing. Rather than entailing transformation in all dimensions of social life, as has been the case with Hinduism, the transformation is expected only in a selected or limited aspect of total social lives that were considered religious in nature or had religious overtones. Hence, while there were changes with respect to one or more of the social aspects, there were other aspects, both structural and cultural, that were common between the converts and the non-converts. The converts, for example, continued with their language, food habits, rules, customs, traditions, etc. that were integral part of the social organization of tribal society. The surrender of the old was thus never total. It is commonly to be seen among the Nagas and Mizos that they have retained the system of clan exogamy even after conversion of Christianity. The transformation thus did not lead to a total breaking away from their erstwhile and traditional community. Neither did it lead to an absorption or assimilation into an alien society. In the case of Hinduization, however, a tribe has to give up many of its old habits like drinking and consumption of beef. However, it is noticed that while the Jesuit priests promote westernized lifestyle to the students in their schools, the Vanbasi Kalyan Ashram tries to maintain the local ambience.

Majumdar (1972) observed that the Rabhas in Meghalaya adopted Hindu gods and goddesses like Kali, Durga and Saraswati after the Hinduization process set in. They also started using Brahmin priests during worships. The Rabhas also abandoned their clan organization, matrilineal inheritance, uxolilocal residence, clan-oriented kinship system and rather vowed for patrilineage. They also abandoned their traditional system of birth, death and marriage customs.

Mukherjee (1994) noticed that due to Kshatrization the Rajbansis of North Bengal have started emulating Vedic rites and donning sacred thread. Bhadra (2004) states that Kshatrization process has affected the status of Rajbansi women a lot. The old system of bride price has been given up and so has been companionate marriage, connubial union, divorce and remarriage, widow marriage, levirate, polygamy, etc. Women have become more confined domestically and their freedom has been curtailed and their status has been lowered in the society.

Xaxa states that though there is enough give and take between Hinduism and tribal religion, it is not an adequate ground for calling the tribes as Hindus. No doubt that the tribes worship many natural objects as the Hindus. As a natural religion, tribal religion shares practices of tribes in America or Africa with Hinduism in India. Yet it is doubtful if the religious practices of tribes in America and Africa can be described as Hinduism and the tribes as Hindu.

Sundar (2009) states that the Christian missionaries had to withstand lot of hardships. They often fought court cases on behalf of the tribes while the British support the unjust acts of the Hindu rulers. Independence and a Constitutional right to propagate proved more congenial to Christian missionary activity than colonial rule.

Sundar assails that though the Hindutva forces like Vanvasi Kalyan Ashram (VKA) blames the Christian missionaries as changing cultures of the tribes, it itself rarely promotes the local culture and it rather stresses on Vedic culture and Hindi and Sanskrit are glorified. However, if they see Christian competition in the use of local adivasi languages, the VKA is not averse to using them either.

Although the Kalyan Ashram publicly claim that one-third to half its workforce is 'Vanvasi' and the ceremonial positions like that of the president and vice-president are filled by tribals, the organizational positions who hold real control are in the hands of non-tribals, upper caste RSS men. As of 2001, the VKA had 842 male and 210 female full timers, out of which approximately half were Vanvasis.

In a recent visit to tribal areas of Thane district in Maharashtra it came to light that the Ekal Vidyalaya scheme launched by the Hindutva forces is giving emphasis on literacy programme for the children belonging to the age group of 6–14 years, along with vocational training and rural development. For this they are taking the village elites into confidence and a committee is formed in every village to supervise the different programmes. It is the village committee which appoints a teacher. The teacher is paid a low amount and allowed to hold classes for the children at his/her home only. The teacher is usually slightly better off who owns a big house where a good number of children can be accommodated. The timing of the school is usually in the evenings so that children can come after dinner. This also helps those children who work as shepherds during the day or those children who take care of the infant brothers and sisters during the day time when their parents away working in the fields. The Ekal Vidyalaya management has evolved a close monitoring system over the schools at various tiers. It operates the entire system through very little external funding. It of course, receives good amount of donations through Non-Resident Indians. Schemes have also been thrown open to adopt the students through funding by individual donors. It also receives financial support from US-based NRIs through India Development Relief Fund (IDRF) and the UK-based Hindu Swayamsevak Sangh. The districts where the work has been initiated are expected to attain self-sufficiency within five years. Unlike the Christian missionaries, the Ekal Vidyalaya scheme is backed up by political parties like BJP and Vishwa Hindu Parishad. Till September 2008, Ekal programme has reached to some 27,000 village all over the country. More than 8,00,000 children have been taking advantage of the education programme alone.

A short visit to the Ekal schools in Thane district revealed that several children have been able to take advantage of the scheme. Many children have been able to improve upon their reading and learning skills. But it is disconcerting to note that religious orthodoxy has been transmitted into them and many non-tribal elements have been forced upon them. Instead of learning to greet through their traditional tribal way, the children have been taught to say 'Jay Shree Ram'. The legends about the heroes they are taught to learn are not the tribal people but figures like Shivaji. The children are taught to identify themselves are as 'Vanvasi' – 'forest dweller' and not the common notion of adivasi or indigenous people as they did identify earlier. The forest dweller identity is a pejorative remark which many of the tribes did not appreciate privately. Besides, the notion of Vanvasi opposes the concept of adivasi – indigenous people, which many of the tribals assert. The notion of Vanvasi also denies the land rights to the tribals by claiming to be the indigenous peoples.

Friends of Tribal Society, another Hinduization agency in the tribal areas is now promoting organic farming and watershed development in many of the tribal regions including Thane district. These are no doubt indispensable in the context of present environmental crisis and developmental needs. But are they the priorities for the poor tribals? Organic farming can be taken up only by those who own a large number of cattle. Artificial watershed development also can be adopted mainly by those who own fairly large area of arable land.

The elite bias of the Hindutva forces has been noted by Froer (2007) in her study of the adivasis of Korba area of Chhattisgarh state. She has of course also noted the local RSS leadership helping out the tribals in regularizing the 'encroached' agricultural lands in the forests areas. Froer is of the view that the Hindutva forces are supporting the 'Swadeshi' – nationalistic agenda so as to counter the intrusion of multinationals as well. In any case the Hindutva forces are backed up by the business class. In the Madhya Pradesh, Sunderlal Patwa, the erstwhile BJP Chief Minister of Madhya Pradesh was the biggest tendu leaf (Bidi leaf) contractor. It should not be missed out that tribal areas in the country are the largest repositors of natural resources and are also the centre of attraction for the neo-liberal forces. The prospects of tribal economy can be accordingly gauged. Marginalization of the tribals in these regions is extremely glaring. In the case of Arunachal Pradesh the percentage of tribal population is rapidly receding. The large number of hydroelectric dams planned for the state will surely be catastrophic for the indigenous people. Already the Subansiri dam project has witnessed the intrusion of more than one lakh outsiders. About 43 dams are in the pipeline for the north-east region. The Hindutva forces in Arunachal Pradesh could not stem the rapid conversion to Christianity in the state. Nor could it tide over the massive ethnic disturbance in Changlang and Tirap districts which have been proclaimed as 'Disturbed Area' by the state administration and no inner line permit is issued to outsiders.

The anthropologists in India need to evolve methods based on political-economy and not remained moored to inane culturological studies causing immense damage to the tribal people. The impact of the cults of Rajmohini Devi and Gahira Guru on the tribals of Chhattisgarh and adjoining areas did not result into national integration at the micro-level, as was suggested by Ajit Danda, former Director of Anthropological Survey of pronouncement of a *Statesman* newspaper reporter that the inauguration of Ram Mandir at Barbil (A mining town of Mayurbhanj district of Orissa) marked the consolidation of monetary forces in a semi-monetized tribal area is a much realistic projection. Forces behind Rajmohini Devi and Gahira Guru were inevitably backed up by the tendu leaf contractors and the big business lobby. Danda (1990) makes no mention of them in his book *Tribal Economy in India.*

Hinduization per se has not brought about any perceptible material gain to the tribal masses. But the introduction of 'desi' education in the western fashion or popularizing western medicine to do away with the evils of superstitions are certainly impacting upon the traditional tribal power structure, particularly at the micro-level. This is leading towards elite cooption and has disabling effect on any form of resistance against intrusion of the neo-liberal forces and economy. Rather NRIs sponsoring many of the Hindutva projects are on the prowl looking for marketing possibilities of the local commodities in the international markets. The union territory of Dadra, Nagar-Haveli, principally a tribal territory has been turned into a safe heaven for industrialization with massive tax exemptions.

Kshatrization of the Rajbansis in North Bengal in no way did help from staving off the British colonizers from declaring large tracts of their lands as reserved forest, protected forest and wildlife sanctuary. Huge territories of theirs were lost to the British tea planters and MNCs. It is to be seen whether the present Kamtapur movement of the Rajbansis supported by the BJP can usher in any material gain to the indigenous peoples. Formation of Jharkhand and Chhattisgarh states has mainly witnessed the consolidation of the BJP power and political control of the non-tribals and tribal elites playing the second fiddle. The BJP government that came to power immediately after the

Jharkhand state formation cleared all pending mining applications put up by multi-national companies withheld by the erstwhile Bihar state legislature. If research on the dynamics of this nature in the tribal regions does not pertain to the sphere of tribal economy, what really does?

References

Aerthayil, M. (2008): *Impact of Globalization on Tribals: In the Context of Kerala*, Bangalore: Indian Social Institute.

Bhadra, M. (2004): "Status of Scheduled Caste Women: A Case Study of the Rajbansis of West Bengal", in *Man in India,* Vol. 84, Nos. 3–4, pp. 285–301.

Danda, A.K. (1990): *Tribal Economy in India,* New Delhi: Inter-India.

Froer, P. (2007): *Religious Division and Social Conflict: The Emergence of Hindu Nationalism in Rural India*, New Delhi: Social Science Press.

Majumdar, D.N. (1972): "A Study of Tribe-Caste Continuation and the Process of Sanskritization among the Bodo Speaking Tribes of the Garo Hills", in K.S. Singh (ed.), *Tribal Situation in India*, Simla: IIAS.

Mukherjee, S. (1994): Khasatrization among the Rajbansis of North Bengal, (Mimeo).

Sundar, N. (2009): "Adivasi vs Vanvasi: The Politics of Conversion in Central India", in D. Kumar and Y. Sunny (eds.), *Proselytization in India: The Process of Hinduization in Tribal Societies*, New Delhi: Aakar.

Xaxa, V. (2009): "Tribes, Conversion and the Sangh Parivar" in D. Kumar and Y. Sunny (eds.), *Proselytization in India: The Process of Hinduization in Tribal Societies*, New Delhi: Aakar.

12

Forest Management vis-à-vis Tribal Economy

Livelihoods Generations for the Reduction of Poverty of the Tribals in Madhya Pradesh

DEBASHIS DEBNATH

India is famous for its natural resources being one of the 12 mega-diversity countries in the world. The Indian civilization is a primary civilization, known as Indus civilization, which has been described by Rabindranath Tagore as *Tapavan* civilization, meaning the very civilization grew in forest, was developed by its indigenous people. India's forest dwelling people are known as *Vanabasi* or *Vanyajati* as well as 'the Scheduled Tribe' (a constitutional category) as their association with the forest from time immemorial. They are enumerated as 48 million living either within or in the vicinity of forest (NCHSE, 1987), which constitute 60–70 per cent of Indian tribals. Out of 445 districts of the country having some land covered under forests, 145 are tribal districts. They still eke out their existence on the traditional livelihoods, viz., hunting-gathering, pastoral nomadism, shifting-hill cultivation and forest artisan, etc., of the total 596 Scheduled Tribes, 75 tribal communities have been identified as primitive tribal groups (PTGs) on the basis of the economic and developmental criteria.

Tribal economy is the survival strategy borne out of the reciprocative interactions with the surrounding ecology and environment. So, the economy is the natural resource-based, be it land, forest or water. Hence, their economic pursuits are hunting, pastoral nomadism, shifting-hill cultivation, artisan and peasantry. Their resources are common property resources, whose ownership is lying with the community based on community institutions with use-rights lying with individuals. Thus, their natural resources are managed by community institution, based on the norms, social rules and belief systems. In the forest economy they are found in collection of non-timber forest products including medicinal herbs, non-traditional timber, fuelwood, fodder and bamboo for their self-consumption and selling the excess in the local market at nominal prices. In the changing sphere they have come in contact with the modern education and technology, which has led them various occupational patterns to adopt like services and business. Being a constitutional category, they are found in the large numbers in government services and also in private services. They can also be seen in small business like petty shops, agricultural and forest products, and crafts, etc.

Tribals and their Economy in Madhya Pradesh

Madhya Pradesh is the second largest state of Indian union and is known as 'tiger' and 'tiger' state. It is situated in the central part of the country and is bestowed with the huge area of dry deciduous forest having huge biodiversity in natural forest. The state has 95,222 sq km of forest land, which covers 31 per cent of the total geographical area of the state. The total human population has been estimated at 60.38 million, who are living in 59,000 villages, out of which 20,000 are forest fringe villages. Madhya Pradesh having 76,429 sq km of forest cover has the maximum forest cover amongst all states/UTs, followed by Andhra Pradesh (68,019 sq km) and Chhattisgarh (55,998 sq km). The forest of the state comprises roughly about 30 per cent of Sal, 30 per cent of teak and about 40 per cent of mixed forest.

Madhya Pradesh has the largest tribal population in India, i.e., 122.33 lakh (20.27 per cent), of the total population of 603.85 lakh as per 2001 census comprising 46 Scheduled Tribes, which is much higher than the national average (8.2%). Total population of the tribals in scheduled area is 66.78 lakh. The growth of ST population during

1991–2001 has been 26.4 per cent, which is 2.1 per cent higher than national average.

The tribal groups are distributed in different cultural zones:

1. Western Cultural Zone which covers the districts of Ratlam, Jhabua, Dhar, Barwani, Khargone, Khandwa, Dewas and Indore, which are inhabited by the Bhil stock like Bhil, Bhilala, Barela, Patelia.
2. Central Cultural Zone which covers the districts of Mandla, Dindori, Balagahat, Seoni, Chhindwara, Jabalpur, Katni, Narshimpur Sagar, Damoh, Umaria, Sehore and Bhopal, which are inhabited by the Gond, Pardhan, Korku, Baiga, Bharia, Nagarchi and Ojha.
3. North-Eastern Cultural Zone covers the districts of Shadol, Sidhi, Rewa, Stana, Panna, Chhtarpur, Guna and Tikamgarh, which are inhabited by the Kol, Biar, Panika, Sour and Pav.
4. North-Western Cultural Zone covers the districts of Morena, Shivpuri, Sheopur, Datia, Gwalior and Bhind, which are inhabited by Saharia.

The highest proportion of tribal population is found in Jhabua district (86.6%), followed by Barwani (67%), Dindori (64.5%) and Mandla (57.2%). Bhind district preceded by Morena and Datia has the lowest proportion of STs (0.5%). Among the tribal population most of them are dependent on forest, so 80 per cent of the forest dwellers come under below poverty line.

Table 1

Tribal Population: Size and Distribution

Tribes	*Percentage of Total Tribal Population*
Bhil	37.7
Gond	35.6
Kol, Korku, Sahariya and Baiga	18.9
Pardhan, Saur, Bharia and Bhumia	3.2
Majhi, Khirar, Mawasi and Panika	2.2
Remaining thirty-three	2.5
Total	100

In discussing the tribal economy of Madhya Pradesh, six tribal ethnic groups have been selected as the representative samples. Of them, Bhil and Gonds are the agrarian communities. The Kol and Korku are dependent equally on agriculture and forest collections. The Sahariya and the Baigas are the 'primitive tribal group' in the category of tribal development in the Tribal sub-plan. Hence they have the pre-agrarian economy or maximum dependency on forest resources. The following table shows the percentage distribution of workers of these six tribal communities:

Table 2

Percentage Distribution of Workers in Four Economic Categories

Economic Category	*All STs*	*Bhil*	*Gond*	*Kol*	*Korku*	*Sahariya*	*Baiga*
Cultivators	46.8	60.7	46.8	12.0	38.8	28.2	32.6
Agricultural Labourers	42.1	31.4	42.5	70.4	54.5	56.9	54.7
Household Industries Workers	1.1	0.3	1, 4	1.0	1.5	0.9	1.8
Other Workers	10.0	7.6	9.3	16.6	5.2	14.0	10.9

The above table shows that tribals of Madhya Pradesh in total are dependent on both cultivation (46.8%) and agricultural labouring (42.1%) due to their poor landholding capacity. The Bhil as an agrarian community has the agricultural livelihoods (60.7%) and has also the economic pursuits like agricultural labouring (31.4%) and business and services (10%). The Gond being the largest tribal group of the state distributed in the largest parts of the state having the 56 sub-groups is an agrarian community. They are cultivators (46.8%) of various categories and also dependent on agricultural labouring (42.5%) in almost equal proportion. The Kol and Korku are dependent on both the agricultural and forest lands. Due to their poor landholding capacity they eke out their existence on agricultural labouring. The Sahariyas and the Baigas survive on collection of forest products and selling the raw materials at very nominal rates in the local *haat* (weekly market). These poor tribal groups have less skills in agricultural operations and highly dependent on daily wage. Twenty to thirty per cent of their earning comes from forest collection. The four tribals - Kol,

Korku, Sahariya and Baiga – are highly dependent on agricultural and non-agricultural labouring.

Tribal-Forest Interfaces

Due to intense pressure coupled with emphasis on industrialization during the past two decades, about 41 per cent of the forest covers of the country have already been degraded and dense forests are losing their crown density and productivity continuously. A large number of India's livestock population grazes in forests, causing serious damage to forest regeneration and productivity. The use of forests beyond carrying capacity and encroachments are the main causes behind the continuing degradation of forests (MoEF, 1999). At present 70 per cent forests have deficient natural regeneration and 55 per cent are prone to fire. By 1980, nearly 4.5 million ha of forests had been diverted for agriculture and other use. However, with the enactment of the Forest Conservation Act, 1980, this process of conversion of forest land for non-forestry purposes has been considerably halted. Per capita forest area in India is 0.064 ha, which is one-tenth of the world average of 0.64 ha. The growing stock in Indian forests is 4,740 million cubic metres with productivity of 0.7 cubic metre per hectare per year against and world average of 2.1 cubic metre per hectare per year. Seventy-eight per cent of the forest area is subjected to heavy grazing, adversely affecting productivity and regeneration. On an average, 51 per cent of the forest area suffers from occasional forest fire. Nearly 10 million ha of forest area is subjected to shifting cultivation. The availability of forest biomass per capita is only 6 tonnes in India against an average of 82 tonnes in other developing countries. Land use changes has taken place at such a rapid rate that area under agriculture which was 118 million ha in 1950 now extends at 142 million ha. The diversion of forest land has consequently removed buffer community areas adjoining forest/grassland (Mukherjee, 2004). Such figures showed that the conventional forestry imposed by British Raj as a result of the demands of the railway companies, which began expanding the railway network in the 1850s, made an adverse impact on biodiversity, natural regeneration, etc. In a nutshell, we can say that the basic causes for degradation of forests are: (i) Over-exploitation or over-extraction, (ii) Over-grazing, (iii) Illicit felling; (iv) Conversion of forest land into agricultural land or others (vi) Forest fire, (vii) Poor management of forest resources, (viii)

Encroachments in forest lands or village commons and (ix) Alienation of people from state management region.

II

Forest Management

Community Forest Management

Community forest management (CFM) refers to community-based activities which are geared towards the sustainable use of forest. The term 'community-based' distinguishes the emerging approaches from an earlier concept of community natural resource management, which refers to communities having full and generally autonomous responsibility for the protection and use of natural resources. CFM is described as a system where a community has "developed institutions, norms, rules, fines and fees to sustain forest resources. CFM characteristically involve one or more communities (social group, village) protecting and using specific forest area" (IUCN, 1996). CFM programme initiative develops and transfers technical, methodological, analytical, social and institutional and policy innovations for more productive, equitable and sustainable forest resource use. CFM particularly targets communities in ecosystems facing environmental stress and degradation. While policies and research have typically discounted the role of local people in designing and implementing solutions for these problems, CFM proposes an alternative approach. The initiative works with those local men and women most directly involved with natural resource management. This often includes the poorest of the rural poor and ethnic minorities, both of which are politically, economically and/or geographically isolated. The programme initiative aims to assist women and men living in ecosystems that face increasing resource exploitation, to manage and use their natural resources sustainably. This is done with recognition that men, women, ethnic groups, and different social classes use natural resources in diverse ways and for distinct purposes. Community forest management involves the governance and management of forest resources by communities for commercial and non-commercial purposes, including subsistence, timber production, non-timber forest products, wildlife, conservation of biodiversity and environment, social and religious significance. It also incorporates the practices, art, science, policies, institutions and processes necessary to promote and support all aspects of community-based forest management.

Sarin (1996) has categorized the community forest management into three types:

1. This emerged out of local initiatives, primarily as a response to the hardships arising from scarcity of forest products.
2. This promoted by the state forest department in collaboration with local communities.
3. Local governance originally sponsored by local government or local civil societies.

Different management systems can be depicted at different points on a continuum, from total state control to total community control in the following manner:

Figure 1

The State/Community Spectrum of Control

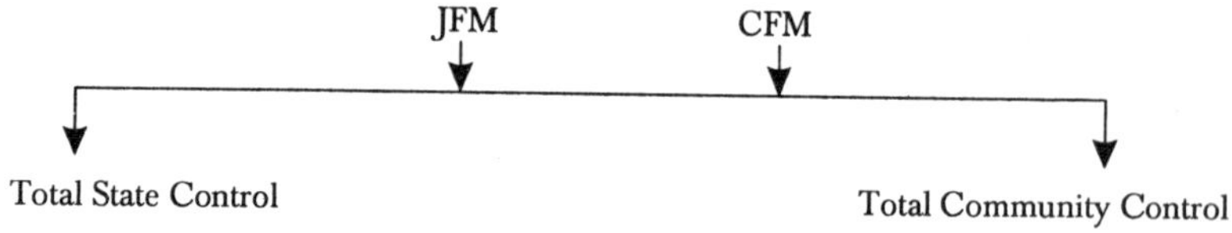

In the present trend forest management system refers to a system comprising the following element:

- A decision-making body and procedures;
- A management plan for the establishment, development, care and reproduction of the forest and its principal species and products;
- A set of rules regarding a set of accepted rules or norms to achieve the goals, viz., efficiency, stability, resilience and equitability;
- A protection system to enforce the rules.

III

Livelihoods Interventions

The term 'livelihoods' connotes the activities, entitlements and assets by which people make a living. Assets in this particular context are defined as not only natural/biological (land, water, common property resource, flora and fauna) but also social (i.e., community, family, social networks), economic (i.e., job, savings, credit), political (i.e., participation, empowerment), human (i.e., education, labour, health, nutrition) and physical (i.e., roads, markets, clinics, schools, bridges). Livelihood interventions are conscious efforts by an agency or an organization to promote and support livelihood opportunities for a large number of people (other than those directly or indirectly employed by them) (Dutta et al., 2004).

In the year 1997 the UK government published the white paper for international development, in which they emphasized 'sustainable livelihoods', which comprises the poverty reduction strategies, quality education, health development and betterment of the surrounding natural environment (DFID, 1999). In this respect the definition enunciated by Chambers and Conway (1992) as "a livelihood is sustainable, which can cope with and recover from stress and shocks, maintain or enhance its capabilities and assets, and provide sustainable livelihood opportunities for the next generation". Sustainable livelihoods began as an approach to maintain or enhance natural resources productivity, secure ownership of and access to assets and income earning activities as well as to ensure adequate stocks and flows of foods and cash to meet basic need (Kaushal and Kala, 2004). Livelihood approaches incorporate assets, strategies and well-being, viewed in the context of risk and individual vulnerability as well as in the context of policies, institutions and processes, which have been bearing on how these assets are converted into flows consistent with livelihood strategies. However, livelihoods framework typically do not lend themselves to analysis of intangible assets such as capability, power, influence and social capital. Later with the effort of United Nations Development Programmes (UNDP), this approach has been clarified to promote a holistic vision of development that includes income generation, natural resources management, people's empowerment, use of appropriate technology, financial services and good governance. Thus SL brings together the thinking and practice of poverty reduction strategies, sustainable development, participation and empowerment.

In the indigenous lands of our country the tribal peoples survive on the collection of the forest produces from inside the forests for their self-consumption and the excess they sell in the local market at nominal rates for their earnings. As these people eke out their existence on the marginal lands and their limited income sources from the nearby forests they remain poor from the hoary past. Looking into the poverty of the tribal communities in India a number of measures have adopted in the planned development programmes in the rural and tribal settings. The impact of livelihoods interventions has been much sound since the implication of the pro-tribal National Forest Policy 1988 through our Joint Forest Management resolution of the 1st June, 1990.

Joint forest management (JFM) is a collaborative management regime, initiated by the Ministry of Environment and Forests, Government of India in the 1990s building a partnership with the local communities for rehabilitation of the degraded forests, with emphasis on protection, management and development of the forest resources by the tribal communities and the women, following guidelines of the National Forest Policy 1988. Later 28 states of Indian union declared the policies and formed 90,000 JFM committees, who took responsibilities for the protection of the state forest lands of nearly 20 million hectares till now. Thus, there was a paradigm shift from centralized, controlled and custodial forest management to democratic, devolving, participatory community-based natural resource management, resulting in orientation from revenue generation to resource development, single benefit to multiple benefits, mono-culture to multiple cropping and above all unilateral decision-making to participatory process.

Poverty reduction and sustainable livelihoods are the two important issues in JFM. The poverty reduction means to achieve the sustainable livelihood which is required to develop continuous employment and income generations, innovation for new economic choices, capacity building for livelihood goals and strategies. This has been followed by implementation with an outcome of equitable benefits sharing and personal and community empowerment.

In the joint forest management, community mobilization for involvement in protection and forestry activities is an essential attempt. The first step was taken in motivating the people for enhancement of the resource stock through decision-making process. The next step is to achieve livelihood goals which comprise the economic and non-economic factors. In this step both formal and informal institutions have significant roles. This step is followed by the livelihood strategies which are formulated on the basis of micro-plan, assessment of community assets, micro-finance, infra-structural development and capacity building. The project is then implemented on the basis of strategies, which provide the benefits to be shared on the equitable basis. This leads to personal and community empowerment which have direct impact on community mobilization and institutional process. In a nutshell, JFM envisages:

- community participation to protect, develop and conserve forest;
- full usufrutory rights to sustain their livelihoods;
- decentralized mechanism in decision-making process;
- a share of the final harvest to the communities to promote and sustain their long-term vision for forest management; and
- develop a sense of belongingness through attitudinal changes.

Livelihoods Generations in JFM and CFM in Madhya Pradesh

As discussed before, the tribal economy in Madhya Pradesh is directly linked with the forest product particularly, the non-timber forest products (NTFP). Increase in human and cattle population coupled with poverty since 1958 had led rapid deterioration of forest in the state. As a consequence, the per capita forest area shrunk from 0.66 ha in 1958 to 0.23 ha in 2001.

Under this socio-economic condition and the burden of rural poor on the natural resources and in pursuance of Government of India resolution, the forest department of Madhya Pradesh passed the JFM resolution of the state in 1991 giving an importance of people's involvement in protection, management and development of forest. The amended resolution in 1995 was passed to give more opportunity to the women and weaker sections along with NGOs involvement. The 1995 resolution had been further revised in 2000 and 2001. A bigger project sponsored by World Bank was also implemented in two phases in the state. The project was designed to benefit tribal and other people living at the forest fringe and particularly those people, who are most dependent (Bhattacharya and Basnyat, 2003).

Since the inception of World Bank aided Madhya Pradesh Forest Project, people's participation has been increased due to income generating activities and resource development work carried out in the villages, with subsequent betterment in the socio-economic condition of the people and poverty reduction (Dasgupta and Debnath, 2008). In the forest area the micro-watershed treatment for soil conservation and groundwater recharging as a part of assisted natural regeneration in the nearby forest areas under (FPC) and rehabilitation of degraded forest under Village Forest Committee (VFC) provided employment to the poor sections. Simultaneously, the plantations of NTFP yielding species, viz., neem (*Azadirachta indica*), mango (*Magnifera indica*), Aonla (*Emblica officinalis*), Mahua (*Magnifera indica*), etc., on the treatment sites. In total, 20,006 ha of forest was planted during this time. Thus employment generation, enhancement of crop productivity and various NTFPs yielding generate livelihoods (Debnath, 1991). Thus, the programme has benefited the landless and poorest through wage employee as shown in following table:

Table 3

Man-days Generated During MP Forestry Project

Year	*Employment (million man-days approx.)*	*Income (in million US$) approx.*
1995–96	2.73	2.17
1996–97	7.17	6.52
1997–98	8.65	8.84
1998–99	12.06	13.7
1999–2000	42.3	45.85

Source: Director, MP Forestry Project, Satpura Bhawan, Bhopal.

Forest Livelihoods

In the JFM programme in the state on attempt was made to achieve the sustainable forest management with the livelihood improvement in the decentralized process. Thus, the benefits were derived in the two major ways; forest endowments (i.e., rights to forest) and forest entitlement (i.e., economic benefits from forest). Thus forest in the state can play an important role as a source of income and a basis for the livelihoods of forest dependent people. The principle service and products from forest include non-timber forest products by collection, processing, marketing, watershed projects for the enhancement of agricultural livelihood and environmental services, i.e., ecotourism and other nature-based entertainmental programmes (Debnath, 2003, 2005a; Debnath and Dasgupta, 2006). The following table shows the types of livelihoods generated in the forest management programmes:

Table 4

Types of Livelihoods Generated from Forest Management

	Livelihooods Pattern		*Types of Livelihoods*
1.	Natural Resource Based	a.	Collection of NTFPs: collection of nationalized NTFPs
		b.	Processing of NTFPs, including medicinal and aromatic plants
		c.	Value addition on processed NTFPs, viz., pickles, morabba, plate making, bidi making
		d.	Marketing of NTFPs, including medicinal and aromatic plants
		e.	Cultivation of mushrooms and medicinal and aromatic plants
		f.	Collection and cultivation of fuel wood, fodder, fruits
		g.	Production of vermicompost and organic fertilizer
		h.	Preparation of bamboo 'thali' and bamboo works
		i.	Production of wood works: toys, wooden utensils, neck-ties, decorative works, wooden idols, human figures, basket-making
		j.	Fishery works
		k.	Piggery, duckery, goatery
		l.	Afforestation and plantation
		m.	Nursery
		n.	Agricultural and horticulture, specially vegetables
		o.	Seri-culture
		p.	Watershed related like contour trenches, stop-dam construction, rafter construction, check-dam construction, tank construction, levelling of land, nullah bandhan (stream living embankments), and percolation tank
		q.	Micro-enterprises, e.g., Dalia preparation, incense sticks, broom making, etc.
2.	Non-natural Resource Based	a.	Tailoring
		b.	Driving
		c.	Grinding flour
		d.	Watershed related
		e.	Infra-structure development, e.g., road construction, school building, livestock shed, etc.
		f.	Paper bag
		g.	Doll-making, mat-making.
3.	Environmental Services	a.	Ecotourism related

Forest Devolution and Equity

In the decentralized process local forest management institutions, viz., forest protection committee, village forest committees and eco-development committee were created to bring the marginalized and poor rural people into the decision-making process providing opportunities in further empowerment and skilled development. In the each Joint Forest Management (JFM) committee all the adult members having the power of casting votes are the members in the general body and the executive body in each JFMC is constituted by 11 members selected or nominated including women and landless labours. The involvement of women in decision-making process has always been emphasized with regard to equal membership right, representation, Participatory Rural Appraisal (PRA)-based planning. In many locations women were consulted at the outset on different issues and sufferings. In many divisions many women's self-help groups have been formed to provide more livelihoods especially on the non-natural resource-based occupations as alternative economic sources. The collaboration with NGOs also was brought into policy for promoting leadership at the local level.

Within these constraints, there have been some remarkable initiatives of individual Divisional Forest Officers (DFOs) in several divisions of enlisting the involvement of NGOs and even developing their district/division level networks to provide 'value added' services in the areas such as

- Training of forest staff and Village Forst Committee (VFC) members in JFM related activities.
- Training for other income generating activities.
- Communication for Village Forest Committee, Forest Protection Committee and Eco-Development Committee (VFC/FPC/EDC) extension and motivation.
- Communication to a wider audience about the transformation taking place through JFM.
- Marketing of forest products for income generating activity.

Since 1992, when the 73rd Amendment of India's Constitution empowered Panchayat Raj institutions (local self-government) to perform a role in the management of local natural resources (including forests) at the village level, Madhya Pradesh has been one of the leading states in the country in implementing the constitutional mandate. However, the linkages between the Panchayats and JFM committees strengthened only when the state resolution was amended in 2001. The new resolution states that the Gram Sabha or village assembly under the Panchayat Raj system also constitutes the general body of the JFM committee. This allows for a more explicit linkage between these two decentralization initiatives. The forest committees have formal links with the panchayats, where the Sarpanch (the leader of the local government) is an ex-officio member of the committee. In addition Memorandum of Understanding (MOU) is also signed by the panchayat as well as the committee and Forest Department. It is expected that linkage between forest committees and Gram Sabha takes place through one of the eight committees of the Gram Sabha, the estate committee, which is expected to act as a nodal committee for the JFM committee and will further develop as a result of the change in legal ownership and of NTFPs, due to enactment of The Provision of the Panchayats (Extension to the Scheduled Areas) Act, 1996. The introduction of Act means that net income from trade of minor forest produce (MFP) will be transferred to the primary societies, thus making the gatherers its owners.

Millennium Development Goals and Livelihoods Generations

Forest Development Agencies

In the new millennium keeping eyes on millennium development goals (MDG), the Ministry of Environment and Forests, Government of India commenced an umbrella scheme of National Afforestation Programme (NAP) in the financial year 2000–01 with convergence in flow of funds under various ongoing centrally sponsored afforestation schemes of this ministry from the Tenth Plan period. It is being implemented through a decentralized set-up at the field level for forest fringe villagers on the pattern of District Rural Development Agencies (DRDA) of Ministry of Rural Development to be called Forest Development Agency (FDA). The FDA is formed of 25–50 JFM villages and all households of the villages needing income generation will be targeted. In the case of FDA it has two-tier structure: at the village level and an apex body. At the village level joint forest management committees (JFMCs) cover all the forest fringe villages. The apex body of the FDA consists of an executive and a general body (MoEF, 2002). Some of the salient features of the FDAs are as follows:

1. Preponderance of the under-privileged committees (constitutionally known as 'Scheduled Castes' and 'Scheduled Tribes').
2. Willingness of people to participate in the conservation efforts.

3. Existence of forest protection committees/eco-development committees.
4. Extent of degraded forest lands.
5. Degree of dependence on biomass resources, etc.
6. Planning at the micro-level and through participatory rural appraisal (PRA) exercise

Under the National Afforestation Programme the plantations have been developed in the following manner in all the divisions:

Table 5

Plantations till 2008

1.	Teak plantations	1,59,602 Ha.
2.	Teak plantation through grant of 12th Finance Commission	5,358 Ha.
3.	Bamboo plantations	20,768 Ha.
4.	Mixed plantations	2,190 Ha.
5.	RDF-cum bamboo plantations	5,167 Ha.
6.	Rehabilitation of degraded forest plantations	13,179 Ha.
7.	Mohini Sagar catchments area treatment	29,724 Ha.
8.	Deposit work plantation (upto 2007)	221 Lac Plants
9.	New Harsood (Chhenra) plantation	73,850 Plants
10.	Maheshwar catchments area treatment	1,158 Ha.

Source: MP Forest Department (JFM/FDA cell).

In consequence, the employment generations took place from pit-digging, nursery works, mulching, manuring, weeding out for the marginalized and landless labours, specially those who are belonging to SCs and STs.

Forest Villages Development Project

For empowering tribals, the major approach in the Tenth Five-Year Plan was to 'resolve the unresolved issues' and 'solve the persisting problems' through continuous on-gong 3-pronged strategy of: (i) social empowerment, (ii) economic empowerment, and (iii) social injustice. Under the 'solving the persisting problems' development of forest villages is one of them. Development of 5,000 forest villages and the 2.5 lakh tribal families living therein continued to remain as one of the weakest links in the whole process of tribal development. Tenth Plan has, therefore, taken up the development of forest villages on priority basis and to ensure extending benefits/services just as provided in the case of revenue villages and reaching a comprehensive package with basic minimum services of food, safe drinking water, health care, primary education, approach roads and other infrastructural facilities. To make it successful, efforts are made towards the development of effective coordination to converge not only the existing services but also the staff and machinery of line departments. In this effort, State Forest Department has played a major role. In Madhya Pradesh there are 925 forest villages, where efforts have been made towards welfare and development of tribals, as over 95 per cent of the tribals living in these villages, with the special central assistance (SCA) by the forest development agencies for improving basic infrastructure facilities such as drinking water facilities, irrigation source development, school building, electricity, roads, alternative energy sources, etc. Under this project the basic issues of the tribal economy have been addressed through agricultural development by land-bunding, land-levelling, improving water-harvesting structures or irrigation sources. The capacity building or skill upgradation measures have also been adopted for income generation and sustainable employment.

Multilayered Irrigation Project under Swarnajaynati Gram Swarojgar Yojana (SGSY)

The Swarnajayanti Gram Swarojgar Yojana (SGSY) is a major poverty eradication plan undertaken by the Government of India to provide self-employment to the rural poor through small industries under implementation since 1 April, 1999. Under this scheme, a special project entitled "Sustainable Employment through Multilayered Irrigated Plantations" was sanctioned for the Madhya Pradesh government by the Government of India, Ministry of Rural Development government of Madhya Pradesh implemented this project on 29 November, 2001 with approved project budget of Rs 8.65 crore, out of which the central share is Rs 6.49 crore (75%) and the state contribution is Rs 2.16 crore (25%) under SGSY. But the total project expenditure was Rs 6.75 crore, which is 97.84 per cent of the total funds received, i.e., Rs 6.90 crore, from central government, state government and miscellaneous sources.

Under this project multilayered plantations of teak, aonla, bamboo, etc., were raised in the upper canopy with under planting of medicinal and aromatic plant species like Rosa grass, Lemon grass, Asagandha. The main objectives of the project were:

1. Sustainable employment to families living below poverty line.

2. Enhancing productivity of degraded forests.
3. Ensuring income to community as per GoMP resolution on JFM.
4. To provide basic infrastructural subsistence facilities for sustainable development.
5. To promote competence building and skill development among Swarozgaries.
6. Ecological amelioration.
7. To train and transfer technology of cultivation, collection, processing, value addition and marketing of medicinal plants and essential oil grasses.

The project was implemented by the MP State Forest Department in 82 villages of the following 10 districts:

1. Sidhi, 2. Chhindwara, 3. Sehore, 4. Guna, 5. Betul, 6. Seoni, 7. Narsinghpur, 8. Mandla, 9. Katni, and 10. Indore.

Under the project total numbers of SHG was formed in the project were 82, involving 893 beneficiaries. In the project the beneficiaries were selected from the vulnerable section, especially ST, SC, women and disabled persons. In the record the less number of women were registered in comparison to the prescription of SGSY scheme of the Government of India. All the beneficiaries were provided sustainable employment with a fix wage per month initially for 2 years from the project. In few districts this was continued from 3 to 5 years due to irregular fund flow. In the project 970 hectares of degraded forest lands were brought under the plantations against the target of 1,050 hectares. In each village each beneficiary was allotted one ha of forest land for the cultivation of the Lemon grass, Aloe vera, Aswagandha, Kalmegh at the lower canopy, looking into the short production period and Aonla, Sinduri, bamboo, eucalyptus, teak at the upper canopy looking into the rehabilitation of the degraded forests and the commercial values of the products. As per Government of Madhya Pradesh JFM resolution in the proposal there was a provision of deduction from the wage for the contribution to the village development fund of the JFM committee for infrastructural development of the village. In the evaluation it was found that only in 50 per cent of the villages the deduction was done. In some villages the amount was utilized for some purposes. In the villages the infrastructural subsistence facilities were provided on the basis of the requirement and availability of the resources. In the project the beneficiaries were imparted training for their competence building for the development of the skills including dealing with banks' account, oil distillation, various cultivation practices of forest crops and maintenance of records and documents, etc. In the project after the plantation through irrigation the development of ecosystem was well-observed by the rising of the groundwater table, soil conservation and moisture retention and enhancement of the canopy in the degraded in the forest lands. In the evaluation 84 per cent of the self-help groups were imparted training for cultivation and processing, value-addition and marketing of the medicinal and aromatic plants within the states and outside the states.

After the detail qualitative assessment and quantitative assessment have been done on the four important aspects of the project upon which the physical and financial performances have been assessed in the project, viz., plantation, training, distillation unit and construction of platforms. The codification has been done on the integral part of the aspects and marks have been allotted. The overall assessment has been done on the sum of the marks allotted to the codification. It has been observed that performances of the 20 per cent SHG are average. The performances of 32 per cent SHGs are good, 8 per cent very good and 40 per cent are excellent (IIFM Consultancy Report, 2008).

Promotional and Commercial Projects under National Medicinal Plants Board

Till 2003–04, no formal State Medicinal Plants Board was formed. But under the guidance of State Minor Forest Produce Federation of Forest Department 17 promotional and 294 commercial projects were sanctioned for the researchers and the farmers, which were worth Rs 1,039.8 lakhs. These projects cover 1,584.14 acres forest in 18 districts. It has established the "Vindhya Herbals", the branded products of medicinal and aromatic plants, at Minor Forest Produce Processing and Research Centre (MFP-PARC), a unit of Madhya Pradesh Minor Forest Produce (T and D) Cooperatives Federations. Both the projects have created livelihoods from collection, processing, value-addition, marketing to micro-enterprise development.

IV

Some Identified Issues in Socio-economic Development of Tribals

Since 1991 the initiatives of the Madhya Pradesh Forest Department in protection and rehabilitation of the degraded forests in the state through participatory process in institutionalization and promotion of the socio-economic development of the tribal communities, various issues have been identified as mentioned in the following:

1. *Dominance of Forest Department:* Though the present attempt for the development of the tribals by uplifting socio-economic condition is participatory, in most of the cases this has been observed that people are not getting opportunities or being oriented in planning, implementation, monitoring and evaluation through participatory process. The forest officials have utilized their administrative rights to run the project in their own controlled mechanism. In many cases their dominance is prominent from the attitudinal point of view.
2. *Preparation of Micro-plan:* The micro-planning is a document for the natural resource management and community development at the grass roots. But even after one decade and half in many cases the proper micro-planning is not available. In few cases these were not developed in the decentralization and participatory process. The in-experienced civil-society organizations or non-governmental organizations who maintain the good relationships with Forest Divisions were given such assignment, but they have not prepared properly. Even in some cases it has been found that the micro-plan is the copy of another.
3. *Excessive Expenditures in Administrative Process:* Instead of much attempt for awareness generation or capacity-building in order to confidence building and self-dependence in the people, the Forest Department has incurred much expenditure in the administrative process rather than human resource development.
4. *Cultural Barrier in Women Empowerment:* Though the women have the significant role in household economy and in fulfilment of the daily requirement, it has been observed that they are not given much opportunity in the participatory process due to cultural barrier created by the patriarchal dominance.
5. *Prioritization of Revenue Earning:* Though the community forest management is people centred activity, in many cases the species were chosen from the point of view of commercial values for revenue earning rather than the natural trees providing multiple benefits like fuel wood, fodder, fruit or food, etc.
6. *Dissemination of Information:* In the era of development communication it is much necessary to disseminate information about the

developmental activities in the village before and after the project or programme for active involvement of the people. But in most cases that has not been done properly.

7. *Allotment of Budget:* Allotment of the budget in most cases has been taken place without need assessment at the village level for the community development at grass roots. Even the allotted budget does not reach in proper time.
8. *Capacity Building:* For making the community development participatory and people-centred the capacity building and skill-upgradation of the people are important, but in many cases this activity is either neglected or limited within papers.
9. *Civil Society Organization:* For decentralization and devolution the civil society organizations have the significant role in planning and implementation of the developmental projects or programmes. In Madhya Pradesh Forest Department has taken initiative in planning and implementation by their own efforts, instead of giving opportunities to the civil society organization or non-governmental organizations in action-oriented programme. The formal involvement of NGOs in assisting MPFD both at the field level and central level was also constrained by the perception of the 'tedious nature' of the process of contacting NGOs in the state and was not accustomed to professional contractual relationships with government agencies that bound them to specific tasks and responsibilities.
10. *Equitable Sharing:* Due to social structure and social organizations in the rural setting the ignorant and poor tribals are deprived of getting due benefits, which are not equitably shared.

V

Conclusion

In spite of the largest forest area and substantial forest cover in Madhya Pradesh the Forest Department has taken a number of attempts of sustainable development of the forest on the triple-bottom line approach, viz., ecology, economy and social and institution. Earlier there was age-old approach and methods of raising plantations of the species for timber production and the revenue earnings on traditional forestry through silvicultural operations of natural regeneration and tending. Since the implementation of the JFM programmes the rehabilitation of the degraded, forest the plantations have been done by the village institutions in the participatory process. Thus the traditional plantation forestry has been overshadowed by the plantations of the natural or indigenous trees for providing multiple benefits in the JFM programme. The watershed management and development has also been initiated for sustainable environmental management of soil-moisture conservation and water harvesting in micro-watersheds. The participatory irrigation management has been undertaken for the tribal peasants for their agricultural livelihoods. The conservation ethos of the indigenous peoples have been taken up into consideration by providing the due values to the indigenous knowledge of species diversity with multiple utility, sacredness of the areas, trees and water-bodies, cultural practices of beliefs and rituals, knowledge and religious affiliation of the medicinal men and its promotion of employment generation. In this manner, the protection of the traditional livelihoods became inextricably mixed up with the promotional livelihoods and alternative livelihoods. Thus the employment generations and the enhancement of income source focused approaches for poverty reduction and achieving sustainable livelihoods. In this context, the decentralized governance has been brought into action through the village institutions, viz. FPC, VFC, EDC, Panchayat and Gram Sabha, non-governmental organizations or voluntary institutions as civil societies, self-help groups or women groups as Dwarka groups. In the process various issues have been emerged. Above all, the combinations of the ecological sustainability, economic stability and social acceptability and institutional sustainability lead the achievements of the sustainable livelihoods in the shorter phase and sustainable development in the longer phase.

References

Bhattacharya, A.K. and B. Basnyat (2003): "Empowering People through Joint Forest Management: A Study from Madhya Pradesh", *International Forestry Review,* 5:370–78.

Chambers, R. and G. Conway (1992): "Sustainable Livelihoods: Practical Concepts for the 21st Century", IDS Discussion Paper 296, IDS, pp. 7–8.

Dasgupta, S. and D. Debnath (2008): *Community Forest Management in Tribal States of India,* Dehradun: International Book Distributors.

Debnath, D. (2003): Social Impacts and Poverty Alleviation in Joint Forest Management Projects in Madhya Pradesh, Proceeding of International

Workshop on JFM from 19th–20th June, 2003 in the Vigyan Bhavan, New Delhi, Dehradun: Indian Council of Forestry Research and Education.

Debnath, D. (2005a): "Livelihood Option for Poverty Eradication through Forest Resources: Experiences from Undivided Madhya Pradesh" in S.N. Chaudhary (ed.), *Human Rights and Poverty in India,* Vol. V, Delhi: Concept Publication.

Debnath, D. and S. Dasgupta (2006): "Livelihood Generation and Poverty Reduction Attempts in Joint Forest Management Activities in Madhya Pradesh", *International Forestry Review,* 2: 241–50.

DFID (1999): Sustainable Livelihoods Guidance Sheets, London: Department for International Development.

Dutta, S., M. Vijay and T. Gitali (2004): *A Resource Book for Livelihood Promotion,* Hyderabad: New Economics Foundation.

IIFM Consultancy Report (2008): Evaluation of Special Project on Sustainable Employment through Multilayered Irrigated Plantation, under Swarnjayanti Gram Swarojgar Yojana (SGSY), (Mimeo).

IUCN (1996): IUCN, Working Group on Community Involvement in Forest Management, Mark Poffenberger (ed.), Washington D.C.: IUCN.

Kaushal, K.K. and J.C. Kala (2004): "Applying the Sustainable Livelihood Approach to Joint Forest Management Projects in India", *International Forestry Review,* Vol. 6(1), pp. 13–18.

MoEF (1999): *National Policy and Macro-level Action Strategy on Biodiversity,* New Delhi: Ministry of Environment and Forests, Government of India, p. 74.

MoEF (2002): Guidelines for National Afforestation Programme and Forest Development Agencies, National Afforestation and Eco-development Board, Ministry of Environment and Forests, Government of India.

Mukherjee, A.K. (2004): "Tracing Policy and Legislative Changes towards JFM" in *Root to Canopy: Regenerating Forests through Community State Partnership,* New Delhi: Winrock International India.

NCHSE (1987): Documentation on Forests and Rights, Vol. I, National Centre for Human Settlement and Environment, New Delhi (Mimeo), (quoted in R. Chambers et al., *To the Hands of the Poor,* 1989).

Sarin, Madhu (1996): "From Conflict to Collaboration: Village Voices", *Forest Choices,* New Delhi: Oxford University Press.

13

Economics of Borrowing in Tribal Areas

A Study of State Intervention through Self-Help Groups

NEETA TAPAN

The word 'tribe' is generally used for a "socially cohesive unit, associated with a territory, the members of which regard them as politically autonomous". Often a tribe possesses a distinct dialect and distinct cultural traits. A tribe, is a social group of humans connected by a shared system of values and organized for mutual care, defence, and survival beyond that which could be attained by a lone individual or family. Tribes are the most enduring and successful social survival system that has ever existed on earth.

The tribal population of India (67.6 million) around 8 per cent of the total population is larger than that of any other country in the world. The rural and urban male population is 3,17,55,930 and 26,07,341 respectively. The rural female population is 3,09,95,096 while the urban female population is 24,00,013. The tribal population of India is more than the total population of France and Britain and four times that of Australia. If all the tribals of India had lived in one state, it would have been the fifth most populous state after Uttar Pradesh, Bihar, West Bengal and Maharashtra. Madhya Pradesh is not only the largest state in India but also has the largest tribal population of the country.

India occupies the second highest number of dams in the world. It is estimated that owing to construction of over 1,500 major irrigation development projects since independence, over 16 million people were displaced from their villages, of which about 40 per cent belong to tribal population. There is no reliable and complete information on the number of tribals displaced in the country since independence. The estimates range between 5 and 7 million – mostly by the dams, followed by mines and industries – approximately one in every ten tribals has been displaced by different developments projects. Such involuntary tribal displacement has led to the sacrifice of collective identity, historical and cultural heritage, and of course the survival support. Consequently, poverty, malnutrition, mortality, morbidity, illiteracy, unemployment, debt bondage, and serfdom among the tribals are markedly higher.

State Intervention for Tribal Welfare

The tribals are part of the Indian society, at the same time they are different. Special policy and programmes are required to address and redress these differences especially in the context of globalization. When we plan for tribal development, we have to regard these differences, take a special note of their situations and capabilities and provide them facilities to develop on the line they want to take. If they have to unfold from within, they must have participation in any development decision. Their felt needs should be transformed in development programmes.

Tribal development policies and programmes in India assumed that all the tribals will develop and will integrate themselves with the so-called mainstream. This has happened only in a symbolic way. In spite of the protection given to the tribal population by the Constitution of India (1950), tribals still remain the most backward ethnic group in India. They rate very low on the three most important indicators of development: health, education and income. The tribals are most backward not only compared with the general population, but also compared to the Scheduled Castes (Dalits), the other backward social group with constitutional protection. While examining the effects of planned developmental intervention on the tribals from 1961 to 1981, it was observed that twenty years of intervention has not made any significant impact in improving the conditions of the tribals. A number of studies suggest that during the 1990s, when policies of liberalization, privatization, globalization (LPG) were implemented in various degrees, income distribution has worsened. Extreme income poverty has affected some 150 million people in India. Tribals make up about one-third of the income poor. An assessment of progress has been less than anticipated. The trade aspects of globalization also alter the context of many issues and areas affecting tribals, in some cases intensifying problems and in other cases affecting the policy actions required to address the problems.

Globalization affects tribals differently. Urban and educated tribals may benefit from the increased opportunities for work that come with the influx of foreign companies and investments. These employment avenues are complemented by greater opportunities to receive education and skills training of a higher quality. The new technologies that define this era, particularly the computer and internet may be accessible to this group of tribals. In general, the liberalization of trade and financial markets also promise benefits for this group, including a greater variety of goods at cheaper prices due to increased competition and much more attractive interest rates to undertake business ventures. Conversely, poor, uneducated, credit-constrained, informal and agricultural sector tribals will benefit in a much less direct manner.

Evidently, the gains of globalization have so far accrued to those who already have education and skill advantage, easier market access and possession of assets for use as collateral to access credit. For the tribals, globalization is associated with rising prices, loss of job security, lack of health care and tribal development programmes. Globalization may also weaken the constitutional protections, in terms of education and job reservations, given to tribals.

Thus, in an era of globalization and privatization, when the entire world economy is undergoing structural changes with wide-ranging ramifications to the developing countries, the fate of tribal people is a matter of concern to administrators and development agencies like NGOs, banks and others. There is a need to ensure sustainable development of tribals through innovative interventions and funding from international institutions and the government. Due to historical reasons, tribal society has not been able to catch up with the changing needs of society. Indifferent and unrealistic policies not only drive tribal people to absolute poverty but also drive them out of their natural habitats. Thus, it was realized that an integrated approach to tribal economic development that is executable and acceptable to the tribals through participatory techniques is the need of the hour. Special policy and programmes are required to address and redress these differences especially in the context of globalization. Outsiders cannot develop tribals; they can become only facilitators if they want to do so. The tribals can participate in their development programmes only if they are considered to be equals and if their unique identities are respected. One such most innovative state intervention to ensure sustainable development of tribals is the self-help mechanism proposed under the Swarnajayanti Gram Swarojgar Yojana (SGSY).

This programme started with the realization that the most critical missing link in the life cycle of the tribals is the credit. The credit needs of the tribals are determined in a complex socio-economic milieu. It has been well-established that despite the tremendous expansion of the institutional credit delivery system over the years and introduction of priority sector lending specifically devised for weaker sections in rural areas, formal credit institutions are still neither attuned nor willing to deal with the section of society requiring small loans and having no creditworthiness or even collateral security to offer. Being economically vulnerable, they often fall into the debt-trap of the exploitative moneylenders. Another point of concern is that in the formal credit delivery system, women have consciously and deliberately been marginalized as they fail to fulfil the banking demands of high discipline in procedures and repayments. Poor women in tribal areas, who are particularly illiterate, burdened with migrant or unemployed husbands, and are employed in unorganized sector with meagre earnings form high credit risk client group for the banks. The formal credit channels are not cognizant of the social objectives of providing credit to such women for whom the dividing line between their consumption and productive needs is highly blurred.

Where the formal commercial channels within the financial sector remained virtually closed to the poor, the state-owned credit institutions in India, including the cooperatives, have failed to reach out to the poor. In addition, the performance of government programmes of poverty alleviation, where provision of subsidized credit was central are disappointing. The subsidy and concessional culture have allowed leakage of benefits to undeserving households. In addition, it has also led to the underestimation of the ability of the poor to save or pay the rate of interest. In contrast to these earlier programmes, which treated the tribals as beneficiaries receiving doles from the government, the self-help groups under SGSY treat them as participants who practice thrift, saving, inter-lending and evolve to the stage of income generation.

This paper attempts to study the credit portfolio of the women SHG members in Jhabua district (a tribal district) of Madhya Pradesh and tries to analyse the findings in the light of tribal society. This paper thus does not touch the bank-borrower regime, instead it attempts to study the patterns of internal lending of SHGs with respect to the age of these groups. It also tries to explore into the borrowing portfolio of the SHG members as to whether any shift from informal to formal sources of credit is visible? The demand profile for credit, amounts of loan and status of repayment of the SHG members have also been looked into.

Sample Selection

The present study is based on a sample of 50 women SHGs drawn from Jhabua district, which is a tribal district of Madhya Pradesh. These SHGs are being run blockwise (12 blocks) in the district under the Swarnajayanti Gram Swarozgar Yojana. Out of 12 blocks in Jhabua one-fourth, i.e., three blocks, Jhabua, Meghnagar and Thandla were purposely selected. There are about 760 women SHGs, which are in the functional state in these blocks. The saving and lending groups were randomly selected from the lists provided by the district agencies and then mapped across the villages in the three blocks respectively. Two women were selected from each SHG. Of these two women, one was purposively selected from the office bearers and the other one was selected from the remaining members by convenience. Thus, in all 150 women were selected to get their responses. A structured schedule was administered on the respondents. Besides, a range of methods like observation, interviews, group discussion, and maintenance of field diary were used to collect primary data.

Major Findings

One of the crucial activities for the group would be internal lending. Initially, loans are disbursed to members out of the savings of the group. At a later stage, the group can access the line-of-credit from the banks and can use the bank loan for disbursement among its members. Internal lending could begin when the group has started meeting regularly and has accumulated savings worth inter lending. A member desirous of taking loan has to apply/ask for loan, stating clearly the purpose of the loan and the amount of loan required. The group would decide the interest rate to be charged, repayment schedule, procedure to be adopted in case of default, prioritizing on objectives in case of simultaneous applications for loan. The major findings regarding the borrowing profile of the tribal women members of the SHGs are:

Tendency to Take Loans

Out of the 105 women who took loan from the SHG, 2.9 per cent took it once, 7.6 per cent took loan twice, 8.6 per cent took for four times, 17.1 per cent took for five times and 60 per cent of them took loan for more than five times.

Size of Loan

Out of the total borrowers, 6.6 per cent of women took loan from Rs 400 to 600, 13.3 per cent of them took Rs 600–800, 11.4 per cent took loan from Rs 800 to 1,000, 4.8 per cent took an amount between Rs 1,000 to 1,200 and 2.9 per cent of the members took loan from Rs 1,200 to 1,400.

Follow Up of Use of Loan

Out of the total SHGs, only 12.55 of the groups follow up the use of loan, while 87.5 per cent of the groups do not follow any such procedure.

Penalty for Default

Out of the total SHGs, 25 per cent of the groups penalize the defaulters while 75 per cent of the groups do not have any provision of punishing those who do not repay loans.

Basis of Instalment

Around 12.5 per cent of the groups determine the installment on the basis of time, 15 per cent of the SHGs on the basis of amount of loan, 50 per cent of the SHGs do so on the basis of the economic status of the borrowers, 17.5 per cent of the SHGs decide this on the basis of income generation of the groups and 5 per cent of the SHGs follow the facilitator's advice in this case.

Timely Repayment

Out of the total borrowers, about 27 per cent of them have returned loans in time whereas 73 per cent of them have not repaid the loans in time.

Reasons Behind Default

Out of the borrowers who could not return loan in time, 9 per cent of them had no regular income, about 12 per cent were unemployed, 21 per cent could not repay loan because of migration, 12 per cent repaid old loans, 25 per cent were unemployed and also migrated whereas 22 per cent had irregular income and migrated.

Objectives of Taking Group Loans

Out of the total borrowers, 57 per cent of them borrowed for household expenditure, 9 per cent for health reasons, 7 per cent for agriculture, 10 per cent for social and religious customs, 9 per cent to repay old loans, and 10 per cent for personal occupation.

Rate of Interest

Out of the total SHGs, 71 per cent of the SHGs charged interest rate at 2 per cent, while 29 per cent of the SHGs charged at 3 per cent.

Status of Borrowing Prior to Association with SHG

Out of 150 respondents, 100 per cent of them borrowed loan from one or the other source before associating with SHGs.

Source of Loan

Out of the total respondents, 80 per cent of them took loan from Sahukar/mahajan, 8 per cent of them took loan from friends or neighbours, and 12 per cent of them took loan from relatives.

Objectives of Borrowing Prior to SHG Association

Out of 150 respondents, 57 per cent borrowed for household expenditure, 4 per cent for health reasons, 20 per cent for agriculture, and 20 per cent for social/religious customs.

Rate of Interest of Informal Sources of Credit

Out of the 150 respondents who borrowed from informal sources of credit, 7 per cent were charged 5 per cent, 21 per cent were charged 8 per cent, 51 per cent were charged 12 per cent and 21 per cent were charged 15 per cent rate of interest.

Present Sources of Credit

Out of the total respondents, 20 per cent women still borrow from sahukar/mahajan or relatives, 20 per cent borrow from sahukar, SHG and bank, 10 per cent from friends, neighbour and bank, 9.3 per cent from relatives, bank and SHG and 37 per cent of the total respondents borrow from bank and SHG.

Bank Linkage

Out of the total SHGs, 80 per cent of them have been linked with banks and 20 per cent of the total SHGs have not been linked with banks.

Use of Revolving Fund

Out of the bank linked SHGs, about 63 per cent of the groups have used the amount of revolving fund for group and individual income generation activities, while 13 per cent of the SHGs have used it in internal lending, 18 per cent of the groups have distributed the amount among the members and 8 per cent of the SHGs have deposited the amount in the bank.

Result of Hypothesis Testing

Chi square test was applied to test the hypothesis that with an increase in the duration of association with SHGs the dependence of the members on institutional or formal sources of credit increase and this hypothesis got rejected.

Reflections

The overall picture that emerges from these findings is that the SHG mechanism has definitely provided a user-friendly banking system at the doorsteps of the poor tribal women. This can be deduced from the facts that the repeated borrowings do establish credit as a missing link in the life cycle of the tribals as accessibility has led to frequent use of credit. The amounts of loan borrowed show that the tribals did need a channel of credit, which can supply small and frequent loans. No follow up, very comfortable interest rates, absence of penalty for default, and justified basis for installment are all such factors which are in favour of tribal borrowing profile. Most of the SHG members have borrowed loan for unproductive purposes and most of the borrowers have not repaid the loan in time, nevertheless there are genuine constraints behind this repayment trend. Prior to association with the SHGs, all the respondents took loan and that too from the informal sources at higher rates of interest. While, consumption dominated the borrowing objectives. The pleasant change visible in the borrowing portfolio of the tribals after SHG association is that they access multiple sources of credit now. Although they still depend on the informal credit channels, however, bank and SHGs have been added to the menu of options. Linkage of most of the SHGs with banks is a positive sign as the amount of revolving fund has been used for group and individual income generation or internal lending. Thus, the borrowing portfolio of the tribal women exhibits signs of financial inclusion to the extent that they have added sources of credit in the form of bank and SHGs, which are not exploitative as some of the informal credit sources. Moreover, SHG is a source of credit and caters to the typical demands of the rural illiterate poor in the most user-friendly manner. Banks, on the other hand, fulfil their productive needs. The mechanism of peer pressure works as a collateral, which solves the demand as well supply side problems of tribal borrowing. Whereas, the rejection of the hypothesis that with an increase in the duration of association with SHGs, the dependence of the members on institutional or formal sources of credit increases implies that the economic status of the respondents is very poor and does not undergo any noticeable positive change so as to enable them to fulfil their needs from earned income. Moreover, the SHGs provide small amounts of loan, which are not enough and have to be supplemented with other sources. Very poor micro-credit users often do not show remarkable improvements in their economic status for a very long time and this becomes clear from the results. It is usually very difficult for very poor people to fulfil their subsistence level needs, save in the groups and repay loans simultaneously unless their employment yields sufficient returns. Thus, it is evident that their employment activity is not generating enough returns as to result in economic betterment and this also implies that the interventions of the facilitator in their income generating activity are not satisfactory.

Problems

The problems encountered by the tribals in the journey of self-help are intrinsic in the nature of the tribal rural society such as:

Existence of Falia

One of the major problems in the success of the self-help mechanism is the absence of clusters or colonies in the tribal areas. There are scattered areas called *falias* in which tribal families live at distances from each other. This arrangement constrains their interaction, meetings and other economic activities. This feature is unique to tribal areas and the other rural areas have an edge over such areas in conducting group activities, as a village is usually a closely-knit unit.

Historical Indebtedness

The extremely poor status of the tribal people throws them into an eternal debt-trap due to dependency on sahukars/mahajans for all kinds of needs. Consequently, association with SHGs and the new borrowing portfolio are not able to make any miraculous change in the situation of the tribals, as paying off old debts obstructs their credit flow.

Employment Oriented Migration

SHGs and bank linkage are not able to give a platform for livelihood until the resulting income generation activity reaches a sustainable level. Till then the tribal poor are compelled to migrate for employment to other areas and this disturbs the whole cycle of thrift, saving, borrowing and repayment. These seasonal jolts break the tempo of SHGs and the groups disintegrate.

Poverty

It is often argued by the practitioners of micro-credit, that the credit can uplift only middle and upper class poor people and can make the very poor people worse off. Tribals are generally extremely poor people and access to credit can help them to the extent of vulnerability reduction temporarily. Credit is fungible and mostly flows into consumption activities and does not result into substantial change in the economic status of the very poor users.

Alcoholism

Most of the respondents reported of alcoholic husband and this trend is common among tribal. The option of SHG gives an easy source of credit for such addictions. The change in the borrowing portfolio of the tribals thus, cannot easily lead to economic betterment.

Defective Agricultural System

Displacement and robbing them off their indigenous and natural resources compels the tribals to fall back upon agriculture labour as the last livelihood support. The traditional age-old lacunas in the agricultural system, however, add to the economic plights of the tribals and diminish the gains arising from SHGs and credit openings.

Delinquency

The tribals are often accused of being delinquent and their criminal or delinquent tendencies lead to the failure of the concept of SHG and its credit plus approach.

Other Problems

Social obligations, backwardness, illiteracy and other such problems divert the group and bank borrowing into wasteful and ostentatious consumption. Family problems and conflicts restrict the tribal women from complete involvement and participation in group-activities. Moreover, illiteracy further worsens their status.

Therefore, the tribals are not able to take full advantage of the SHGs and the new opportunities because of multi-faceted problems which are either generally applicable to the rural areas or are unique features of their communities.

Suggestions

The problems, which are inbuilt in the structure of tribal society, can be solved through executing the very philosophy of Self-Help Groups and improving the level of handholding of the groups.

Facilitator's Support

The facilitator's support in all the group activities like conducting of introductory sessions, formation of SHGs, organizing of meetings, appointment of executive members, maintenance of record, grading, training and capacity building, bank linkage, and income generation can surely lead to successful and systematic evolution of groups. Continuous support, monitoring and hand holding by the facilitator can help the tribals overcome their constraints.

Interventions in Meetings

Positive interventions of the facilitator in the meetings are essential to enable the tribals to engage into meaningful dialogue and prevent the meetings from becoming a few minutes affair of collection, lending or repayment. Moreover, this can ensure regular attendance and repayment of loans.

Change in Mindset through Interactive Sessions

Once the facilitator is present in the meetings to address and to moderate the session, the socio-economic issues can be discussed at large. Such interactive sessions can be used to raise issues like literacy, age at marriage, fertility, contraception, gender sensitization, social evils, politics, environmental awareness, etc. In this way, these meetings can be helpful in changing the attitude and mindset of the tribals and make them more enlightened.

Backward and Forward Linkages in Income Generation

The most important step in empowering the tribal poor is making them economically self-sufficient. Credit can act as an effective link only when it is used for productive purposes. Availability of raw material, training, packaging, warehousing and transport facilities and marketing support are the backward and forward linkages essential for income generation activity to become profitable. Such interfacing, networking and support system should be provided by different agencies to the tribals for the success of the concept of SHGs.

Cooperation from Banks

The tribals are very apprehensive of the formal credit channels, especially the banks, which require lots of paper work, collateral and other formalities. The bank linkage through SHGs leads to an ice breaking between the two parties. So, the banks should be extra-congenial and extend all possible support to the tribals to enable a two-way relationship, which can benefit both the sides. Groups ensure repayment ethics and so the process of financial inclusion of the tribal poor can take off if the banks are supportive.

Conclusion

Hence, it is evident that the tribals are exposed to threats of further aggravation and marginalization in the process of LPG. If globalization were superimposed on a poorly-educated and poorly-trained tribal people, particularly in Indian states with poor systems of governance and infrastructure, it would not lead to growth nor reduce poverty.

Self-help group is a mechanism, which helps to implement globalization with a human face. While keeping the social fabric and identity of the tribals intact, SHGs can use financial and social intermediation to empower and integrate the tribals in the mainstream more easily. The indigenous resources, knowledge and skill can be used to give gainful employment to these communities through building a support system of backward and forward linkages in income generation. The illiterate and unskilled tribals can be involved in training and capacity building programmes to face the challenges of the market age. Finally, empowering the tribals through giving them options of formal credit delivery, reducing their vulnerability, and fulfilling their typical credit needs is in itself a step towards improvement. With proper care taking, sustainable provision of options and opportunities will slowly pave the way for self-sufficiency.

References

Fried, Morton H. (1975): *The Notion of Tribe,* Menlo Park, CA: Cummings Publishing Company.

Nair, T.S. (2001): "Institutionalizing Microfinance in India: An Overview of Strategic Issues", *Economic and Political Weekly,* January 27.

Pathy, Janganath (1998): "Impact of Development Projects on Tribals" in Joshi Vidyut (ed.), *Tribal Situation in India: Issues in Development,* Jaipur: Rawat Publications.

Sah, D.C. (1998): "Displacement and Rehabilitation", in Joshi Vidyut (ed.), *Tribal Situation in India: Issues in Development,* Jaipur: Rawat Publications.

Streeten, Paul (2001): *Globalization: Threat or Opportunity,* Copenhagen: Business School Press.

14

Tribal Economy at Crossroads

Needs for an Appropriate Intervention

S.K. PANT

India's experience with planned development has rather been a mixed one. On one hand it has succeeded in pushing the economy to the frontiers in many areas, helped her to emerge from being a net importer to becoming an exporter in may core sectors, from being a despondent and dependent economy to emerging as a self-reliant and independent country and from being a poor and an impoverished state to becoming a vibrant thriving and power economy, in the last few decades.

However, the inability of the planning to address many critical issues and more specifically the failure to distribute the fruits of development evenly to all of the regions and to all sections of the society has become the biggest disappointment to the planners (Seventh and Eighth Five-Year Plans, 1992–93; Swaminathan, 1996; Economic Survey, 1996). It has, in the process, triggered a chain of ancillary and counter-ancillary reactions that has resulted in a lop-sided development that finally precipitated with the emergence of developed pockets in some of the regions. These developed pockets, with the passage of time, metamorphosed into urban centres, as was envisaged of them, virtually stifled off the whole process of growth and development activities in other regions by attracting both physical and non-physical resources (Prabhu, 1998; EPW Foundation, 1994). This incidentally also laid genesis for rural to urban migration which kept on inclining with the passage of time, thereby, putting severe strain on the fragile urban resources and subsequently threatening to derail the whole process of development (Pant, 2002).

Unfortunately, these anomalies and disparities have not remained confined to one specific domain only but has it cut out across caste, region and gender lines as well. It simultaneously, isolated a vast majority of population from the main stream of development and that has also escalated the problem of skewed development and despite governments' numerous attempts and forays, through various programmes, schemes and social interventions, the problem not only persists but kept growing in volume and magnitude and continues to haunt the planners and social thinkers.

Amongst the many deprived sections, the tribes are, perhaps, one of the foremost groups who have paid an unprecedented amount of price and wrath of the development during all these years.

The Tribals: A Profile

The tribals, who roughly constitute about 8 per cent of the total population of the country, are regarded as the oldest ethnic group. Their distinct socio-cultural milieu makes them as a distinct group with a separate identity. These factors along with the geographical conditions of their habitations, impose upon them isolation from the main stream of national life and insulation from the currents of change. Their primitive mode of production and practices further pushes them down on the social-hierarchy and drives them to live under conditions of abject poverty and conditions of extreme backwardness (Pandey and Pant, 2008).

The Britishers were the first people who made an attempt to break their isolation through extension of their administrative apparatus. However, their attempt was loaded, more, with self-interest rather than being a philanthropic one because the opening of their areas to outsiders made their positions further vulnerable and weak and paved way for the systematic exploitations of their forest resources and other natural vegetations. Ever since then, tribal development has become and has been a subject of great attention for academicians, planners and administrators. Many impressive schemes and programmes have been conceptualized and launched with the view to address and ameliorate the socio-economic conditions of the tribals. After independence, the governments endeavour has been to bring the tribes to the mainstream of development. The subsequent provisions in the preamble and State Directive Policy in the Constitution project their commitment and subsequent amendment in the clauses of the various acts reaffirms their will to implement it. However, with the passage of time, it has become clear that all these provisions, schemes and interventions have only provided marginal difference or relief to the general majority of tribal population; it has, on the contrary, fractured this rather homogenous group further and has given rise to a new class of elite with advanced education and training, who have now joined the government to manage the administrative apparatus generally in their own favour.

The Current Status

The current status of the marginalized sections of Indian society provides a very disappointing picture. Studies by various scholars have shown that, over the years, though there has been an upward movement in their socio-economic status, however, the gap between them and the rest of the population has, by and large, remained quite substantial (Mahadev, 2003).

Despite over six decades of planning, unfortunately, the tribes, today, have remained the most disadvantaged section of the society. On the educational front, it could be seen that though the overall level of tribal population may have risen over five-and-half time, since 1961, however, the gap between them and the remaining population which was 15.5 per cent in 1961 has subsequently inclined to about 18 per cent by 2001!, thereby indicating that the bulk of the remaining population has so far remained, largely, isolated from it. Further, the situation on female's education has also been quite deplorable, where the gap has inclined to almost two-times (from 9.8% in 1961 to 18.9%) during the same period.

Table 1

Literacy Rate of General Population and ST Population During 1961–2001

Year	*General*			*ST*		
	Male	*Female*	*Total*	*Male*	*Female*	*Total*
1961	34.4	13.0	24.0	13.8	3.2	8.5
1971	39.5	18.7	29.5	17.6	4.9	11.3
1981	46.9	24.8	36.2	24.5	8.0	16.4
1991	64.1	39.3	52.2	40.7	18.2	29.6
2001	75.3	53.7	64.8	59.2	34.8	47.1

Source: Eleventh Five-Year Plan 2007–12, Vol. I, Planning Commission, New Delhi:, p. 113.

The study of dropout rates among the Scheduled Tribes has also been a major worrying aspect. The study reveals its shocking state. About 42 per-cent of the SC student dropout by the time they complete the primary level, the corresponding figure for other group being 29 per cent for the year 2004–06, and at the elementary level almost 66 per cent of the SC student dropout and this figure is particularly startling for girls where almost 67 per cent of them dropout. Further, the study shows that hardly about 21 per cent of the SC students complete their high school level of education, the corresponding figure for other group being 51 per cent (Table 2).

Table 2

Dropout Ratio 2004–05

Year	*Sex*	*Primary (I–V)*			*Elementary (I–VIII)*			*Class (I–X)*		
		All	*ST*	*GAP*	*All*	*ST*	*GAP*	*All*	*ST*	*GAP*
2004–05	Boys	31.8	42.6	10.7	50.4	65.0	14.6	60.4	77.8	17.4
	Girls	25.4	42.0	16.7	51.3	37.1	15.8	63.9	80.7	16.8
	Total	29.0	42.3	13.3	50.8	65.9	15.1	61.9	79.0	17.1

Source: Eleventh Five-Year Plan 2007–12, Vol. I, Planning Commission, New Delhi, p. 113.

Occupational Structure

The study of occupation also presents a very dismal picture as about 82 per cent of the tribal workers, both in rural and urban areas taken together are engaged in the primary sector of whom about 45 per cent are cultivators, 37 per cent are agricultural labourers. The corresponding figures for all cultivators being about 32 per cent for cultivators and 27 per cent for agricultural labourers. All this clearly goes on to show that the incidence of ST's dependence on primary sector has still been very high which also projects the fact that not much has changed in the occupational scenario for them despite of the fact that many new advances have been made in agriculture which has benefited some sections, during all these years of development.

Extent of Poverty

Poverty is yet another indicator that adequately reflects the extent of development or lack of development that a particular group or region has been subjected to. If the incidence of poverty shows a declining trend over the period of time, the group or the region appears to have been benefited from it, however, on the contrary, if the incidence of poverty inclines, over the period of time, then the impact of planning is said to be felt adversely.

The study of people living below the poverty line, over two-time periods in 1993–94 and 2004–05, shows that while there has been a uniform decline in the proportion of people living below the poverty line for both rest of the population and the tribals, however the incidence of decline was much sharper steeper for rest of the population than that of tribals. Further, the study also shows that poverty was more rampant in rural areas where even in the year 2004–05, about 29 per-cent of the rest of population and over 47 per cent of ST was still living below the poverty line. All this implies that poverty alleviation programmes are skewed or biased towards urban areas or are ill-conceived and fails to address the core issues of poverty uniformly.

Table 3

Population Living Below Poverty Line

Category	*1993–94*		*2004–05*		*Percentage Decrease (1993–94 to 2004–05)*	
	Rural	*Urban*	*Rural*	*Urban*	*Rural*	*Urban*
All	37.3	32.4	28.3	25.7	9.0	6.7
STs	51.9	41.1	47.3	33.3	4.6	7.8
GAP	14.6	8.7	19.3	7.6	4.4	1.1

Note: Includes ST Population.

Source: Perspective Planning Division, Planning Commission, New Delhi.

Tribal Representation in Central Services

Apart from initiating various welfare programmes for tribals, the government also provided reservation for tribal in the central and state government services. The ST's representation, which was about 5.49 percentage in 1994, had gone up to 6.54 a mere 1.05 percentile increase during the last decade which was well below their population share in the total population. The analysis also shows that the proportion of ST's in class A and B categories has gone up from 2.9 per cent and 2.8 per cent to about 4.1 per cent and 4.6 per cent respectively, yet it was still well below their stipulated mark of 7 per cent. However, it could be stated that the reservation policy has only marginally affected their socio-economic status, though much was expected of it. It further goes on to show that bulk of the recruitment has taken place in group C and D which were low skilled-based services whereas not much has changed in the group A and B services which require greater skills and competence. All these goes on to show that external interventions, no matter of any magnitude or volume, could produce development on sustainable basis as compared to the intervention coming from within. Hence, greater effort should now be placed not only on incapacitating them but also encouraging them to develop a mechanism of their own which encourages them to develop the leadership from within themselves, help them to take independent action, make plans for themselves that are based on the local requirements, etc. It is against this backdrop, that the role of micro-finance plays a crucial role.

Table 4

Percentage of ST Representation in Central Government Services (As on 1.1.2004)

Group	*1994*			*1999*			*2004*		
	All	*STs*	*% All*	*All*	*STs*	*% All*	*All*	*STs*	*% All*
A	59,013	1,727	2.9	93,520	3,172	3.4	80,011	3,311	4.1
B	1,03,198	2,902	2.8	1,04,963	3,512	2.4	1,35,409	6,274	4.6
C	23,81,613	1,28,225	5.4	23,96,426	1,45,482	6.1	20,40,970	13,6,630	6.7
D	10,23,285	62,945	6.2	9,49,353	66,487	7.0	8,02,116	53,776	6.7
Total	35,67,112	1,95,802	5.5	35,44,262	2,18,653	6.2	30,58,506	1,99,991	6.5

Source: Eleventh Five-Year Plan 2007–2012, Vol. I: 114.

Need for Credit for Tribals

As has already been stated that the tribals have all been subjected to large-scale exploitation by non-tribals. Even though a series of measures have been initiated after independence to ameliorate their economic conditions, the degree of exploitation has remained unabated. The development of tribal economy has been seriously hampered by the lack of infrastructural facilities, viz., transport and communication, adequate organized/monetized market system, adequate organizational base, etc. In addition to this, the money-lenders, traders, intensive industrial/mining activities in the tribal belt, inefficiency and callousness of state owned agencies as also the high degree of land alienation and indebtness have impoverished the tribals (Karmarkar, 1999).

What has come has a rude shock to them is that they have also lost their rights and controls over the resources and property on which they have been depending for generations. Thus, denied of their assets and unable to participate in the developmental activities in and around their areas, the tribals have been forced to live in the state of perpetual penury which invariably results in their large-scale migration as a coping mechanism.

II

Micro-Finance: Concept and Practices

In the development paradigm, micro-finance has evolved as a need-based policy and programme to cater to the as far neglected target groups (women, poor, rural, deprived, etc.). Its genesis and evolution is based on the concern of all developing countries for the empowerment of powers as well as the alleviation of poverty. Development organizations and policy makers have included access to credit for poor people as a major aspect of many poverty alleviation programmes.

Micro-finance, thereby, is a provision of broad-based range of financial services such as deposits, loans, payments, money transfers, and insurance to low income households and their micro-enterprises. The basic purpose being to provide access to financial assistance including credit to the poor to enable them to start expand micro-enterprises to breakout of poverty. Micro-credit enables the poor to be thrifty and helps them in availing the credit and other financial services for enhancing their income and subsequently their living standards.

For several decades, many economies, including the Indian, experimented with subsidized credit for the poor; however, it only resulted in increasing the non-performing assets (NPA). It was then realized that the core issue of poor was the access to credit rather than the cost of credit (Srinivasan and Sriram, 2003). It has now been increasingly realized that micro-finance can be a critical element of an effective poverty reduction strategy by enabling the poor to smooth their consumption, range risks better, build their assets gradually, develop their micro-enterprises and enhance their income earning capacity. It can also be an effective way to assist and empower the women and above all can contribute to the development of overall financial system through integrations of financial markets.

Profile and Growth

The micro-credit programme, which was formally introduced in 1992 with a modest pilot project of linking around 500 self-help groups (SHGs) has made rapid stride in India is exhibiting considerable democratic functioning and group dynamism. The micro-credit programme in India is now the largest in the world. The programme envisages organization of rural poor into SHGs for building their capacities to manage their own finance and then negotiate bank credit on commercial terms.

There are a variety of micro-finance organizations in government as well as non-governmental sectors. Leading national financial institutions like the Small Industrial Development Bank of India (SIDBI), the National Bank for Agriculture and Rural Development (NABARD) and Rastriya Mahaila Kosh (RMK) have played a significant role in making micro-credit a real movement in India. The size and types of implementing organizations range from being very small to moderately big, involved in savings and or credit activities for individuals and groups. These groups adopt a variety of approaches; however most of them tend to operate within a limited geographical range. There are few exceptions like PRADHAN, ICECD, MYRADA, SEWA, etc., who have been successful in replicating their experiences in other parts of the country and act as resource organizations. (Figure 1)

The regional distribution of SHGs spread indicate overwhelming performance in the southern region (65%) followed by eastern region (11%), western region (11%), central region (10%) and northern region (3%). As the banking system in the country does not have any rural outlets of their own, on a large-scale, the banks have shown interest to patronize SHGs and channelize their resources through them.

There are a number of distinctive models of micro-finance, reflecting the fact that micro-finance has evolved differently in different environment. Some countries tend to rely on one particular

Figure 1

Development Process Through Micro-Finance

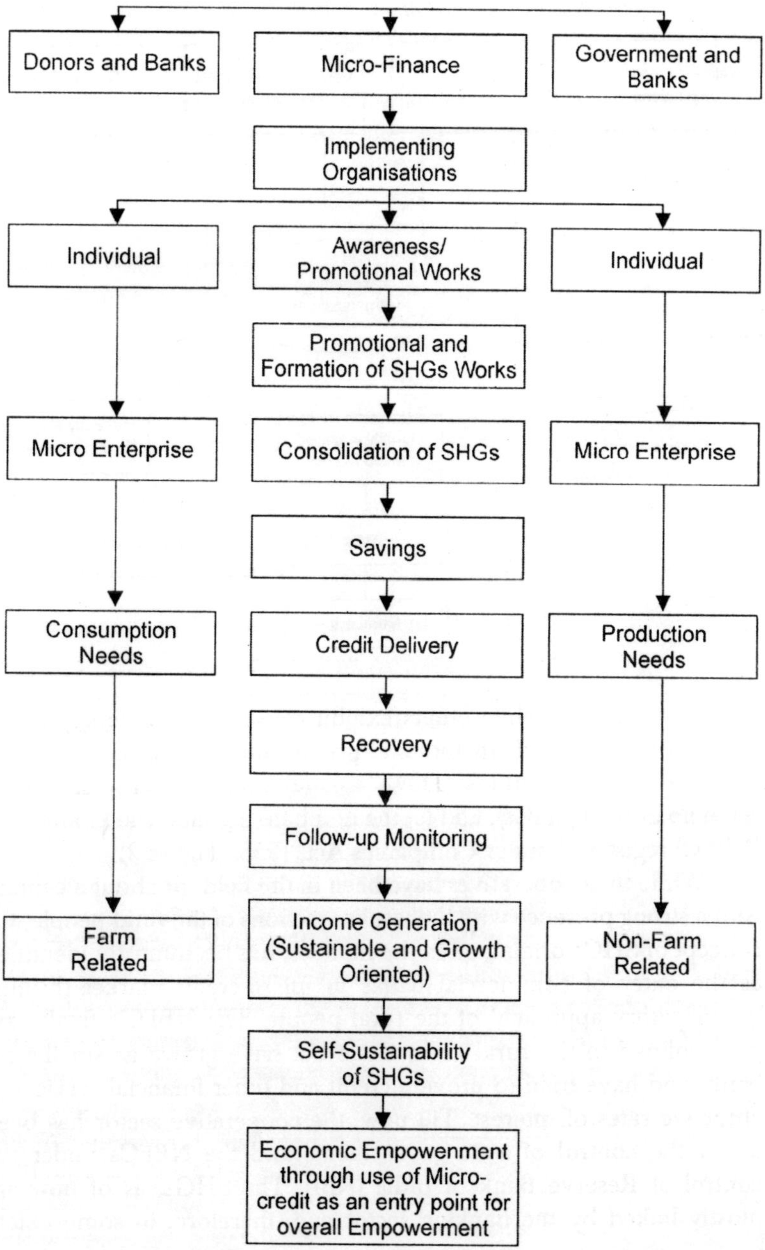

Figure 2

Micro-Finance Interventions through Different Organizations

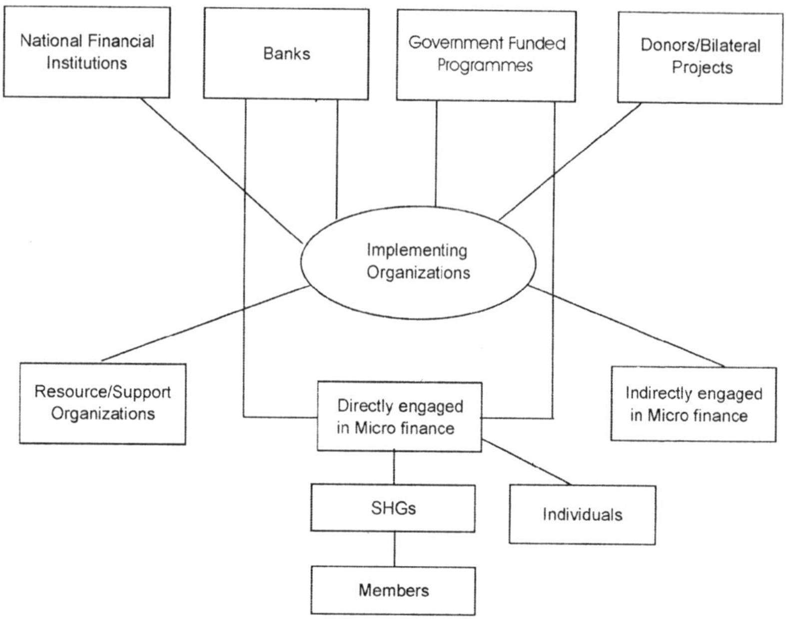

model or method, while others exhibit considerable diversity in the range of models used. In India, at present there are three important types of such institutions. These are: (a) the cooperatives, (b) the self-help groups (SHGs), and (c) the non-banking financial Companies (NBFC) registered under Companies Act, 1956. (Figure 2)

While the cooperatives have been in the field for about a century with a strong presence with the weaker sections of the rural people, the concept of SHGs originated in the nineties, has been mostly identified as the entry of commercial banks in micro-credit market through 'participatory approach' of the rural people. The NBFC's finally are not confined to the rural areas alone but have grown as small-scale banks and have tried to provide credit and other financial services at attractive rates of interest. Till now, the cooperative sector has been under the control of state governments and the NBFCs under the control of Reserve Bank of India (RBI). The SHGs, as of now are mostly linked by the banking sector and, therefore, to some extent guided by the rules and regulations of RBI and central government. Hence, it could be stated that micro-finance/credit institution have a relatively safer mode of operation and could be held accountable in case of defaulting.

In India, the geographical distribution of both SHG-bank linkage and the MFIs is highly skewed. The southern states account for the bulk of the SHGs. However, in recent years, SBPL has been making inroads into the regions with large percentage of rural poor. About ninety per cent of the SHGs that are linked to the banks are that of women. Thus SHGs also provide an opportunity for the developing capacity and empowering the women, besides addressing the issue of poverty and employment.

How the Self-Help Group (SHGs) could be Useful?

A self-help group, which is the most crucial base of micro-financial institutions, is nothing but a small economically homogeneous and cohesive group of rural people who have agreed to voluntarily coming together for the following purpose:

1. to save small amount regularly;
2. to mutually agree to contribute to a common fund;
3. to meet their emerging help on mutual help basis;
4. to have collective decision-making;
5. to solve conflicts through collective leadership; and
6. to provide collateral free loans with terms and conditions decided by the group.

On account of their nature of configuration, the members of the SHG's very quickly strike alliances among the members, which help to allay their fears, apprehensions and suspicions about each other. This enables or facilitates their working as a cohesive unit and also helps them elect their leader from within through democratic means as a result of which the chances of their succeeding are fairly high, though the incidence of failures cannot be ruled out. However, it has been brought out by many studies how the formation of SHGs has helped the group to function successfully on a sustained basis and help the group to come out of the poverty through micro-level enterprises.

However, despite the success of micro-finance institutions, their access has, so far, been very limited. Various estimates show that barely about two per cent of the world's roughly 500 million small entrepreneurs have access to financial services. Thus, in order to make the working of micro-finance institutions self-sustaining, their access has to be enlarged to more rural people. The question then is how the micro-enterprise institutions are geared to provide short-term capital to small business in the informal sector that becomes sustainable.

Modus-Operandi of Micro-Finance Institutions

Micro-finance institutions provides loans to very poor families or groups or individuals to start small enterprises. The loans are provided without any guarantee but based on trust. Each borrower must belong to a five member group. But the repayment responsibility rests on the individual borrower. However, the group makes sure that its members repay the loan. MFIs encourage the borrower to save small amount for the group and this serves as an insurance of amount for any emergency.

However, despite the huge success, the working of these institutions has drawn severe criticism from several quarters. The recent Andhra Pradesh fiasco is a glaring example in which the MFIs were implicated for charging exorbitant rates from the poor on hand and resorting to unethical means of recovery. They have also been accused of adding to the problem of farmer's suicide in the state. Likewise, their weekly repayment schedules has also been attacked because it puts a lot of pressure on the members to maintain regular repayment cycle as a result of which the members many a times resort to borrowing from informal agencies to repay the MFI loans to retain their access. Thus, micro-finance model have both the virtues as well as the vices and if operated with skill and caution have the capability and potential of bringing about major transformation in the lives of the rural poor by providing credit access to them.

Future Strategy

The planned development has clearly brought for many lessons that could be drawn and the foremost being that planning has not been able to address many critical issues and tribal development has been one of the foremost among them. What has really been ironical is that despite of massive investments, incentives and other interventions, the outcome has not been to our expectations. What has also become a matter of deep concern is that the trickle-down effect has not commensurate with the amount and volume of efforts the government has been pouring in. What has crystallized, over the time, has the emergence of an elite class, also identified as a creamy layer, while the bulk of the population has so far, remained, more or less, isolated from its impact. Thus, it could be said that external social intervention strategies, so far adopted, have only succeeded in fracturing this relatively homogenous society into elite and non-elite classes. All this clearly highlights the limitation of external support that has failed to take note of the actual grass root needs of the people. Thus, there is a need to adopt an alternative model that not only takes into account the internal demands of the people but also promote the concept of indigenous capacity building, empowerment and leadership into the system.

Alternative Model

It is in this context that role of micro-credit and micro-level institution needs to be redefined and the chance of their getting success appears to be much brighter for the following reasons:

1. the intervention/support from outside is bare minimum;
2. micro-finance works on principle of joint cooperative action;
3. it works with a small group with homogeneous background thus promotes communal harmony; and
4. there are no stringent official bindings on borrowers and the accountability solely rests on group.

Besides this, the SHGs homogeneity also helps in promoting brotherhood fraternity, encourages people to discuss, share, and articulate their ideas and thoughts, which helps to develop a sense of belonging and confidence in them – a skill or virtue they so far lack. Another factor that favours them is that the whole process of planning and development is managed by the group through their internal leadership which, with the passage of time, gains experience and perception.

The basic strength of micro-financial model lies in its ability to function in the most diversified and hostile informal sector where formal institutions fail to operate. This sector, on account of its diversity and multiplicity, provides a very complex platform where no formal rules could be implemented. This uniqueness of micro-finance institution enables them to tap vast resources of rural masses and help them to become financially viable. Micro-finance also addresses the issues of gender empowerment which has so far remained the most neglected section. Hence if the micro-finance institution's working is supervised and monitored effectively and an element of transparency is installed into their working, these institutions can provide the much needed thrust to the rural economy and vibrancy into the whole economy.

Scope

The relevance of micro-finance institutions, in these parts or regions of the country that are normally identified or addressed as the BIMARU states and incidentally have the highest incidence of poverty and regional backwardness, need not be emphasized. The poor state of infrastructure supplemented with low industrial base and subsistence agriculture provides an ideal plank for migration of rural households to other parts of the country. The presence of micro-finance institutions would have multiple positive spin-off effects in the region. The foremost being the issues of rural credit which is so badly needed by the rural people. It has been well-documented in various studies that though micro-finance may have attained phenomenal success; however their reach still has hardly been two per cent of the total volume of requirement. Their presence would not only provide an alternative course to the rural poor households who till now have to rely on local moneylenders and who, in return, charge exorbitant rate from these helpless lots. As a result of which they subsequently fall in the debt-trap, and also help in breaking their hegemony. Besides this, the formation of SHGs would also help in promoting spread of ancillary industrial activities through micro-level enterprises thus setting the base of secondary sector.

Thus, it could be said that micro-finance institutions have the capacity to contribute in solving the problem of inadequate housing and urban services as an integral part of poverty alleviation programme.

Notes

The evolution of Indian micro-finance can be broadly divided into four phases:

Phase I: The Cooperative Movement (1900–2000)

During this phase, the credit cooperatives were the vehicles to extend subsidized credit to villages under government sponsorship.

Phase II: Subsidised Social Banking (1960–1900)

The failure of cooperatives forced the government to focus on taking measures such as nationalization of banks, establishment of Regional Rural Banks (RRBs) and setting up of apex institutions such as National Bank for Agriculture and Rural Development (NABARD) and the Small Industrial Development Bank (SIDB), including intuition of a government sponsored Integrated Rural Development Programme (IRDP). While these steps helped the government to reach out to masses, however, the period was also characterized by large-scale misuse of credit thereby creating a negative and wrong perception about the credibility of micro-borrowers among bankers, thereby further hindering access to banking services for low income people.

Phase III: SHG-Bank Linkage Programme and Growth of NGO-MFIs (1990–2000)

The failure of subsidised social banking once again triggered a paradigm shift in the delivery of rural credit with NABARD initiating the Self-Help Group (SHGs) Bank Linkage Programme (BLP), aiming to link informal women's groups to formal banks. This helped the programme to increase banking system outreach to otherwise unreachable people and initiate a change in the banks outlook towards low income families from 'beneficiaries' to 'customers'. This period was thus marked by the extension of credit at market ratio. The model generated a lot of interest among newly emerging micro-finance institutions, largely of non-profit origin, to collaborate with NABARD, under this programme. The macro-economic crisis in the early 1990s that finally led to the introduction of economic reforms of 1991 resulted in greater autonomy to the financial sector. This also led to the emergence of a new generation of private sector banks who became important players in micro-finance sector a decade later.

Phase IV: Commercialization of Micro-Finance

In the first decade of new millennium post-reforms, the rural markets emerged as the new growth drivers for MGIs and banks, the latter taking interest in the sector not only as the part of their corporate social responsibility (CSR) but also as a new business line. On the demand side NGO-MFIs increasingly began transforming themselves into more regulated legal entities such as NBFCs to attract commercial investments. MFIs set up after 2000, saw themselves less in the development mould and more as business in the financial services space, catering to an untapped market segment while creating value for their shareholders. This overriding shift brought about changes in institution legal forms, capital structures, sources of funds, growth strategies and social alliances.

References

Economic and Political Weekly Foundation (1994): "Social Indicators for Development for India: Inter-State Disparities", *Economic and Political Weekly,* Vol. XXIX, No. 21: 1,300.

Economic Survey (1996–97): Ministry of Finance, Economic Division, Government of India, New Delhi.

Eighth Five-Year Plan (1992–97): Planning Commission, Government of India, New Delhi.

Karmarkar, K.G. (1999): *Rural Credit and Self-Help Groups, Micro-Finance Needs and Concepts in India,* New Delhi: Sage Publications India Pvt. Limited.

Mahadev, M. (2003): "A Critical Reflection on Development of Scheduled Castes", *Journal of Social and Economic Change,* Vol. 5, No. 1, January-June, Bangalore.

Pandey, Janak and S.K. Pant (2008): "The Marginalized Dalits: Disadvantages in Learning" in *Perspectives on Learning Disabilities in India,* edited by Komilla Thapa, Geerdina M. Vander, Aalsvoort and Janak Pandey, New Delhi: Sage Publication India Pvt. Limited.

Pant, S.K. (2002): *Gender Bias in Girl Child Education,* New Delhi: Kanishka Publishers and Distributors.

Prabhu, Seetha (1998): "Social Sector in Economic Development", *Journal of Social and Economic Change,* Vol. 1, July-December, Bangalore.

Seventh Five-Year Plan (1985–90): Planning Commission, Government of India, New Delhi.

Shylendra, H.S. (2006): "Microfinance Institutions in Andhra Pradesh Crisis and Diagnosis", *Economic and Political Weekly,* May 20, Mumbai.

Srinivasan, R. and M.S. Sriram (2003): "Microfinance: An Introduction", IIIB, *Management Review,* Bangalore.

Swaminathan, D. (1996): "Inaugural Address", National Seminar on Rural Water Supply and Sanitation, Sponsored by Rajiv Gandhi National Drinking Water Mission, New Delhi and organized by Centre for Development Studies, Thiruvananthpuram, June 20–22. (SPD)

Index